THE
FRUIT
YOU'LL
NEVER
SEE

GAIL BRENNER NASTASIA

CONTENTS

PROLOGUE

Not even law school could change the fact that I was trash. The truth had never been as clear to me as it was one afternoon in estates class. During my second attempt at a Juris Doctorate, I doodled geometric designs in my notebook while the professor paced the front of the room. He was lecturing about the rules of consanguinity—how property passes after one's death. I had little to offer in any discussion of property, or family, for that matter. After my mother's death six years earlier, her kids, Chrissy, Philip, and I, had to scrounge for the money to have her body cremated. That wasn't in the rules. Likewise, my mother's siblings had to do the same for their mother, who died just a few days after mine.

My thoughts were interrupted by Professor Conlin's voice, his words so entirely out of place I was sure I had been mistaken.

"White trash," he said.

My head snapped up. I waited for more.

"Yes," he said. "Even white trash has to adhere to the rules." The comedic example that followed included a trailer, loud white beer-drinking men, women who weren't afraid to fight, and dirty, barefoot kids. Although my family was a different brand of trash, we fit the description in our own way. And as we'd never owned property, I would've gladly accepted the hereditary gift of a trailer over debt.

Rationally, I knew Conlin didn't know anything about my history; nobody did. Still, I was sure he'd looked directly at me while turning the phrase. Several of my classmates laughed at the professor's illustration. As good as I'd gotten at pretending, I couldn't even crack a smile. I stayed frozen. I wondered how they'd respond if they knew they were laughing at me—that my mother was a junkie, that I'd been on my own since my early teens, and that I'd learned how to make money by doing things with men.

I considered getting up for a pretend trip to the bathroom—I really needed a cigarette—but that was a sure way to draw attention. Instead, I kept my gaze fixed on the front of the room, afraid my shaky hands or red-hot face would give me away. With my back erect, and hands folded on the table, I sat quietly in my chair, willing the stillness to render me as invisible as it had when I was a kid.

My classmates probably had it easy, I thought. They likely came from money, had families who cared, and parents who didn't abandon them. Of course, it was just as likely that we had some things in common—for one thing, we'd all been presented to the world in one way or another. Although my family didn't have traditions like the coming out party or quinceanera, I, too, had undoubtedly been introduced to society. But, because my parents and other family were absent during my transition into womanhood, it was my Aunt Julie who made the introductions.

1

FOUR CENTS SHORT OF A NICKEL

~1981~

I hear Aunt Julie on the front stairs. She's in a rush, taking two steps at a time. A few seconds later, the door swings open, bringing in a sudden stream of midday light.

"Shut the door!" Little Nana, my great-grandmother, yells. She can't see the TV with the glare.

Ignoring her, Aunt Julie stands in the doorway, her dark silhouette against the bright backdrop. A few inches taller, she could pass for my mother.

"Gail, come outside quick. I have to tell you something!" She's excited and short of breath. I follow her out to the front porch, out of Little Nana's earshot, and into the warm spring day.

"Do you want to take a ride and smoke a joint?"

I answer quickly. "Let me get my shoes." In all my eleven years, my only wish has been that she take me with her.

Even though Aunt Julie lives here, I don't see her often because she's mostly out. When she does come home, she brings a force of life that ricochets off the nicotine-stained walls. For however long she stays, it feels electric until her bedroom door closes, and she shuts all that energy up in there with her.

Some days she comes out of her bedroom and disappears into the bathroom for hours; the curly yellow telephone cord is the only evidence that she's in there. Eventually, she emerges to the sound of a beeping horn and passes by Little Nana and me on her way out through the living room. A quick flash of bare legs and shoulders and she's gone, leaving behind the faint smell of Prell shampoo. Sometimes I get to the window in time to see the back end of a car or truck pulling away from the curb, its windows down, music blaring.

I know Aunt Julie isn't quite right. A part of me has known for a long time. When I was little, after she walked out of the corner store one day, I heard a guy say: "That girl is four cents short of a nickel." That was long before she started sneaking me hits from joints in Little Nana's backyard. Still, I don't care what anybody says—she's my idol.

Aunt Julie slides into the rusty old pickup truck first. Her smooth, tanned skin seems out of place against the torn, stained fabric of the long seat. The driver keeps his eyes on her as she scoots sideways into the middle of the bench. He looks her over, from her tube-topped chest, down the length of her body, to the exposed skin of her legs beneath cutoff jean shorts. I want to dress like her, but I can't do that with hand-me-downs from Little Nana's landlord; I have to make do with a t-shirt I knot on the side, and little girl shorts, the kind with an elastic band around the waist.

When I jump up to take my place beside her, I see that the driver is older than Aunt Julie, much older, I think, probably even thirty.

As she introduces us, I see his eyes move over my body the same way they moved over hers. He stares at my chest. I cross my arms and look away; I've already seen enough of his straggly, black hair and pot belly to know I don't like him. But I do like the attention. I want guys to look at me the way they look at Aunt Julie. Even though I'm ten years younger than her, and my chest is already larger, I'm nowhere near as pretty. I wonder how it'll feel to be twenty-one like her, beautiful and sexy, with straight white teeth and shiny hair.

The man drives around the outskirts of Gloucester, through Riverdale and Bay View, while we pass a joint among the three of us. Aunt Julie stubs the joint halfway through and leaves it sitting in the ashtray in front of her. He turns back to the highway and drives south over the A. Piatt Andrew Bridge, away from downtown Gloucester.

As the Rolling Stones scream through the speakers, I sink back into the breeze that blows through the truck's open windows. I'm thinking about the last time Aunt Julie took me out with her a few weeks ago. We'd gone to a party with one of her friends. When we got to Gloucester's Stage Fort Park, a dozen people were sitting in a circle around a blazing fire. Each of them was holding a red plastic cup.

I found a bare rock where I sat, stared at the fire, and waited for the joint in circulation to get to me. I didn't know what to say to anybody—I was, by far, the youngest one there. Aunt Julie left me to go talk to a man near the partially hidden keg of beer.

I'd only been sitting for a few minutes when a guy to my left spoke.

"I'm Danny," he said. "And you are beautiful." I glanced in his direction, convinced he was talking to somebody else. But he was looking directly at me.

I turned back to the fire.

"Do you want a beer?" he asked.

"Sure," I said, even though I hate the taste of beer. I watched Danny walk to the keg. Thin but not too skinny, his arms and legs were muscular like a guy who plays sports. I couldn't help but notice that his shirt was tight against his chest.

I turned to the fire when he was done pouring, so he wouldn't see me watching him.

He sat on the ground beside me and handed me the cup.

"Thanks," I said.

"So, where have you been all my life," he asked. I couldn't help but smile. When I really looked at him for the first time, I noticed that even though his face was smooth, it was definitely a man's face. At least twenty, I guessed. His blonde hair was grown past his ears and was parted down the middle, and his eyes—God, his eyes—were the bluest blue.

Aunt Julie was suddenly on my other side. "That's my niece," she said. "Isn't she pretty?"

"Gorgeous," he said, already getting to his feet.

"Do you want to go for a walk?" he asked, holding out his hand.

I guzzled the beer and let him pull me up. His hand was warm. It felt strong wrapped around mine. Safe.

We walked hand-in-hand away from the cannons toward the playground.

The further away we got from the fire, the harder it was to see the path. It had to be close to midnight.

Danny did all the talking. He didn't ask me any questions. I'm glad he didn't ask my age. He never even knew my name. All I learned about him is that he worked in construction and planned to have his own business someday.

I could hear him talk as we walked, but I wasn't listening. My mind was on what was about to happen and if it would be like what I saw Aunt Julie and my godfather, Dennis, do together on the pullout when I was a kid. I wondered if it meant Danny would be my boyfriend.

When we got to the see-saws, he led me off the path to a lone tree close to the woods. We were far enough away from the group, so they couldn't hear us, but close enough to still see the glow of the fire.

Danny pulled his shirt over his head and spread it flat on the ground. He was quiet as he sat down and pulled me onto his lap. He kissed me on the lips. Then with his tongue. He wasn't forceful; in fact, I think he was trying to show me how. I was glad; I didn't want to do anything to make him not like me.

We'd been kissing for a few minutes when he moved from beneath me and laid me down where he had been sitting. He leaned over and kissed me again before he unbuttoned my jeans. He pulled them—and my underwear—down to my ankles, yanking just one leg over my foot. He was kneeling before me, leaning forward to kiss my stomach. I held my breath and stayed perfectly still. I could feel the mosquitoes biting my bare legs.

Danny stood to take off his shorts. I couldn't see his naked body in the dark, but I knew I wanted him to put his clothes back on. I wanted to return to the party but didn't say anything. He pushed my legs apart and lay on top of me. His thin shirt was no match for the roots, sticks, and rocks digging into my back and legs. He pushed against me, trying to force himself inside, but my body wasn't ready for him. I stayed quiet. I was sure I'd soon make the same noises Aunt Julie had made with Dennis. Still, I put my hands on his chest just in case I needed to push him away.

He kept trying as the mosquitoes feasted on me.

"You have to stop," I said quietly. "It hurts."

"It'll only hurt at first," he said. "I promise. Then it will feel good."

I tried to hold back my tears, but I couldn't stop them. As much as I didn't want to disappoint him, I couldn't help it.

He finally moved off of me when he saw that I was crying.

I pulled my clothes back on and wiped my face with the back of my hand.

"I'm sorry," he said as he helped me up. He tucked his shirt into the back pocket of his shorts.

"Do you want a shoulder ride?" he asked and kneeled so I could climb on. I cried again on the way back to the party, knowing I'd made a terrible mistake.

When we returned to the group, Danny sat on the other side of the fire. He wasn't looking at me anymore.

AUNT JULIE'S FRIEND turns off the highway at the first exit and onto a small dirt road. He drives a short way into the woods, far enough so that I can't see the street in the side mirror, and puts the truck in park.

Aunt Julie and the man whisper to each other so softly I can only make out a word or two of the conversation: "my niece" and "she's young."

I close my eyes and let the music on the radio move through me. It seems so far away. The weed is working its magic.

"Here, take these," Aunt Julie says, nudging me with her elbow. When I open my eyes, I see that she has five round, white pills in the palm of her hand.

"What are they?"

"Just take them. They'll make you feel good."

"But what are they?"

"Percs. I promise you'll like them." I can tell she's getting impatient.

"All of them?" It seems like a bad idea. I've only taken Valium and Xanax, no more than one at a time.

"Yeah," she says, pushing a half-empty bottle of Pepsi into my hand. I take one and then another. I don't like soda, and the bubbles with the pills make me gag. The third one gets stuck in my throat, and I almost throw it back up but force it down with more liquid. It leaves a bitter taste in my mouth. I wait a few minutes to take the last two. Aunt Julie watches and waits before taking five of her own with one big, admirable gulp. I can't wait to be grown up enough to do the same.

The man whispers something to her.

"No, let's finish smoking this first," she says, relighting the joint. She isn't whispering anymore.

My body is again drifting back into the comfort of the place the weed has taken me when suddenly, I'm overcome by a wave of nausea. I open my eyes but stay quiet and wait for it to pass. A second wave follows quickly behind it. "Oh my God, Julie, I'm gonna puke."

She reaches over me and opens the door. "Come on. You need some air," she says.

Aunt Julie holds back my hair as I heave, doubled over in knee-high weeds. When I'm done, she lights a cigarette and hands it to me before lighting one for herself. We finish our cigarettes before getting back into the truck.

"Is she okay?" I hear the man ask as I climb in behind Aunt Julie. He sounds concerned.

"No, she's not."

The man holds onto the steering wheel with both hands like he's driving, but we're not moving. He looks straight into the trees while he asks through clenched teeth, "Is she going to take care of me?"

"No," Aunt Julie says. "My niece can't do it now; she's sick."

We sit for a moment in silence before the man mumbles something, forces the idling truck into gear, and peels out of the brush onto the paved road—his rage crowds around me in the small space of the cab.

I glance at Aunt Julie; it's not like her to be so quiet. She's smiling. At first, I don't know why, and then I understand completely. They made a deal, she and the guy, ten pills for me to do something with him. Of course, she knew I'd get sick if I took all those pills.

Still, even though I know she used me, at least I got to go along for the ride.

2

HITCHED

~1975~

I wait impatiently by the door until my father blows the horn of his old red two-door sports car. The sound is like a starting gunshot, and the race with my sister, Chrissy, is on.

"It's my turn to sit in the front," I yell, trying to push Chrissy away from the passenger-side door. "You got it last time," I say, out of breath.

"No, sir, you did," she says.

The flip of a coin decides who will copilot. It should be me since he's my father, not hers. She has her own and doesn't share him with me. So what if she's known my father the longest; it's only because, at seven, she's two years older.

I win the coin toss and slide into the front seat. Although I used to see him most weekends before we moved to Newburyport, my father feels much like a stranger to me. He and my mother have been apart for as long as I can remember. My mother rarely even mentions him. All she's told me about my father is "he's a good guy and a great dancer." I've overheard her say, "he's never paid a penny in child support," but she'll never be "one of those mothers who bad-mouths the father to their kid."

I know little about what it was like when my mother and father were a couple, although I know they were married. "We got hitched at the city hall," my father told me on one weekend visit. "We went up to New Hampshire and tied the knot in front of the Justice of the Peace. I had to make an honest woman out of her," he laughed.

Since no pictures were taken, I made up a story about their wedding. In my imagination, my mother's twenty-year-old skin is smooth and clear. Her eyes are bright. Her long, straight hair is parted down the middle, and one side is tucked behind her ear the way she always keeps it. She's wearing the ruffled white short-sleeved shirt she wears in a picture of her holding me when I was a baby. The top hangs loosely over her thin body and denim skirt. My father is next to her, just a couple of inches taller. His full, dark hair falls past his ears to meet thick sideburns that make him look like Elvis. He plays with the wide collar on his button-down shirt, having trouble standing still. My father, who likes to play pool and keep pigeons, agrees to be my mother's husband. My mother, who loves to read and play Scrabble, agrees to be his wife. Since I've never seen them so much as smile at each other in real life, I'm not surprised they didn't last.

My father isn't the kind of guy to hug me or give me piggyback rides, but he's nice enough. He hardly ever gets angry, and being with him means time away from my mother's boyfriend, Phil, and our noisy home for the day.

Besides Phil being at home, I wouldn't mind staying there if I didn't feel so lonely. Debbie, Phil's oldest daughter, is the only adult who notices me when I'm at our apartment. I'd be surprised if any of the other people who hang around even know my name is Gail.

But something unusual happened last week. They noticed me. I had gone to look for my mother in the living room. Although it was the middle of the day, I could barely see who was in the room; the sheets covering the windows to "keep nosey people out of our business" made it dark inside. While standing in the living room doorway, I watched cigarette smoke swirl in the air and tried to make out the faces of the half dozen men and women who lounged on our mismatched furniture. At first, none of them paid me any mind.

After realizing my mother wasn't among them, I stretched my arms and legs to either side of the doorless frame and pressed my hands and bare feet flat against the smooth painted wood. My tiny body being a perfect fit for the space, I quickly shimmied my way up. For a moment, I forgot all about the living room crowd and my mother.

"Holy shit," said a guy before sucking on the long neck of his sweating bottle, "she's a fucking monkey." Some of them looked at me and laughed.

A guy sitting in the chair next to Long Neck handed him a joint. "Keep going!" he yelled as though he were watching a race and had money on the horse that was me. I climbed until my head hit the top of the frame, leaving me nowhere else to go. I wished I could keep climbing forever so they'd keep watching.

"Do it again," said a woman's voice as I dropped to the floor. I did it again and again until they grew bored of me, and I went back to being invisible.

WITH THE WINDOWS down, I can smell low tide long before I see it. The odor makes me think there must be dead things wrapped in the seaweed the water leaves behind. It keeps me from eating anything that comes from the ocean.

The smell also tells me we're almost to the bridge that leads to downtown Gloucester. Freddie's Lobsta Land is on the left, and Nichols Candy is on the right as we head into town. I've never been inside Freddie's, we don't go to expensive restaurants, but we sometimes stop at the candy store. Not today, though; we don't have much time.

Today, my father is bringing us to Gloucester to see his mother, Nana Raizin. I'm glad we're going to my grandmother's house and not to Boston to visit with Nana Raizin's family—Aunt Annie and her kids. I'm not comfortable around the Boston relatives. I'm not really part of that family; I can't be because I'm not Jewish like them since my mother isn't. That's the rule. They're nothing like my mother's family. They own things, and I've never seen them drink or smoke. I don't even think they say bad words.

"Hey, you guys wanna hear a dirty joke?" my father asks as we drive over the Annisquam River. Chrissy and I look at each other and roll our eyes—we already know the punch line. "Two white horses fell in mud," he says, laughing like it's the first time he's heard it.

I'm watching out the window as we drive over the bridge. Since it's summer, I see lots of green and blue from the highest point, where it seems like we're on top of the world. Still, as pretty as it is, I can't help but wonder what it would be like to fall from the railing into the water below and become invisible for real.

By the time my father pulls his car alongside the curb in front of Nana

Raizin's gray and red house, I'm already starting to feel more relaxed. My neck and back aren't sore like at home, where people always come and go. My grandmother never has company, so it'll just be the four of us.

Nana Raizin's house makes all those around it look small. The front porch is bigger than our entire apartment. She owns the place but lives only on the bottom floor and rents out the upstairs. Even though she doesn't live on both floors, I'm sure she's rich.

My grandmother gets up from her recliner when the door opens and comes to greet us. She's tall like my mother, bigger though, thicker around the middle. Her yellow hair has been freshly colored and curled. She's always made up—red lipstick and all—even if she's got nowhere to go.

"Mamala!" she says and bends, so her eyes are level with mine. She holds my face in her hands before kissing me on the cheek. She greets Chrissy the same way. I think she's so happy to see us because she's lonely. Nana Raizin doesn't have a husband. My father was just a baby when his father died. She remarried and had another boy, but her second husband died when my father was still a teenager. She's lived alone ever since.

I don't feel like I belong here like I do at Little Nana's, but I love that it is as perfect on the inside as it is on the outside. Here the windows are tall, the ceilings are high, and the rooms are bright. Everything is clean and in its place. The wallpapered walls are free of nicotine stains, and there aren't any roaches. The furniture matches—the wood dark and shiny— including Nana Raizin's four-poster bed, which sits where a dining room table should be.

The bedroom my father and uncle shared as kids is off the living room at the front of the house. The room seems to be exactly as it was when they were kids, with two twin beds separated by a nightstand. If Chrissy and I ever stayed here, this is probably where we'd sleep, but we never do. Even though this place is much bigger than Little Nana's, my father says there isn't room for an overnight.

"Are you hungry?" Nana Raizin asks. It's always her first question. "Do you want a hot dog?"

"Yes," Chrissy and I say at the same time.

My father stretches out on the couch as we follow Nana Raizin into her yellow kitchen. We sit at the table while she puts hotdogs in a pan of water on the stove and two onion rolls in the toaster oven. When they're done, she takes the hot dogs out, slices them down the middle, and then in half so they'll lie flat enough to fit on the rolls. We have pickles and chocolate milk with our hot dog sandwiches before playing in the yard.

The yard is as big as the house. We spend most of our time outside climbing the enormous maple tree that will shed so many leaves in the fall, Chrissy and I will spend an entire Saturday raking and bagging them.

Three or four hours after our arrival, Nana Raizin calls us back into the house. It's time to go home. She reaches into her wallet, hands each of us a flat dollar bill, and lets us pick a treat from the top drawer of a small cardboard chest she keeps in her bedroom. Today, I choose a set of Jacks with a red rubber ball, and Chrissy selects a Fun Pad.

Chrissy gets the front seat on the way back to Newburyport. It's dark outside. I'm quiet and tired from the day. I'm thinking about who will be at our apartment, whether they'll be loud, and if I'll be able to sleep. I wish I could stay with my father. He's been talking about moving away but hasn't said anything about taking me with him. I wish I knew why he doesn't want me. I think he loves me, even though he doesn't say it. I wonder if he was happy when I was born, whether he held or kissed me goodnight. I don't remember, and I don't ask. There's only one thing I know for sure—my being in the world isn't enough to make him stay.

3

SHACKING UP

~1976~

Stepping into Little Nana's dark, smoky apartment feels like coming home. She sits up on the couch when we come through the front door, the main entrance that opens into the living room. With the daylight behind us, it's hard to see her face. The light from the television is reflected in her glasses.

"Hi," Little Nana says as she reaches for a cigarette on the table next to her. She doesn't come to hug us—we don't do that sort of thing—but somehow, I know she's happy to see Chrissy and me.

As my eyes get used to the dark, I can see that her couch isn't made up for sleeping yet. Later, Little Nana will pull her sheet out of the closet and cover herself with the blanket that's draped over the back of the couch. She's always slept in the living room, where she says she can "see who's coming and going." She'll also set up my cot in the middle of the room, on top of the oval, braided rug. Chrissy—being older than me—gets to sleep on the frameless twin bed against the wall opposite Little Nana's couch.

"Hi, nan," my mother says, coming in the door behind Chrissy. "Can I bum one of those?" she asks as she takes the few short steps to the coffee table. Without waiting for an answer, she shakes out a cigarette from Little Nana's soft pack. She lights it and turns to leave. She's in a rush because Phil is waiting in his station wagon.

"See you guys on Sunday," she says. "I love you more than I can say." She blows a kiss, and then she's gone.

I'm not sad that I won't see my mother until Sunday. It's been a month since we last visited with Little Nana, and I miss being here. My father can't bring us anymore now that he lives in Texas. I don't know how far away that is, but I haven't seen him in the months since he left. Hopefully, now that Phil has a car, we'll be able to come here every weekend. Little Nana likes it when we're here. If she had enough room, I bet she'd let Chrissy and me stay with her all the time.

As it is, she's only got one bedroom, and that belongs to Aunt Julie. She's my mother's youngest sister. I've never asked why she lives with Little Nana instead of with Big Nana, her mother, but I'm pretty sure it's because Big Nana is so mean.

Aunt Julie just turned sixteen; she's ten years younger than my mother and ten years older than me. She's one of the reasons I like coming here. Well, she and her new baby, Mary Lee.

"Hi, nana," I say, moving quickly through the living room and into the kitchen, where I can see the baby sleeping in her crib at the foot of Aunt Julie's double bed—the only space big enough to put another body—even one as tiny as Mary Lee. Aunt Julie isn't here. "Don't wake her up!" Little Nana whisper-yells. She knows where I'm headed.

I go to the bedroom, kneel beside her crib, reach through the bars, and run the back of my finger along Mary Lee's soft cheek. I'd sing to her if she were awake. I love being a big cousin.

When I finally leave the bedroom, Chrissy is sitting at the kitchen table, eating a bowl of cereal and reading the back of the box. Beside her is the tall dresser where Little Nana keeps her clothes and whatever food doesn't fit in the kitchen closet. On the first of every month, Little Nana walks to Cape Ann Market with her steel, two-wheel shopping cart and a list. We always know when she's gone shopping. On top of the bureau, we find foods she gets especially for us, including a fresh loaf of Wonder bread that's double-bagged to keep the roaches out. Today, there are two boxes of cereal, Stella Doro cookies, Pinwheels, peanut butter, and a brand-new jar of Fluff. She's been to the store.

"What do you want for supper?" Little Nana asks from her place at the table. I knew she'd ask that. It's one of my favorite things about being here; nothing changes.

Tonight, she'll roll her short, gray hair in pink plastic and foam curlers and be asleep by seven o'clock. When she wakes at two or three in the morning, she'll tiptoe into the kitchen to make her coffee. She'll sit at the table smoking cigarettes and playing solitaire until the rest of us wake up.

Even when she drinks her wine, Little Nana is the most dependable person in our family. On those nights, she closes the drapes at five, wraps her couch with the fitted sheet she washes by hand in the sink, fluffs her flimsy pillow, and takes off her glasses. With her Raleigh Filters and orange plastic round ashtray on the coffee table beside her, she pours the wine into a small glass, stopping halfway. I never see her refill the glass, but it stays halfway full.

When she's done drinking, Little Nana falls into a sleep so deep that not even the loud ring of the telephone is enough to wake her. But, by the time I roll off my cot, the glass is washed, and she's sitting at the kitchen table with her rollers gone, shuffling her worn deck of cards.

"Do you want some cereal?" Little Nana will ask when I enter the kitchen. She'll pour my Cookie Crisp or Captain Crunch, and I'll watch her lay her cards out on the table while I eat.

ON OUR SECOND day at Little Nana's, Chrissy and I head outside to play after Saturday morning cartoons. Aunt Julie didn't come home last night, and the baby is asleep, so there's no good reason to stay inside. And, even in the summer sun, it's cooler in the shaded yard than inside Little Nana's apartment. We're constructing an onion factory using the slide of the neighbor's broken swing set as a conveyor belt. After searching for what we call "mini onions" in the overgrown sumac-filled yard, Chrissy, the two neighbor girls, and I take to our posts along the rusty slope: separator, cleaner, inspector, and packager. We'll sell the onions and make a fortune like the *Beverly Hillbillies*.

"Chr...ail," Little Nana yells through an open window at lunchtime. She's always mixing up our names, making them sound like one. We both spring into action—as always, it's a race to the door. I'm determined to win, even though I'm barefoot. I never wear shoes if I can help it. I take the steps two at a time and push the tenement door open, slamming into the entrance to Little Nana's first-floor apartment directly behind it. Moving quickly, I must shut it again to open Little Nana's door. I'm just stepping over the threshold when Chrissy pushes the outer door behind me.

"Jesus, you're going to break something," Little Nana yells from the kitchen.

"I win," I say to Chrissy as she steps into the room.

"Whatever," she says.

Rounding the kitchen corner, I stop short when I see Big Nana, my mother's mother. She's sitting at the table with an open beer can in front of her. She must've gotten here while we were playing outside.

Big Nana glares at me as I move slowly into the room. She hates me; I'm sure of it. Of course, I'm looking at her, too—her stringy black hair falling against the cheeks of her sagging, pale face. I'm trying to find a trace of the teenager whose picture hangs in Little Nana's living room. In the photo, young Big Nana has thick, wavy brown hair that frames big dark eyes, and her features are soft against smooth, clear skin. That girl is long gone.

Little Nana is Big Nana's mother, although it's hard to believe they're even related. For one thing, Little Nana is nice, and Big Nana isn't. Sometimes she seems nice; she'll even talk to me, ask me about school or something, and then say, "You're a spoiled brat, just like your mother."

The Nanas also look nothing alike. Little Nana is tiny, not much bigger than me, and Big Nana is big. She's so big, it's hard to imagine that she was ever inside Little Nana's belly. Of course, that's how they got their nicknames, who they've always been to us. To other people, Big Nana is Mary, and Little Nana is Lillian.

Little Nana is spooning food onto our plates.

"Wash your hands," Big Nana says. I guess it's her way of helping without having to get up. I push my bangs back with my wrist and let the warm water wash away the backyard before turning to wipe my face on the short sleeve of my t-shirt, a habit I've been punished for more than once.

"I don't want that much," I say when Little Nana hands me the plate.

"Just eat it," she says. "You're too skinny—you'll wither away to nuthin." I take it, knowing she'll never make me eat more than I want.

After Little Nana pushes the plate into my hands, I follow Chrissy into the living room. The Nanas stay in the kitchen. Chrissy sits on Little Nana's couch and sets her plate on the coffee table. I sit in my swivel chair, just a foot from the TV, and balance my plate on my lap.

We've only been inside for a few minutes, but I can tell something isn't right—Big Nana is hardly ever here on the weekend.

I look over at Chrissy to see if she notices it too. She's holding a forkful of macaroni, looking past me at the television. Chrissy avoids problems, unlike me. Big Nana always says I don't know how to mind my own business.

It's impossible to see either Nana from my chair, but I know what they're doing. Little Nana is in her seat, with her back to the hallway that leads to the living room. Her chair is closest to the telephone and bathroom. Big Nana is in her chair at the other end of the table, the one closest to the refrigerator, and her twelve-pack of red-and-white beer. Each of them has a cigarette lit, their packs in front of them—Winston for Big Nana, Raleigh Filters for Little—with matches on top.

"She's been gone for three days," Big Nana says. "Who knows who she's shacking up with." She's talking about Aunt Julie, I can tell. I can't help but overhear. They're only a room away, and there's no door separating us.

"She can't take care of that baby," Little Nana says quietly. She sounds like she might cry, but I never know what she's feeling. We don't talk about things like feelings.

"I'm going to call," Big Nana says.

I don't know who she's planning to call, but it doesn't sound good. I want to run into the kitchen and tell her not to do it. Aunt Julie will come home; I want to say. I don't move.

A moment later, a chair slides back, and the refrigerator door opens. I guess that it's Big Nana because she's closest to it. I know it's her when I hear the opening crack and hiss of a fresh can of beer.

Sitting with my lunch still in my lap, I hear the telephone dial turn again and again. After a moment, Big Nana repeats what she said to Little Nana. "My daughter left three days ago. Her baby is here with my mother and me, and we're too old to care for her." I can tell she's talking to a stranger because she calls Aunt Julie her daughter.

Big Nana is quiet; the other person must be talking.

"We don't know who the father is," Big Nana says, breaking the silence.

I never thought about Mary Lee's father or that she even has one. Aunt Julie has never mentioned him. Of course, Mary Lee has a father. I'm pretty sure everybody does. But I don't know any fathers who live with their kids: I don't live with mine, Chrissy doesn't live with hers, and Phil's kids don't live with theirs.

I move the macaroni on my plate around with my fork. I'm not hungry at all.

After she hangs up the phone, Big Nana calls for a taxi.

Everything is normal when my mother and Phil pick us up to go home. Little Nana is on her couch watching TV, and Mary Lee is next to her in the carrier.

A WEEK LATER, we're back at Little Nana's. I open the door to find the living room empty. The TV is off.

"Nana," I yell from the living room.

"I'm in here," she says.

Chrissy doesn't follow me into the kitchen. Little Nana is sitting in her usual place at the table with a cigarette in her right hand. Her white porcelain coffee mug is next to the ashtray, and her playing cards are in front of her. I walk past her to the bedroom. There's a space where the crib had been. Mary Lee isn't here. No Aunt Julie or Big Nana.

"Where's Mary Lee?" I ask. I feel like crying. I wish my mother had come inside with us like she did last week.

"She's gone," Little Nana says. She counts in her head as the cards slide against each other—one, two, three—and she flips over the last card.

Where is she? Did Aunt Julie take her? Did they go to Big Nana's? I can't make sense of it.

"DSS had to come and take her." I don't know who DSS is, but I want them to bring my cousin back. "Julie can't take care of a baby," she says, "and I'm too old."

Little Nana crushes her cigarette in the ashtray. "Mary Lee is in a foster home now." My heart is pounding so hard it feels like it might break through my chest. I don't know what a foster home is, but this is Mary Lee's home.

"For how long? When is she coming back?" I look around the bedroom for evidence of my baby cousin. There's none; everything of hers is gone. It's like she was never even here.

"I don't know," she says without looking at me. And that's that.

Either Little Nana doesn't have any answers, or she doesn't want to tell me. I can't think of anything else to say. I go to the living room, where I turn the TV on, but I'm not watching. I'm wondering what will happen the next time we have to move—the next time we don't have a home—and whether Little Nana is also too old to care for Chrissy and me.

4

CHANGES

~1978~

My mother opens the door to the kitchen of our new second-floor apartment on a warm day in June, just before my eighth birthday. A lingering bouquet of Pine Sol and bleach hangs in the air as evidence of the love she's put into getting the place ready. Chrissy and I will sleep here tonight instead of at Little Nana's, where we've been for the last few months.

My mother said Phil isn't coming here to this apartment. He's not her boyfriend anymore. In fact, she doesn't have a boyfriend at all. It'll be just the four of us: my mother, Chrissy, me, and Philip, my new baby brother.

I'm happy Phil's gone, but I wish his kids were still part of our family. Before the breakup, they were my sisters and brothers. I don't know what we are to each other now since my mother and Phil weren't married. If I don't get to see them, of the six kids, I'll miss Dawn and Debbie the most. Dawn is closest to my age—just two years older—but I didn't see her often. She spent most of her time with their mother.

Debbie, who's Aunt Julie's age, used to babysit for us when we lived in Newburyport. When I was with her, I never felt invisible. While babysitting, she'd search through her chest of bell-bottom jeans, colorful flowered shirts, and thick wooden clogs to find a tie-dye t-shirt to drape over my small frame. While blasting the Beatles' "Yellow Submarine" on the radio, she'd tie a bandanna around my waist to cinch the shirt and then another to cover my hair. After adding a pair of clip-on earrings that made my earlobes ache, and a string of bulky wooden beads around my neck, I'd be dazzling. She'd step back and admire her work. "Perfect. You. Are. Beautiful," she'd say, as though it were a matter of fact. She'd blow me a kiss, and we'd sit on the hardwood living room floor for "royal" tea. I'd become a princess, sipping tea with the queen.

Our new apartment is in Gloucester, near downtown, where most apartment rentals are. Of all its different parts—East Gloucester, West Gloucester, Bay View, Magnolia—this is the best place to live for people like us who have to walk or pay to get around.

This place is right next to the boulevard, close to the fort where the fishing boats come in, where men wearing Chamois shirts covered in fish scales, ripped jeans, and rubber boots unload their catch. In this part of town, the smells of freshly baked cookies from Mike's Pastry, and bread from Virgilio's Bakery, mix with the stink of fish.

We follow my mother through the rooms of our latest fresh start. "Look at the size of this kitchen," she says, smiling. Her cheeks are flushed, and her eyes are clear. There's a bedroom off the kitchen that contains only a twin bed and a large, empty wooden crate. "This is your room, Gail," she says as we walk through. Ten steps, I count, as we cross to the other side.

From my bedroom, she leads us through a small hallway to the living room and another larger bedroom to the right.

"And this is yours," my mother says to Chrissy. "Philip will be in here with you for now, but you won't even notice." Philip is a little more than a year old. In this room, along with a twin bed and dresser, there's a crib in the corner.

Back in the living room, there's a couch that turns into a bed. It's open and made up for sleeping. There are cigarette butts in the ashtray on a small, round wooden table next to the couch. I can tell my mother has already slept here.

"Check out these built-ins," she says as she waves a hand toward the white, thickly-painted wooden drawers with shelves that go all the way to the ceiling. My mother loves built-ins.

"And this bay window," she says, stepping in front of it. I'm next to her. Chrissy is on my other side. I can't remember the last time my mother smiled the way she is now. She's often sad because she hasn't been a good mother. "It's hard," she says, "when you don't have a great example." And, like me, she grew up without her dad.

My mother was named Jacqueline for her father, Jack, although everybody calls her Jackie. People say my mother is the "spitting image" of her father, just as they say about my mother and me. The few times I met Grampie Jack, I could see my mother in his round face, aquamarine eyes, and wide smile.

Grampie Jack moved away after my grandparents' divorce and, like my father, rarely visited. He isn't a big part of my mother's story except for his leaving, and like my father, he gets a pass.

Big Nana said Grampie Jack didn't send money—and neither did her second husband, who gave her two more kids—so the family stayed poor. The seven of them were forced to move into a garage where they hung sheets from the ceiling for privacy.

"There were two beds for the kids, one for the three girls and one for the three boys," my mother said. "If one of my sisters wet our bed, I'd drape the sheet over the footboard so it'd be dry again by nighttime. In the morning, we'd pray at a makeshift altar and then rummage through the dirty clothes barrel for the least wrinkled, best-smelling outfit to wear."

They'd been living in the garage for a year when Big Nana began to tell people about her talking statues. Somebody decided she should be hospitalized, and the kids went to live with Little Nana. As the oldest of six, it became my mother's job to care for her younger brothers and sisters during the two years Big Nana was gone. The way she talks about having to mother them makes me think they wore her out and that my mother was done with kids by the time Chrissy and I came along. Maybe that's why she's always trying to get away from us.

My mother looks beautiful standing in front of the window, watching the sunlight shimmer across the ocean. Everything is better now. Not only are we back in Gloucester, but there's a beach just a minute away. "It'll be different this time," she says out loud. She's right—I can feel it.

IT'S BEEN A month since we moved into our new place. I'm sitting at the kitchen table. Chrissy is outside, and Philip is taking a nap. My mother is standing in front of the sink. She's not the same as she was when we moved here. In the beginning, she burned candles and incense and played music on the radio while she cleaned. Some nights she'd cook dinner. We had milk for cereal and, sometimes, even Hostess cupcakes.

Today, my mother's not cleaning or singing along to the radio. The sink is filled with dirty dishes, but she's not washing them. Soiled clothes have spilled onto the linoleum from a basket next to the stove—laundry my mother will have to taxi to the laundromat. The trash can is overflowing, and another full, tied bag sits next to it. There are no snacks in the cabinet, and the refrigerator is empty except for some eggs and half a bottle of Pepsi.

There's a Highlights magazine in front of me, but I'm not looking for hidden pictures. I'm watching my mother. She moves from the sink to the middle of the kitchen. With the back of her hand on her forehead, her shoulders slumped, and her eyes closed, she speaks to the room: "Please help me, God, I can't take it anymore."

And then, like an answer to her prayer, there's a knock at the door. She moves fast, as though her salvation might leave as quickly as it has arrived. My mother's body blocks the visitor from my view, and the two of them whisper before the door closes.

Afterward, she again moves through the kitchen, although this time, her back is straight, and her shoulders are upright. As I catch a glimpse of her face, I notice her changed expression. Just a few minutes ago, her jaw was clenched as she bit her bottom lip; now, she seems relaxed. I don't know why she's changed, but I'm glad about it.

With her fist closed around something, my mother goes to the silverware drawer, removes an object, and announces, "I have to go to the bathroom." When the door shuts behind her, I somehow know that when it opens, she will have changed yet again.

I stay and wait because it is so rare to get her alone. The apartment is quiet. I try to focus on my magazine, but I can't. She's been in the bathroom for so long that I have to pee. I sit on my foot to hold it in.

When the door finally opens, my mother smiles, and I forget being mad that she took so long. I ignore my need to use the bathroom and the ache it's causing in my belly. Finally, she's here, happy, and I just want to be with her.

She glides to the counter, turns on the radio, and lowers the volume from where it had been during last night's party. Her hips sway from side to side, and she's snapping her fingers as she closes her eyes and tilts her head back to face the ceiling. And upon the very same sticky floor, dishes still piled high, she begins to move her feet while she sings "ch ch ch ch changes" along with David Bowie. She turns toward me and stretches her arms in my direction, inviting me to join her. And, of course, I do.

5

NOBODY LIKES A RAT

~1978~

The rickety staircase on the left side of our apartment building hugs the outside of my bedroom wall, so I can hear everybody coming up the stairs. There are people here all the time now. At night, I try to guess who is on the stairs by their footsteps.

"Mom, somebody's here!" I yell from my bed whenever I hear the thump of heavy work boots or the squeak of rubber soles.

"Go to sleep!" she yells back before I see Aunt Julie, one of Phil's kids, or a stranger pass by my bedroom door on their way to the living room party.

If it's before bedtime, I sometimes slip into the living room behind the most recent guest, find a spot in a corner, and sit quietly on the hardwood floor. Scrunching my body into the smallest package possible, I try to keep myself invisible so I can stay. I sit quietly, watching while one of the visitors, David or Neil, or Terry, balances a tray on their knees and breaks up a tight bud to roll a joint. I can't look away. I'm lured to the process like a fish to a worm.

First, they remove the seeds and stems. Then they sprinkle a generous amount of the leaves into a small piece of paper, roll gently with equal pressure with their thumbs, and finally lick along the edge to seal the seam. The more experienced will then hold one end, put the entire thing in their mouth, and slowly pull it out between moistened lips to make sure the seam is tight and won't unravel when lit. I study the way they work so that someday, I'll be able to roll the best joint they've ever seen.

On the nights my mother goes out, somebody usually stays with us. Tonight, Aunt Julie is in charge. I can hear her in the living room talking to Dennis. It's just the two of them. Philip and Chrissy are already sleeping. I'm in my bed but far from asleep.

Aunt Julie laughs.

"Come on. Let's have some fun," Dennis says. He sounds more like a boy than a man.

"You want to play with me?" Aunt Julie asks. She laughs again. I can tell she's in one of her good moods. They can change so quickly. On her good days, when we're at Little Nana's, Aunt Julie will let me stay in her room, sitting cross-legged on her bed while she gets ready to go out. She'll slide on a pair of cutoff jeans and then pull a tight t-shirt over her braless chest before undressing again and starting over with a different outfit.

"Do you think this looks good?" she'll ask, turning from side to side, pulling the tube top down to show her cleavage and then up again to expose her flat belly. She'll look away from the vanity and twist her neck, trying to glimpse her jeans-covered backside in the mirror. "Do you think these make my ass look big?"

"Yes, Julie."

"No, Julie."

I try not to upset her, so she'll let me stay.

When she's at our apartment, Aunt Julie talks to me in whispers, telling me things like she got high with her boyfriend and let him go down on her. I don't ask what those things mean. I just listen and give her my attention so she'll keep giving me hers.

When her mood turns dark, she'll sit with her legs folded under her on the couch or floor, brushing her straight, auburn hair for hours. Or she'll become as still and quiet as a statue.

Dennis and Aunt Julie are smoking a joint. I know the smell as well as I know what it feels like to be hungry. I strain to see them, but they're out of my view. Although there was probably once a door separating my bedroom from the small hallway between the rooms, now it's just an open space. I turn around, so my head is where my feet are supposed to be, but I still can't see them.

I remember the blue wooden crate at the foot of my bed. It's been tipped onto its side and acts as a table with its opening to the wall. I slip into the space beside my bed frame, squeeze my small, thin body through the opening, and into the box. It's dark inside, but there's a crack in the wood. Through it, I can see them on the pullout.

They're lying on their sides, facing each other. Aunt Julie's tube top is around her waist, and her breasts are completely exposed to him. He rubs one of them with his hand and then leans over to lick it. She closes her eyes. He stops and reaches for something I can't see. Aunt Julie sits up while Dennis holds something in front of her. She tucks her hair behind her right ear, presses one nostril closed, and sucks something up the other nostril. Dennis does the same before reaching between her legs.

He removes the rest of his clothes after helping Aunt Julie with hers. The only thing left on him is a pair of white tube socks with red stripes that circle just below his knees. His body is hairy and pale next to her smooth-tanned skin. "Mmmmm," is the only sound Aunt Julie makes when he puts his head between her wide-spread legs.

My stomach is tight, and I know I shouldn't see this. But I can't move. My heartbeat is so loud I think they might hear it over the low hum of voices coming through the radio. I should get back in my bed, but I'm frozen. He gets on top of her and moves up and down until they're both making noises I've never heard. From my position, all I can see of Aunt Julie is her legs wrapped around him. At first, his movements are slow and gentle, but then their naked bodies hit against each other so fast and hard I'm sure it must hurt. When my eyes close, I can still see the red stripes of Dennis' socks moving up and down.

When I wake up, my neck is sore, and something is digging into my back—a book or an old shoe. I'm still in the crate. It takes a few seconds for me to remember what I saw. I look through the crack again, but there is only darkness and quiet. I climb back up onto my bed and lie awake. I think about Dennis' hands on Aunt Julie, what they were doing, and whether I should tell. The scene plays over and over in my head for days, but the only voice I hear is Phil's saying: "Nobody likes a rat." So, I keep it to myself.

6

SYMBOLS

~1979~

It's a weekend afternoon, and my mother has sent me down to Dennis' basement apartment for rolling papers. As much as I don't want to go, I'm excited at the chance to do something for my mother since she rarely asks for my help.

The door creaks open slowly when I tap on it with my knuckles. Dennis is lying on a small couch, and his feet are crossed over the arm. He's shirtless, and his jeans are loose around the waist and baggy at the knees like he's been wearing them for a long time. He doesn't show it if he's surprised to see me standing there.

"Mom needs papers," I say from the doorway. The air is so thick with the smells of rotting fish and stale beer; I can almost taste it. Dennis is one of the guys who work down at the wharf when he isn't stumbling around or passed out drunk.

"Come in and shut the door," he says as he sits up, pushing his blond hair behind his ear and away from his face. It's greasier in the front from his dirty hands. He pats the stained cushion on the seat beside him. "Have a seat."

"No thanks," I say, moving into the room just far enough to get what I've come for. It's not that I'm afraid of Dennis since he's pretty scrawny, but I don't like him. Not one bit.

For one thing, it's gross how he passes out at our place while sitting on the couch or in a living room chair, snoring, his chin on his chest, with a thin strand of saliva leaking out of his open mouth. Also, I think about what he did with Aunt Julie every time I see him. But the worst thing about Dennis is how he smacks me on the butt when I walk too close to him. It's impossible to stay out of his reach in our tiny apartment. Other people laugh when they see him do it. Sometimes, I think I should laugh too and lighten up as he says, but I don't think it's funny.

Dennis' living room is crowded with the loveseat, a coffee table, a folding chair, and a small TV on a metal stand. An overused piece of fly paper hangs in the corner above the couch. The only picture in the room is a yellowed poster of a large-breasted blonde woman whose tight shirt is unbuttoned to the bottom of her rib cage. I figure Dennis doesn't have any family since he doesn't have any pictures of them, but then again, we don't have any family photos in our apartment either.

He pulls a Marlboro from the pack and lights it. When he starts moving things around on the table in front of him, an empty can tips onto its side; and the noise scares a few flies off of an old pizza crust next to it. I see the familiar bright orange book of Zig Zag rolling papers before he does. It's next to an ashtray, a ceramic statue not more than four inches tall.

I take a step closer. The statue looks like a woman's head, with a wide-stretched mouth wearing bright red lipstick. Dennis notices me looking and flicks his cigarette into the gaping hole. He ignores the ashes that fall onto the table.

"Do you know what that means?" he asks, pointing at the ashtray with a nod of his chin.

"What?" I ask.

"This ashtray. It's a symbol. Do you know what a symbol is?" I don't know, but I don't want him to think I'm stupid.

"Kind of."

"It's when one thing stands for something else." He smiles. "I'll tell you what it means, but you can't tell your mother." The way he squints his eyes into slits makes my stomach ball up, but I want to know all the things adults know.

"I won't tell her," I say.

"Okay," he says as he pulls a few rolling papers from the book and hands them to me.

"It's a symbol for when a woman sucks on a man's dick. It's called a blow job."

I grab the papers out of Dennis' hand and run back up the stairs, leaving his door open. My mother doesn't ask what took so long, and I don't tell her about the ashtray. Again, I'm no rat.

A FEW WEEKS later, my mother tells me I'm going to be baptized. Philip too. She says that Dennis is going to be our godfather. Dennis, of all people. Maybe she'd choose somebody else if I told her what he said about the ashtray or the things I saw him and Aunt Julie doing, but I keep quiet.

Lucia will be our godmother. I don't know her very well, but like Dennis, she spends a lot of time at our apartment. She's pretty, and she seems nice enough, but I don't understand any of it. We've never even set foot in a church as a family, Catholic or otherwise. Still, for a day, at least, my brother and I will have my mother's attention.

The next day, the five of us, my mother, Dennis, Lucia, Philip, and I, walk the mile or so to Our Lady of Good Voyage Church. Chrissy is staying with Little Nana since she was baptized when she was born.

I can see the bright blue peaks of the church long before we get to the door, where we are greeted by a man with hair so white it matches his robe. He's tall and thin, and his pale skin makes me wonder if he ever leaves the church.

As soon as he tells us where to stand, the priest looks at my mother with what I can tell is a pretend smile. Before he closes his eyes, he says some things to her and my godparents-to-be. He taps his forehead, chest, right shoulder, and left with his right hand. "Let us pray."

I think I'm supposed to close my eyes like everybody else, but I don't want to miss anything. This is the closest I've ever been to God. I look at Dennis, who's wearing what has to be his nicest t-shirt, loosely tucked into a less-than-clean pair of jeans. He shifts from one foot to the other—it's probably the closest he's been to God, too. I look from him to one of the stained-glass windows and then at the life-size wooden Jesus on a cross behind the altar, where we form a semi-circle. All I can think about as I look at his bloodied hands is how much that must have hurt.

"Gail." My mother's whisper gently nudges me back into the church. The priest is looking at me. He holds out his hand for me to come forward. He traces a cross on my forehead with his thumb. He lifts my chin, tilts my head back, and pours water over my forehead. "In the name of the Father, the Son, and of the Holy Spirit, you are baptized," he says. The ceremony is repeated on my brother.

We walk across the street to Destinos to celebrate with submarine sandwiches when it's done. What makes the day so special, more than the subs or all-you-can-eat pasta salad, is the time I'm spending with my mother. Maybe church is a good thing, after all.

Now, I'm part of God's family, whatever that means. What I can't understand is how Dennis fits into the whole thing—how he can be a godfather. He isn't anybody's father, and it doesn't seem like he has much of anything to do with God. For that matter, neither do I. And God doesn't have much of anything to do with me.

7

EVERYBODY'S KIDS

~1980~

I have a feeling it's only a matter of time before we have to leave this apartment. There are people here all the time now. Often, the partying starts early in the day. The radio gets louder as day turns into night and empty cans pile up on flat surfaces. The more drunk and rowdy the people become, the more they try to yell over each other. They mix up their words and repeat themselves. Everybody seems to be having fun, and then, all of a sudden, somebody gets pissed.

"What the fuck. Who took my lighter?"

"Stop your whining," comes the slurred response of a different voice.

In these moments, my shoulders rise to meet my ears, the muscle on the left side tighter than the right. My jaw and hands are clenched. My body is getting ready, either for a fight or to scurry to the closest hiding place. I sit still and wait, folding into myself, keeping my eyes down. I listen for what comes next—the sound of chair legs sliding back hard and fast on the kitchen floor, a table flipped on its side, beer cans and ashtrays crashing around it, or the click of a lighter wheel.

And then: "Thanks, man."

But today, it's quiet enough to work on my math homework. I'm lying on my bed, stomach down, propped up on my elbows, when I hear my mother's voice.

"Gail," she says. "I need you to do me a favor." She's standing in my bedroom doorway.

"What?" I ask.

"A guy owes me twenty dollars, and I need you to walk to the other end of Main Street, near the movie theater, to get it. Can you do that?"

"Yes," I say, trying not to sound as eager as I am to show her how grown-up I can be.

Within minutes of instruction, I'm out the door, down the stairs, and on my way. I move beyond the pastry shops in the West End of town and hurry past the wave of loud voices that spill out of The Rigger, one of the downtown barrooms.

I'm less than halfway to my destination when my feet begin to drag. I'm frustrated that my legs won't move faster.

I tie my sweater around my waist and count the numbers on the buildings, so I know how many more there are to go. "Eighty-six, eighty-eight...." I think I'm almost there.

Finally, after what seems like an hour, I'm standing on the sidewalk looking at the house. I can't see inside because the windows to the first-floor apartment are completely covered.

I walk slowly up the unfamiliar stairs. I don't know who will greet me. A large rock stops the outside door from closing all the way. I push the door open only enough to squeeze through. My mother told me to knock on the door to the left, where I can hear country music playing inside. I'm careful to be quiet, so he won't open his door until I'm ready.

I take a deep breath and knock twice. While I wait, I think about running back down the steps and telling my mother that nobody was home. Instead, I knock again, louder this time. There's the creak of a chair and then heavy footsteps. A skinny old man with a wrinkled face, wearing only a pair of graying jeans and work boots, opens the door.

"You look just like your mother," he says as he steps back and gestures for me to come in. I hear my mother's voice, "Say thank you."

"Thank you," I say, putting out my hand. The man snorts a chuckle and places the bill in my palm.

"You act like her too." I'm halfway down the stairs when he says the last word.

There's enough chill in the early spring air to put my sweater back on. Near the halfway point, realizing how thirsty I am from the long hike, I stop at CVS and use some of my mother's money to buy myself a Pepsi and a bag of chips. And for her, a Hershey bar and pack of Marlboros. She'll be so happy, I think.

I move quickly the rest of the way home. I'm in a race with the sun, afraid to be alone in the shadows.

Finally, I make my way back up the stairs. My mother rushes toward me for the money. She's smiling until her eyes shift to the brown paper bag in my hand. Her eyebrows come together as her smile disappears. Once close enough, she snatches the bag from me. She reaches in and fishes out its contents. She holds what's left—fifteen dollars and some change in one hand, the candy and smokes in the other. The empty bag falls to the floor.

"What the fuck did you do?" she asks.

She turns and leaves the room but comes right back and stands before me.

My neck is tight, and a lump is blocking my throat. I don't know what to say. My mother has never spoken to me this way. I keep my eyes on the floor.

"I'm sorry. I-I didn't know, and I was thirsty and...." The shock of unexpected pain stops me, and for a moment, everything is quiet. I don't make a sound. My right hand instinctively goes to my left arm, just below the shoulder, where it has taken a blow. I look first to where her fist had landed and then at her. Her eyes are wet, and her hand is still clenched. She looks wounded, which confuses me since I'm the one who got hurt.

"You punched me?" I ask. Although it's more a statement than a question. She's never hit me before. The words open something in me that I can't close. I begin to wail, and I can't catch my breath.

My mother leads me to the couch, where she cries and rubs my back. When she speaks, it's barely above a whisper. "I'm so sorry. I'm sick, and I really needed that money. All of it. I'm sorry, Gail. I'll never hit you again. I promise."

THAT'S WHEN I started taking things. Now I crave the rush that comes with reaching my hand into my mother's pocketbook or somebody's coat pocket for a five-dollar food stamp or handful of change. Sometimes I stuff unused workbooks from my third-grade classroom into my backpack, my heart pounding as I try to beat the class back from recess for a few minutes alone in the room. I love the smell of fresh ink and the feeling of bound pages in my hands. I use the things I steal to impress the Italian neighborhood girls.

When I take something—anything—I feel powerful. At least until I get caught. But even that doesn't stop me from needing to do it again. I watch and listen, waiting for any opportunity to make something mine.

It's Saturday morning, a few weeks since I went to collect the money for my mother. I'm the first one awake, and I have to go to the bathroom. I tiptoe into the kitchen and past Neil, a snoring, drunken houseguest who's sleeping upright in a kitchen chair with his head resting on his shoulder. As I move by him, I catch sight of a familiar green bill sticking out of his shirt pocket. The folded bulge of cash sends a current through my body. It makes my heart race the way it does when I'm afraid, but here, I'm in control.

Every step closer to where he sits makes me feel more alive. I feel like I'm moving in slow motion when my finger and thumb grip the edge of the fold. The money slides easily into my hand, and he's still out cold as I creep back into the safety of my room.

I unfold the booty in the early morning light—three ten-dollar bills. It's the most money I've ever seen, never mind held in my hand. After tucking the bills under my pillow, I fall asleep thinking about how I'll spend them.

"What the fuck! I had thirty bucks, and it's gone." I can hear Neil yelling in the kitchen.

"Are you sure?" a female voice asks. It's Debbie, once my sister—now his girlfriend.

"Positive. I had it when I went to sleep."

I'm sure they won't suspect me, a kid. But I don't move from my bed just in case. My mother is with them in the kitchen.

"Jackie, do you think one of your kids took it?"

"No way. Chrissy and Gail wouldn't do that." She's as positive I won't steal as I am that I won't get caught. Philip is just a toddler. Their voices are quiet. I hear bits of the conversation before I hear Neil's footsteps coming toward my room. My mother and Debbie are right behind him. Almost as soon as he's standing above me, Neil grabs my pillow. He yanks it from my grip and exposes the bills stashed there.

"The shit's a little thief," Neil says as he reaches for the cash. I can't think of anything to say. I feel sick. I look from my mother to Debbie. Both of them look surprised and disgusted; neither of them says anything.

Early afternoon, I'm still in bed. I'm watching the dust swirl in the sunlight that peeks around the broken plastic blind hanging in my window. I can't face any of them. I wish my father would come and take me away from here, but I don't even know how to reach him. I would call Little Nana or even Nana Raizin if we had a phone.

Somebody else has come into the apartment, and Neil is telling them the story. He talks loud enough for me to hear every word.

"So, I wake up in the kitchen, who the hell knows how I ended up there, and I go to grab a smoke and notice my money is gone. It was right here in my pocket with my smokes." I can picture him pointing to the pocket on the breast of his wrinkled button-down shirt. "And I start thinking, I know I had it when I passed out. I wasn't that plastered."

"What the fuck," Dennis says, laughing. That's who came up the stairs.

"I says to Jackie, did one of your kids take it? And she's like, no way would my kids steal. Well, I wasn't born yesterday. Nobody else was here. So, I march into Gail's room, and there it is, under her pillow. First place I look." I can almost hear him smiling at his brilliant detective work.

My mother doesn't say a word. Debbie doesn't either.

"Holy shit," Dennis says. "That kid's got balls."

In the early spring, just nine months after moving into the boulevard apartment, Chrissy and I don't go home after a weekend at Little Nana's. She says our mother went out on Saturday afternoon and left Philip with Aunt Julie. Maybe our mother asked Aunt Julie to watch Philip, or maybe she didn't. She really didn't have to; we're everybody's kids and nobody's kids.

Little Nana's hands shake as she tries to hold a match to the end of her cigarette. The windows of our apartment had been left open, she says. Our street, Western Avenue, is busier in the warmer months, and lots of traffic moves past the apartment toward the ocean. I guess somebody looked to the second floor and saw Philip—a barefoot, red-headed toddler—sitting on the sill of the screenless window, facing the water, kicking his heels against the gray wood siding. I wonder if my brother picked that spot for the view.

Little Nana turns away, and there's a crack in her voice when she speaks. "Philip is in a foster home." Although I'm older now, and I know foster homes aren't supposed to be forever, I can't help but wonder if, just like Mary Lee, he won't come home again.

8

PORTUGEE HILL

~1980~

Walter, my mother's new boyfriend, is sitting on the yellow plastic couch with his legs crossed, holding an open newspaper on his lap. I'm not surprised he's here; he'd been staying with my mother on the pullout couch before we left the old place. His boots are on as though he's just stopped by for a visit, but I have a feeling he's not going anywhere.

Chrissy and I have been following my mother on a tour of our new apartment. We had started in the kitchen, where the bathroom is built into the corner like somebody threw it up at the last minute; two of its walls stop at least a foot from the ceiling, which is slanted like all the other rooms. My mother says that's because the place used to be an attic. Inside, there's just enough room for the stand-up shower, toilet, and a small sink. We then walked to my mother's bedroom on the opposite side of the kitchen and now, through another doorway, into the living room.

I'm still next to the entryway when I hear a kitten meow. It's coming from my right, underneath a table that holds a small television. Chrissy is already sitting on the floor, reaching toward the sound. After taking a few steps into the room, I can see the kittens. They're in a cardboard box, and the two are standing on their back legs, scratching at the inside.

Chrissy is holding the gold kitten when I pick up the black and white one and sit cross-legged beside her. We've only been in our new home for less than twenty minutes, and I already know everything has changed.

We've never had pets before, and gently cradling the bundle in my arms, I have a sudden urge to cry.

"That one's a boy," my mother says from the doorway.

"We named him Handsome," Walter says, peering over the paper. We? I think. My chest feels heavy. Now I know for sure Walter's here to stay.

The kitten in Chrissy's lap looks like a tiger. "That's Baby," Walter says.

"The girl," my mother adds.

I turn my attention back to Handsome. I want to be happy about this new home and the soft furball in my lap, but I can only think about Walter being here. What I know about him is that he drinks a lot of beer, he swears more than anybody I've ever heard, and he can be violent. I also know my mother will always choose him over me. It's already happened.

One day, at the old apartment, a bunch of people were in the living room. My mother was sitting next to Walter on the couch. His arm was slung over her shoulders, the swastika tattoo showing on his bare forearm. He coughed, handed my mother a joint with his free hand, and said, "Holy shit, this is good weed." My mother took in a deep hit, gave it to the person next to her, and leaned her head into Walter's chest, resting her arm and hand on his thigh.

Just like Phil, he was taking my mother away. He'd been sleeping at our apartment every night; it was too much. I had to show him that I was more important.

My mother glanced at me when I walked into the room. I took her silence as a good sign; at least she didn't tell me to leave. I tucked my hair behind my ear and made my way into the group gathered around our coffee table, an old lobster crate. With my bare feet silent on the wooden floor, I moved quickly to beat my nerves.

When my mother saw me so close, climbing onto the couch toward her lap, she looked surprised.

"Oh, Gail, not right now," she said, holding up her hand to stop me as the roomful of drooping, glassy eyes watched. I tried to move around it, but her hand moved too.

"You love him more than you love me!" I yelled and ran from the room.

"Gail, come back." I heard her say. "Stop being so dramatic." But I didn't go back. Instead, I cried on my bed and waited for her to come and tell me she was sorry. She never did.

I put the kitten back in the box. There's a lump in my throat, but now is not the time to be sad. This is a homecoming. At least it is for Chrissy and me. My mother says Philip won't be moving home right away but that it won't be long. I hope she's right; I've only seen him once in the three months he's been in the foster home.

The bedroom Chrissy and I will share is at the front of the house, farthest from the apartment's entrance. To get to it, we had to pass through the kitchen, living room, and Philip's bedroom. It's already furnished with two twin beds and a long dresser, leaving just enough space to get around. I claim the bed in front of the window, which means Chrissy gets the one under the slant. Our slant is splattered with small dark spots that remind me of rain clouds. My mother says it's mold from moisture in the walls and that there's nothing we can do about it. "I was lucky to find a place with three bedrooms," she says.

When the tour is over, my mother returns to the living room and Walter. Chrissy plays with the kittens. I go outside, stand on the top of our apartment stairs, and turn my face toward the hot summer sun.

From way up here, I loom above the pastel-colored houses of our neighbors. I wonder if we'll fit in. According to my mother, the area is known as "Portugee Hill" because so many Portuguese people live in this part of town, just like a lot of Italians live in the West End. My grandfather is part Portuguese, which means we are too. Maybe we do belong, but I'm not convinced. This neighborhood looks like it's meant for normal families, and we're anything but normal.

WE'VE BEEN IN the new apartment for a few months, and it hasn't been so bad having Walter here. Unlike Phil, he makes my mother laugh. She thinks it's funny when he tips his coffee mug onto its side to signal her for a refill. Walter likes to turn things into games. In the potato peeling game, he is the only contestant. The winning peel is the one that comes off in one continuous piece. My mother and Walter also prank each other by dumping cold water over the bathroom wall onto their unsuspecting partner while the other showers. The trick, they say, is to calculate carefully, to plan for what they call a "premeditative dousing." They fill the weapon in advance and hide it until the time is right. Otherwise, using the kitchen faucet will scald the person showering and tip them off as to what's coming.

Walter is also young. He's nineteen. My mother is twenty-eight. "What he lacks in age and experience, he makes up for with energy and enthusiasm," she says. Phil was older than my mother and always complained about pain in his back. He tilted forward at the waist when he walked. His big belly seemed to push his pants down, exposing the top of his crack whenever his t-shirt rode up. Walter is thin, fit, and taller than my mother, who is at least five-eight. He looks a lot like John Cougar with his dark shoulder-length hair parted on the left, which, if not tucked behind his ear, will fall over his face leaving one dark blue eye exposed.

Walter might even be the reason my mother has a job for the first time in my life. She's working at Action, a program that helps people pay their utility bills. She found out about the job while she was applying for assistance. Some days Chrissy and I walk to Action's second-floor office on Main Street and help sort paperwork and copy important documents on the Xerox machine. Other times, we play and make copies of our hands and faces instead.

During work visits, I watch my mother sit at her organized desk with her shoulders back and head high, eyes clear and bright. She greets people with a smile when they arrive. She listens and looks them in the eye when they speak to her. Her jeans and long-sleeved sweatshirts have been replaced with blouses and slacks. I'm fascinated by the way her fingers glide over the typewriter keys. I hear her tell somebody she types eighty words per minute. Until now, I didn't even know she knew how to type. Seeing her this way, I notice my own back straighten, and my eyes meet those of her co-workers I've come to know.

Everybody here loves my mother, and although I recognize her, in some ways, this woman is a stranger to me.

MY FAVORITE THING about living on Portugee Hill is the small wooded area behind our house. Even though it's really in the middle of a bunch of houses, the trees and bushes are overgrown enough to provide cover.

A thin path has been worn into the brush, maybe by a girl like me who needed a place to be alone.

I walk a few steps in, and there's a rock to my left. It's a perfect size. The boulder is half my height with a flat surface, just wide enough for me to stretch out on my back or sit cross-legged with my lessons spread out in front of me. There are enough leaves to hide me from the world but not so many as to block the sun. Before moving here, I never had a private space of my own.

Now, as I sit on my rock wrapped in the cool air of early spring, I think about how everything is finally falling into place: Philip is home, our family is together, and it doesn't seem like we'll have to leave this apartment any time soon.

It's time for me to get to work. Since early fall, after a sleepover when my friend Serena's mother brought us to her college, I've known what I'm supposed to do. While sitting at the back of the classroom that day, pretending to be one of the students, I felt like I was exactly where I belonged.

I open my dictionary to where I last left off and continue copying each word and definition into my notebook. When it's time for me to start college for real, I'll be ready.

9

ON THE WAGON

~1980~

I'll be ten tomorrow. Even though we don't have birthday parties, I can't wait to be in the double digits. When the phone rings, I'm sure somebody is calling to wish me an early happy birthday, maybe Little Nana or Debbie. Or my father, whom I haven't seen since we moved here a year ago. I answer because my mother is out, and Walter is still at work.

"Hello," I say.

"Hello. Is Waltie there?" It's Walter's father. He's speaking so softly that I can barely hear him. I cover my other ear with my hand.

"No, I think he's still at work."

"Tell him to call me," he says. There's a click and then silence. I'm still standing in the living room with the receiver in my hand when the shrill noise of the busy signal forces me to pull it away from my ear. I don't understand why he didn't say happy birthday. Walter's father has never been short with me. Neither of his parents has. For Christmas last year, they came with a bag full of presents for all of us. In fact, Walter's whole family has been like our family. At least, it was before the last time we went to his parent's house in Rockport.

They were all there that night, Walter's brothers, Kevin and Rich, and his sister, Beth. We took a taxi to the house and played Yahtzee around the long farmer's table in the kitchen. Everybody was having fun, drinking and laughing.

But like the parties at home, the more they drank, the louder their voices became. Soon they were talking over one another. I don't know how the fight started, but somebody threw a bottle. Walter's mother had blood on her sweater. She was screaming that Walter had thrown a Hibachi at his father, and his father's nose was broken. What I saw of his father's enraged, bloodied face from behind the living room chair where I crouched with Philip, something sure looked broken to me.

The four of us escaped by taxi; my mother, Chrissy, Philip, and I piled into the back seat. Near the end of the long driveway, we saw Walter's shadowy figure stumbling toward the main road, away from the house.

"Stop the car," my mother said to the driver.

As soon as Walter got in the front seat, he started talking in his loud drunken way. "Look at my fucking finger, Jackie. He broke my fucking finger." Walter's index finger was bent at a strange angle and looked at least three times the size of the others. "Holy shit, I can't fucking believe that son of a bitch broke my finger," he said again and again during the ride home, his hand and clothes covered in blood. Philip wouldn't stop crying.

That was a few months ago, and Walter's been "on the wagon" since. I'm afraid to tell him to call his dad for two reasons: I'm not his favorite person, and it sounds like bad news. Walter isn't great at handling things, and even sober, he's got a short fuse. Just last week, he blew up at me over a sink full of dishes. And that time, he did more than yell.

I'd been in the kitchen. My mother was nearby, standing in the doorway to the living room. "It's not my turn," I said, crossing my arms over my chest. "I did them last night."

My mother sighed and looked away. "I don't care whose turn it is. Just do them." Her voice was barely above a whisper. "It's Chrissy's turn," I said again.

My mother walked back into the living room, where Walter was watching TV. Being sober, he was the most patient version of himself. "I want to put her head through a fucking wall Jackie," he said, knowing I could hear him. I could picture her rolling her eyes.

But then she must've seen something in him—maybe he was bouncing his knee up and down fast, the way he does when he's agitated—because she came back into the kitchen with a new urgency in her voice. "Just do them," she said through clenched teeth. Just as she finished the sentence, Walter rushed past her. I could hear him come up behind me at the sink, where I was standing, refusing to get my hands wet. I didn't turn around—I didn't want him to see the fear on my face. He was close behind me when he yelled, "Just do what the fuck you're told and stop giving your mother a hard time!"

I said something—I always say something. I can't help it. My mother was still somewhere in the room when he snapped. I felt the wind from his fist as it sailed past the left side of my head and hit the wall above the sink. The sheetrock gave way to a hole that exaggerated the size of his knuckles.

Even after he'd left the room, my neck stayed stiff and my jaw tight. When I turned to see my mother standing in the doorway, she asked, "Why do you always have to piss him off like that?"

MY MOTHER IS still out when Walter gets home, so I have no choice but to give him the message. When he goes into the living room to return his father's call, I stay near the kitchen sink, where I can listen in. There isn't much to hear. "No," Walter says. And then, "What the fuck." I jump when he slams the receiver onto its cradle. Walter's eyes are wet as he passes through the kitchen on his way out the door. He doesn't acknowledge me. When he returns a half hour later, he's carrying a brown paper bag.

Later that night, I overhear Walter telling my mother that his youngest brother, Kevin, has committed suicide. They pass a joint back and forth as Janis Joplin blares through the stereo. Although he takes regular swigs from a bottle inside the paper bag, my mother doesn't say anything about his drinking.

I slip past them and into my bedroom, where I stay for the rest of the night unless I have to use the bathroom. I know enough to keep out of the way. Walter doesn't like me on a good day, and today is not a good day.

10

BROKEN

~ 1981 ~

Alita and I became friends when we moved to Portugee Hill. She lives on the top floor of an apartment building just a few houses away from ours. The apartments are close enough that we can wave to each other from our kitchen windows. Alita's parents are separated like mine, but her mother doesn't have a boyfriend, so it's just the two of them since she doesn't have any siblings either.

We have plans to hang out. We'll probably play Atari before going to Caesar's store for penny candy and then to the Friend Street playground. We need to get in as much fun as possible before summer ends and we start sixth grade.

I'm here so often there's no need to knock when I get to the door. Besides, Alita is expecting me. She starts talking as I walk into her bedroom. "Look what I have," she says. The tip of a joint is pinched between her fingers. She's holding it sideways in front of her face as though she's trying to see through it.

"Oh my God. Is that what I think it is?"

"Yup."

"Holy shit," I say. I can't believe she was able to get her hands on a joint before I could. "Where did you get that?"

"My mother had some," she says. Do you want to smoke it?"

"Of course," I say. I can't stop smiling.

After she gets a spoon and a small jar of peanut butter from the kitchen—to mask the smell of weed as we've heard—we walk the short path to my rock. Her mother will be home from work soon.

Alita gets to light it because she's the one who got it. When the flame from the lighter ignites the paper, she sucks in her breath, pulling the smoke into her lungs and making the weed pop and crackle.

She coughs. When she hands the joint to me, I turn it so the lit end is beneath my nose. I breathe in the smoke before I take it into my lungs for the first time. I squeeze the tightly rolled joint between my thumb and finger like I'm squashing a bug. My lips close on the end, and I suck as hard as I can. I expect it to feel like smoking a cigarette, but it's harsher. The rush of smoke burns my throat as I cough out the hit. The second time around, I go slow.

Just a few minutes later, everything feels heavy. My hands, my legs, my head—all are dead weight. And the best part—my mind isn't racing. Not one single thought of my mother's pretend migraines or that happy-drunk Walter is nearly gone. I'm not thinking about how neither of them has a job or that we're back to slicing off a chunk of orange government cheese for sandwiches when we have bread and eating Kix cereal for dinner when we have milk. All that, and I'm not afraid of anything. Now I understand why everybody loves getting high. I can't wait to do it again.

TURNS OUT, I like smoking pot even more than smoking cigarettes. I've been a daily cigarette smoker since I tried one for the first time a couple of months ago. That day, I had the apartment to myself. Philip was at daycare, and Chrissy was at a friend's house. While rummaging through my mother and Walter's bedroom, I found an open pack of Marlboros and a book of matches in the top drawer of my mother's dresser.

I took one out of the cardboard box and breathed in the smell of fresh tobacco. I held the cigarette between my fingers, like I'd seen it done, and rubbed the filter with my thumb before lighting it. It made me feel grown up. After a few practice puffs, I closed my dry lips around the filter and sucked in until the tip burned a bright hot orange. The thick smoke passed smoothly into my lungs as though I'd been doing it my whole life. I was born to be a smoker. I stayed on my mother's bed, chain-smoking and thumbing through Walter's Hustler magazine until it was time for somebody to return home.

The only problem with smoking is that I don't have any money, so the only way to get cigarettes is to steal them. When I'm behind Caesar's penny-candy counter, I slip a pack into my jacket pocket when he looks away.

I also take them from my mother. If she sends me to the store for two or three packs, I put them on the corner of the washing machine when I get home. I push one of the packs into the pile of dirty clothes next to the washer and cover it with a t-shirt or towel. A day or two later, I dig for my prize once I know it's been forgotten. On the rare occasion that she notices a missing pack, I help her find it in the pile.

Pot is another story; it's much harder to come by. What I can get is what I steal from Walter's stash. It's mostly roaches, small pieces of leftover joints. But sometimes, there's a baggie full of big, beautiful green buds—enough for me to break off a small amount and roll a skinny joint. Of course, I'm always worried he'll catch me, and as he'd say, there'll be hell to pay. Some days I have more reason to worry than others.

Like today, I can hear the Doors playing "People are Strange" from the bottom of the stairs. Walter is singing sloppily along. The Doors are one of his go-tos when getting "shit-o'd," a Walterism; his favorite term for getting intoxicated, obliterated, shit-faced, fucked-up, plastered, or just plain old drunk.

I take my time going up the stairs. I'm high and late getting home. We were riding around getting stoned with some older guy that my once-sister, Dawn knows, me in the back, her steering from the passenger seat. As with all the guys, she shows him some cleavage, and he lets her do whatever she wants.

Walter is still working at the wharf during the day, in the freezer or lumping fish. At night, he's often drunk, more so in the year since his brother died. I can usually tell whether he's got a buzz by looking at him, but if I can't see it, all I have to do is ask him what we're having for dinner. If he ignores the question or says something like, "What do I look like a fucking waiter?" he's probably sober, and I know enough to lie low. If Walter's answer is funny, like "great big booooowls of nuthin," he's either drunk or well on his way.

On rare occasions, he'll drink only enough to get a warm glow, and the rest of us will get a good night's sleep. More likely, though, he'll drink too much, which means there's a good chance he'll become violent. We kids will go to Little Nana's in a taxi. The next day we'll come home to more broken furniture. If he got arrested, my mother will bail him out. She'll try to hide the bruises he gave her, so sober Walter won't have to bear witness to the realities of drunken Walter.

I think that's why my mother is out most of the time. There's usually a note on the kitchen table when I get home from school, written to everybody, in her flawless handwriting: "I'm at the store. Be back soon. P.S. I love you more than I can say." When she is home, she's often in her dark bedroom with a sheet folded over the metal curtain rod, lying on her back with a cold, damp facecloth draped over her eyes. She says it's migraines. Walter says she's a dope-sick junkie.

The worse things get between my mother and Walter, the more run-down our apartment seems to become. At first, I didn't know why the wood under the kitchen floor swelled like a sprained ankle and broke through the linoleum. Now I know it was from the washing machine. The floor is uneven, and sometimes when the washer shakes, the hooked drain hose pops out of the kitchen sink and onto the floor. The hose thrashes around, blowing out dirty laundry water with force so powerful that it's nearly impossible to catch hold of. My mother says the water keeps making the floor worse, and the only way to stop it is for one of us to sit on the washer during the spin cycle to prevent it from shaking. I'm not the best person for the job—I'm so skinny and light, the washer doesn't even notice when I'm there.

I used to think that's where the cockroaches lived, in the rotting kitchen floor, like ants in an anthill. Then, one day, I heard my mother scream from the living room. She had taken the hairdryer out from the living room closet, plugged it in, turned it toward her wet hair, and switched it on. Along with warm air, out came a family of roaches that had been living in the dryer's motor. Now I know they live pretty much everywhere.

Like my mother, I do everything possible to avoid our apartment. I spend a lot of time babysitting for Debbie. These days, she's as absent as my mother, and I want to be the big sister to her kids that she was to me. Even though my mother and Phil, Debbie's father, have been separated for almost four years, she'll always be my sister. Her kids—Sage and Tommy—are my niece and nephew. When I babysit, Debbie sometimes leaves me with the kids for days. When the food starts to run out, and Tommy won't stop crying because he's lost his pacifier, I'll go to the apartment next door and use their phone to try and track her down. No matter how hard it is at Debbie's, I'd still rather be there than here at home.

Chrissy stays away as much as she can, too. She spends most of her time with friends. When she is home, she hides in our bedroom.

Poor Philip is trapped. At four years old, he can't get away on his own. I would take him with me if I could, but it's hard enough for me to find places to go. He comes to Little Nana's on the weekends, but other than that, he's stuck. He doesn't even get to come with Chrissy and me when we go with Nana Raizin since she doesn't know him. His father and other siblings—all adults now—are doing their own thing. All I can do is wait until I'm old enough to get a place, then he can come and live with me.

After a deep breath, I open the door to the kitchen. As soon as I step inside, I'm hit with the smell of burnt marijuana.

"Thank God," I whisper when I see Charlie sitting in the living room chair. Walter is always better when his friends are here, especially Charlie, who's funny and by far my favorite.

"What's that terrible stench?" Charlie asks with a grin when he sees me.

"It's your breath blowing back in your face," I say, smiling; sure, I've won this round of our ongoing battle of wits.

"No, Gail," he squeaks out around the hit from the joint he's holding in, "because of you, there is no wind." He beats me every time.

"There's the little pot thief now," Walter slurs. I ignore him and continue walking through the room toward my bedroom. My mother is sitting near him on the couch. Her glassy eyes are half-closed.

"Hey," she mumbles. "How was school?"

"Fine," I say as I pass by them. I keep my head down, so she won't see that my eyes look like hers.

11

ABANDONED

~1982~

Chrissy, Philip, and I have been at Little Nana's for five days by the time my mother finally calls. We were only supposed to stay for the weekend. Chrissy talks to her first. When it's my turn, I take the receiver and listen politely.

"I'm in detox," she says. "I'm sick, and I need to get well." *No shit. It doesn't take a rocket scientist to figure that one out.* "You guys will stay with Little Nana until I get out and get another place. We have to leave our things at the apartment, so we don't take the roaches with us," she says.

I don't tell her that I know we've been evicted. How could I not know the rent hasn't been paid for months? She and Walter were arguing daily about money—him drinking it and her shooting it. Nearly every Friday after Walter got paid, he'd get drunk and pass out. My mother would roll him for whatever cash was left from his paycheck so she could get high. The next day he'd think he spent it all.

Of course, we also hadn't had a phone for at least a year. No cable. The electricity had been shut off several times. Still, I don't want to hurt her with the truth of my knowing.

"We'll start over once I'm clean and healthy. It'll be different when I get out," she says.

"Okay." I wish I could say more. I want to say, "I love you and always will, no matter what." But I don't say anything; she doesn't deserve it.

I hold the phone against my ear and listen to her same old tired story, biting my lip to hold back the sting of tears. Screw her for not being here. She's always had a choice between her kids and dope, and she chooses to get high every time. I hand the phone to Little Nana and go outside where I can be alone.

On the front stairs, I light a cigarette and think about all that's happened in the last year—too much.

The worst of it started last spring, almost exactly a year ago. Alita was killed in a bike accident. She'd just turned twelve. We didn't even have the chance to be twelve together; my birthday wouldn't happen for three months. We were also in a fight and hadn't spoken for a week. Maybe she wouldn't have been on that bike if we hadn't been fighting. Perhaps she'd still be alive. Anyway, after Alita's death, I pretty much stopped going to school altogether. The truant officer filed a report with the court, and she's been trying to catch me since.

Then, in January, I was arrested for the first time. Three of us left our sixth grade, second-period class, and let ourselves into a vacant apartment. When we got to the attic, one of the girls pulled out a joint and lit it. A few minutes later, we heard the footsteps and voices of the police, who were on their way up the stairs. We were locked up at the Gloucester Police Department until our parents came to get us. I was charged with breaking and entering, trespass, and possession of drugs. I pled no contest to the charges and started reporting weekly to probation.

Since then, I've racked up a few more arrests. Just like when I was a kid and took the money out of Neil's pocket, the adrenaline rush of taking something that doesn't belong to me still makes me feel alive. Although now, it's worse than ever. No store is safe from my sticky fingers. A pack of gum, a notebook, tampons, ice cream—in the moment, anything will do. I can't even resist the lure of shiny coins or a pack of smokes in the console of an unlocked car.

I also had sex which wasn't as big of a deal as I thought it would be. The boy was twelve like me, and even though I had hoped for more, I knew he wouldn't want to be my boyfriend any more than Danny had.

I know some people matter, and some people don't. I'm one of the ones who don't—a throw-away. Part of it, I think, is that I'm unlovable. I'm argumentative, and I'm a thief. I'm always looking for a fight. I don't think I want to keep people away, but I can't seem to help it. These days I only hang out with people who are like me.

A COUPLE OF days after my mother's call, Chrissy and I take a taxi to the abandoned apartment. We don't have anybody to bring us, and we're still too young to drive at fourteen and twelve.

The place is eerily quiet. It doesn't feel like home anymore—just a few small rooms with slanted ceilings, three flights up from the ground. There are no lights and no heat. The cats are gone; I don't know where, but what they've left behind in the litter box stings my eyes. There's a rotten smell coming from inside the dark refrigerator. Our kitchen table is still here, and the sink is filled with dishes. The pile of dirty clothes next to the washing machine is still waiting to be washed.

Our bedroom looks the same as when we last slept here, with sheets and blankets still on the beds. Moisture has curled the edges of the posters we hung to cover the mold. Now, brown-greenish spots have joined the black and taken over most of both walls. We pick through what remains of our lives here and gather all the pictures and belongings we can carry.

After closing the door behind me for the last time, I stand on the porch as I did when we first moved here. I look over to the apartment window where Alita used to be. And I think about our other neighbors. While they were fishbowls to us, we were on stage for them. Throughout the past two and a half years, while we saw them eating dinner and watching television through their brightly lit windows, they saw a drunk Walter stumbling up and down the stairs. They watched people come and go, including the police, who often took a handcuffed Walter back down with them. I'm ready to say goodbye to those who witnessed it and did nothing—good riddance to them and this miserable place.

12

A MATTER OF TIME

~1983~

"Do you want to make some money?" Aunt Julie asks in her quietest voice, although she's terrible at whispering. Doesn't matter. We're in the kitchen at Little Nana's, and my great-grandmother is in the living room. She can't hear over the television anyway.

"How?" I ask, although I have a pretty good idea. I've known for a long time that my aunt does things with guys for money and that my mother does too. I'm thirteen, not stupid.

"We'll see," she says with a grin that always makes me uneasy.

"What do I have to do?"

"I'll tell you when we get outside."

Once on the porch, she turns to face me and starts talking as soon as the door closes. "All you have to do is give him a hand job," she says. "It'll be quick, too, because you're so young and pretty. I promise."

Behind her, parked on the street below, I can see a navy-blue double cab truck. It's shiny and looks new. Even though the back window is in view, the tint is too dark for me to see inside.

"I don't know, Julie." I'm already starting to feel sick thinking about it.

"Don't worry," she says. "Let's just go for a ride and see what happens."

I slide down the hot iron railing, meet Aunt Julie at the bottom of the stairs, and follow her to the waiting truck.

When she opens the passenger door, a gust of cool air, along with the scent of pine, escapes from inside. I welcome the air conditioning on this hot August day, and the smell is a big step up from the cars of most of her friends. It's so clean inside I feel like I should take off my shoes. Aunt Julie slides in first, her jeans smooth against the black leather seat. I climb up and sit next to her.

She flattens her hair with her hands and starts talking before I have a chance to close the door. "My niece is young, you know." She sits on the edge of the seat and turns the rearview mirror to face her. The small tree that hangs from it swings back and forth. She licks her thumb and finger and runs them along the hair that frames her face to tame the flyaways. She speaks without looking away from the mirror. "She's worth a lot."

"Yes, I see that," he says, although his accent is strong. He looks past Aunt Julie directly at me through the space behind her. I wear hand-me-downs as usual, but today I look mature in tight, green Jordache jeans and an off- the-shoulder black sweater.

The man is thin, probably tall. He's older, for sure, older than my mother, I bet, but surprisingly, he's not gross. He's not even ugly. His hair is slicked back away from his face the way most of the Gloucester Italian men keep it. I appreciate that he doesn't wink at me—I hate when guys do that.

"She's pretty, too," Aunt Julie adds.

He nods. I look out the window and pretend to be interested in a young-looking girl pushing a baby carriage.

By the time we get to his house, I know the man's name is John, he's Italian, and he's married.

John pulls into a driveway and then into the garage of a neat, one-story house just past the boulevard. He leads us through a doorway and into a kitchen that's as clean as his truck. Like him, we take off our shoes before stepping onto the tiled kitchen floor. There's a placemat in front of each of the four chairs surrounding a glass table. The counters are spotless. I've never been inside a house in this part of town, and I feel out of place.

The living room is as immaculate as the kitchen. I'm careful not to touch anything. It looks more like a showroom, not lived in at all. The plush white carpet still has lines from a vacuum cleaner, and my white socks look dingy against it. There are splashes of gold in the fixtures and frames, and everything is polished and bright.

We follow John into another living room. This one we can sit in. I choose a mint green overstuffed armchair, where I sit so close to the edge of the cushion that my knees touch the ottoman. I'm ready to move quickly if I have to.

When John leaves the room, Aunt Julie hands me a Valium. "Here," she says, "this will help." She drops the pill into my shaky hand. I put it on my tongue and gratefully swallow it dry like I've learned to do in the year I've been taking them regularly.

"I don't think I can do this," I say quietly.

"You can," she says. "Think about all the money you'll make."

John comes back with a drink in each hand. Kahlua sombreros. I take the glass and ease back on the chair. Money sure does sound good. I'll be able to buy my own pot. Cigarettes too. That way, I won't have to steal them from my mother and her boyfriend or take Little Nana's. It's not like Little Nana has a ton of money. Her social security check barely lasts through the third week of the month; still, she'd never tell me no.

If I can do this, maybe I can even make enough cash to get my own place. Since our most recent eviction, we've been living at a campground in West Gloucester for the last month. The four of us, my mother, Walter, Philip, and I, share a room in one of the cabins. Chrissy, now fifteen, has been spending most nights at a friend's home.

We'll stay at Camp Annisquam until my mother gets another place from which we'll inevitably be evicted. That's how it goes every time; my mother stops doing heroin for a while, gets an apartment, things are good, and then they're not. We never have more than a day or two of warning before it's time to move again.

The Valium is starting to work. I slide back until my head rests against the chair and stretch my legs out in front of me. Everything is beginning to seem possible. I take a big gulp of the sweet drink and trace the heat from the cold liquor down my throat behind closed eyes.

"Gail," Aunt Julie says from far away. Her voice startles my eyes open. I've forgotten where I am until I see John standing in front of the couch. Aunt Julie is still sitting next to where he had been before I closed my eyes. They're both looking at me.

"Let's go to the other room," he says.

I don't say anything. If I want to be treated like an adult, I need to act like one. I take another sip of the drink and put it down on the side table. The glass hits the surface hard, splashing thick liquid onto the rug. I ignore it and push myself up and out of the chair. I'm swaying a little. My legs feel so rubbery, I'm surprised they can hold me up. I don't remember telling them to move, but I must have because I'm following John.

As we walk toward the end of a short hallway, I hear the music video that Aunt Julie is watching—Prince is singing about having class. For a moment, I feel something, my stomach tightens like an angry fist, and then it's gone, thanks to the booze and Valium.

A few seconds later, it's quiet. John has shut the door behind me, and he's moving toward the window to close the blinds. We're in a bedroom that is as perfect as the rest of the house. It looks like something out of a magazine. The same thick white rug covers the floor, and the dark wood furniture looks sharp against it. A king-sized bed is centered between two tall windows. It's covered with a puffy floral comforter that matches the curtains, and there are more pillows on this one bed than we have at Little Nana's or any apartment we've ever lived in. Most are different shapes and sizes, so the bigger ones are on the bottom. It makes me think John must be okay to live in a place like this.

"You want to sit?" he asks, pointing to the foot of the bed just a few feet in front of me. He sits as though to show me how it's done. I'd been caught up in the room and again forgotten why I was here with my cloudy head. I don't want to look at him, but I have to. He looks down at his lap when I do glance in his direction.

I think about changing my mind as I move toward the bed. But there's no turning back now. *Grow or go, Gail. It's time.* I take a deep breath and hold it until I'm sitting on the bed to John's left. I leave enough space between us so he'll have to reach for me. My feet dangle above the floor.

"What do you want to do?" he asks, still without looking at me. His accent is so thick that he's hard to understand.

"I don't know," I say, unsure of my choices.

"Can I touch you?" he asks.

"No, I don't want you to do that."

"Do you want to touch me?"

"Okay."

"With your mouth?"

"No."

"With your hand?"

"Okay."

"Okay," he says before standing. John looks down as he unfastens his belt, unhooks the clasp, and unzips his pants. I chew on my thumbnail and keep my eyes on the floor at his feet, away from this private act of undressing, until I see his slacks around his ankles, their crisp creases bent. The clinking sound of his belt buckle hitting the floor is amplified by the silence in the room.

When he sits back down, John closes the gap between us. I glance in his direction and then back down at the floor. He's close enough for me to smell the clean scent of his aftershave and hear his quick, shallow breaths. He's waiting for me.

"I'm sorry," I say, "I don't know what to do."

He reaches over, takes my hand, and puts it on his penis. He wraps his hand around mine. He squeezes until the pressure is as firm as he likes. Then, he moves my hand in his, slowly at first, and then faster. As his breathing quickens, I don't make a sound. I'm focused on the dresser against the wall in front of the bed. It's long with fancy handles and little drawers across the top. Perfume bottles are arranged there, and a jewelry box—his wife's things. I wonder where she is and if she has any idea what's happening on her bed while she's away.

John finishes quickly with a noise that makes me think he might cry. Maybe it was so fast because he likes how my small hand feels against him—a hand that will take eighth-grade quizzes come fall.

He picks up a towel I didn't know was there and cleans the sticky mess off my hand before wiping himself and pulling up his pants. We're both quiet. I wait on the bed until he's dressed. John still doesn't look at me when he hands me forty dollars from his front pocket—a twenty-dollar bill and two tens.

In the bathroom across the hall, I stare at my reflection in a mirror surrounded by giant round movie star light bulbs. I thought I would look as different as I feel, older, maybe. Deformed. But I look exactly the same.

Gratefully, people won't be able to see the truth of what I am now. My cheeks feel hot. I push the lump in my throat back down and reach for one of the fluffy pink towels that hangs next to the sink. I wet the corner and scour my right hand like a doctor scrubbing in for surgery. I splash water on my face before running my wet hands over my hair. When I'm done, I fold the towel lengthwise and hang it on the bar with the damp part in the back so the wife won't notice anything out of place.

Once back in John's living room, I hand Aunt Julie her ten-dollar cut. "I knew you could do it," she says, smiling. I sit in the chair I left just half an hour ago. When I pick up my drink, the ice cubes still clink against the sides of the glass. Aside from a new video playing on the screen, everything is the same as before. It all seems normal; I can almost pretend I was never in John's bedroom. But if I'm being honest with myself, I'm glad to have gotten the whole thing out of the way; it was only a matter of time.

13

RENDEZVOUS

~1983~

During the second week of eighth grade, just a few weeks after leaving Camp Annisquam and moving into our newest apartment, I gather the courage to call John on my own. It's been a couple of months since our first meeting, and Aunt Julie doesn't know that he slipped me his number the last time we saw each other.

I make the call from Little Nana's. She's on the couch watching soap operas, and Aunt Julie is out. John is glad I called, he says, before we plan to meet at a nearby cemetery.

I pop a Valium I bought from Russell, the lonely middle-aged guy who lives upstairs from Little Nana. He always has plenty for sale. He keeps asking me to let him touch me for them—a trade-off—but with all the money I'm making with John, I don't need to take him up on the offer.

After smoking a joint in Little Nana's backyard, I walk to our rendezvous spot. The street is quiet, but I can't help but think that somebody will see me getting into an older guy's truck. I let my bangs hang, covering my face, and hope it's enough of a disguise. This time, Aunt Julie isn't here to provide an explanation.

When John arrives, I climb into his truck as quickly as possible. We say hello, but don't speak again until we're at his house. He's the first to break the silence.

"Do you want a drink?" he asks. He's walking behind me through the kitchen.

"No, thank you," I say over my shoulder. I want to get this over with. I walk directly to the bedroom and take my place at the foot of the bed.

John doesn't close the door; he doesn't need to—we're the only ones here. He's standing just inside the doorway when he looks me in the eye for the first time.

"Can we have sex?" he asks.

In an instant, I'm aware that we are alone. Nobody knows I'm here. I'm in a house with a man I don't really know. His house, his bedroom. He can do whatever he wants, and I'm certainly not strong enough to stop him. I'm wondering if I can get past him.

John must see something in my expression because he steps out of the doorway, making enough space for me to get by. It's enough to show me that I'm free to go and he's not a threat.

"I can't," I say.

"Please. I won't hurt you. I promise."

"No," I say again. But I'm thinking about it. What difference does it make? I can't imagine anybody wanting me as a girlfriend now, not after the things I've already done. At least John is nice to me.

We meet in the middle. I agree to take off my shirt before I please him.

I compromise more every time we meet. First, I take off my bra. After that, I let him touch my breast with his hand. And the next, his mouth.

TURNS OUT, JOHN always wants to see me. By the end of October, we're meeting a couple of times a week. The more I allow, the more money he gives me. I'm making so much that it's getting harder to explain whatever I buy. Not that anybody ever asks.

Although I've never seen a normal family up close, I'm guessing ours doesn't compare. Shouldn't a mother know when her child is in trouble? My mother is oblivious. I dare her to pay attention—to recognize how fucked up my life has become. I want to tell her where I'm getting the money. I will if she'd just ask.

At first, I hid the big things. Then I started wearing new clothes underneath an old outfit when I went home like I did when I used to steal them. Gradually, I wove the new things into my once-pathetic wardrobe.

Now I bring my purchases home in bags.

One of the bigger upsides to having money is that I can buy my own weed. I'm off Walter's radar now that I'm not stealing his anymore. I also have plenty of pills—they're easy to find with money. I'm taking Valium or Xanax most days. They give me a little bit of peace. Within minutes of a hit or half an hour of swallowing a pill, my hands quit shaking, and my shoulders relax.

The best thing about being high is that I stop worrying about my mother. I've known for at least a year that she's addicted to heroin, shit that's on a whole different level than the drugs I use. She finally confessed before going into her last detox. Now it's common knowledge. Aunt Julie knows, and Big Nana, even Little Nana says stuff when she thinks I'm not listening.

Thanks to my mother's friend Kathy, I also know heroin can kill people. Last year, I was at a party with Aunt Julie when I learned that little tidbit. After choking down a couple of beers, I had to pee. I found the bathroom and knocked on the door.

"Just a minute," a raspy female voice said. I immediately recognized it as Kathy's. She and my mother have been heroin buddies for years.

I danced in the hallway until I couldn't hold it any longer. "I have to go!" I yelled through the door, over the noise of the party.

I rushed in as soon as the lock disengaged, closed the door behind me, and sat to relieve myself. There was just enough room for us in the small space. Kathy wordlessly continued her task as I did my business.

With the vanity opposite me, I could see my face in the mirror above the sink on the right side and Kathy standing closer to the wall to my left. A torn cigarette filter, a lighter, and a small empty packet lay on the counter in front of her. Her sleeve was pushed past her elbow, and a long elastic band was tied around her upper arm. With her right hand, she stuck the tip of a needle into the small piece of cigarette filter she had already placed in a spoon. She pulled up the syringe's plunger to draw a brownish liquid that had absorbed into the filter like a sponge. I was fascinated.

After tapping a vein on the crook of her arm, she inserted the needle. I winced and briefly looked away. The drug's effect was instantaneous. I looked back just in time to see her fall against the wall and watch the blues of her eyes disappear, leaving only white. Her lifeless hand fell from the needle, which popped out of her arm, and shot blood across the mirror.

"Hey!" I yelled, trying to stand while pulling up my pants.

Her eyes opened suddenly. She quickly pulled the tourniquet from her arm and covered the hole with her finger. She grinned and said, "Shit, that stuff's good."

It all clicked at that moment—why my mother went out so often, why she spent so much time in the bathroom, and why we never had any spoons. Now that I know what my mother does in the bathroom, I hate when she goes in there. It makes me wonder what will happen to us if she dies and whether Chrissy, Philip, and I will be able to stay together. All I can do is save up some money and be ready just in case.

CHRISTMAS IS A week away, and I've finally agreed to let John have sex with me. That makes today a two-ten-milligram Valium day. I swallow them before we get to his house. He doesn't offer me a drink anymore. We go right from the garage, through the house, to the bedroom.

I wait while John removes the decorative pillows from the bed, stacking them neatly on a chair in the corner of the room. When he closes the blinds, I pull off my jeans and underwear and quickly get under the blanket. He strips off all his clothes, lays them neatly on a chair in the corner, and pulls the blanket back just enough to slide in beside me. He tries to touch me, to get me ready, or to make it seem like we're on a date, but I push his hand away.

John gets out of bed, goes into the bathroom across the hall, and returns with lubricant on his fingers. He rubs it on himself before getting back into bed. I'm looking at a print of Jesus hanging on the wall on my side of the bed—the wife's side—while he moves over me. In the picture, Jesus is wearing a crown of two-inch thorns, and there's blood oozing from the cuts on his head. Still, even though he's being tortured, his eyes are bright blue, and his rosy pink cheeks are smooth.

"Is this okay?" John asks as he presses himself against me.

When I don't respond, he continues to push his way in. It hurts more than it did when I had sex the one time before; of course, that time, I was with a boy, and this time I'm with a man. I almost tell him to stop. Instead, I hold my breath and wait for the pain to pass. It does. I notice the pretty swirling pattern on the ceiling. I can feel him on me and in me, but I'm thinking about other things, like what would happen if his wife came home and how I wish I could tell Aunt Julie. How I wish I could tell somebody.

After a few minutes, John's breathing becomes quick and shallow. His body is rigid before he shudders, grunts like an animal, and collapses on top of me, his body so heavy that I struggle to take a full breath.

"I'm sorry," he says and rolls off of me.

I jump up as though he's been holding me down. All I want is to get away. Before John can catch his breath, I'm dressed and on my way to the bathroom.

This time I don't look at myself in the mirror. There's nothing there I want to see. This time I take a perfectly folded pink facecloth out of the closet, wash him off of me, and leave it on the counter next to the sink in a ball. So what if his wife finds it? That's his problem, not mine.

John pays me before we leave his house. He doesn't look at me when he hands me one hundred dollars. "Thank you," he says while pressing the folded bills into my hand, as though I'd held open a door for him instead of letting him fuck me. I don't respond. If he had wanted more from me than a warm, young body, or if he was unhappy with my performance or lack thereof, he doesn't say. That's good because I couldn't care less.

We don't speak during the ride to the Main Street arcade, where I'll have him drop me off. While he watches the road, I watch the ocean and think about what I can do with all that money.

14

SPLINTERING

~1983~

When I get home from school, Rena, our family social worker, is sitting in one of the living room chairs in our new apartment. My mother is in the other. Since most of the place can be seen from the kitchen entry, my mother was able to skip the usual parade of rooms, but that also means Rena sees me at the same time I see her. It's too late for me to walk back out the door.

The woman is clearly uncomfortable. She's sitting as straight and proper as the low deep wooden chair allows. She's still wearing her brown wool jacket, and the handles of her purse are hanging loosely around her forearm. The mere sight of her makes my neck and shoulders stiffen—her visits tend to happen right before the splintering of our family.

What's unusual about this visit is that my mother is here at three o'clock in the afternoon. She's usually gone before I wake up and still out when I get home. If she does stop in during the day, she often goes directly into the bathroom to get a heroin fix before leaving again. She must have had notice of this visit, which is strange in itself because, in the three or four years that Rena has been supervising our family, she usually shows up unannounced. Also, Walter isn't here, and lately, he's been home more than my mother.

"Rena needs to talk to you," my mother snaps and stubs out her cigarette in the ashtray sitting on the flat arm of her chair. She doesn't look at me. I'm in trouble, but I don't know why. I haven't had any new arrests, and if this had anything to do with stealing, I'm sure the cops would be here instead of social services.

Rena stands. "I'd like to speak with you privately," she says. "Let's go outside." I follow her out the door and down the back stairs.

Rena's small, beige social-worker car is parked along the curb on the opposite side of the street. I'm not surprised I didn't notice it on my way in; it blends in with its surroundings, much like Rena. She unlocks the doors and drops down into the driver's seat. I hesitate after opening the passenger door. Maybe this is a trick. She could be taking me away. If I had any other option, I'd take it. Unfortunately, I don't, so I slip into the worn seat beside her.

She speaks as soon as I'm seated.

"How are things going?"

"Okay, I guess."

"Are you going to school?"

"I went today," I say, grateful for this rare truth. Some days I still go to classes and pretend I'm an ordinary girl talking about things like clothes, boys, and music. Occasionally, I raise my hand, hoping for a correct answer that seldom comes because I'm so far behind.

"I'm having some concerns," Rena blurts, turning slightly toward me in her seat. The stupid brown handles of her purse are still hanging at her elbow.

Thankfully, I'm already looking down when she continues.

"I've gotten some information from your doctor that you've had sexual intercourse with a man over forty."

The feeling of being underwater comes on so quickly that I instinctively take a deep breath and hold it for a moment, fearing I might drown otherwise. It feels almost the same as when I pocket a pack of gum and hear the store security voice behind me say: "Stop right there." Except this is worse—so much worse.

"That's not true," I finally say after at least a minute of silence, my voice weak and unconvincing. Rena is watching me. As always, I'm grateful for my hair, a wall that hangs between us, blocking my face from her view. Despite being a great liar, I'm afraid my expression will give me away. Be cool, I think, as I focus my attention on the cuticle of my right thumb, and bite at the ragged edge as though it's a task that requires my undivided attention. My heart feels like it might beat out of my chest.

"Okay," she says. "But, it's a serious allegation, and I'm required to follow up."

I don't respond. My head is spinning. I saw my doctor a month ago for a urinary tract infection, but I don't remember whether or not he even examined me. Is it possible for my doctor to know I had sex with a man? I don't see how he could. And how could he know his age? I mean, I don't even know how old John is. It doesn't matter; either way, Rena knows something, and it's pretty damn near the truth.

She doesn't say anything else. She's known me long enough to know I'm done talking. After just ten minutes in her car, she lets me go.

Instead of going inside, I sit on the cold granite slab staircase at the front of our building, light a cigarette and watch Rena's taillights disappear around the corner. I have a feeling my denial won't be the end of this. It might not be the worst thing, though. Maybe my mother and I will finally have a real, honest conversation.

A FEW DAYS after Rena's visit, my mother and I take a taxi to see my doctor for an itchy rash that has spread from between the fingers of my right hand, to my arm, and now to my face. It's the first time we've been mostly alone since Rena dropped the bomb.

We've just gotten into the back seat when my mother turns to look me in the eye. She lowers her voice and says, "You're not in any trouble, but we need to go to the police station tomorrow." Her words are clear, and her tone is even, as though, like Rena, she's practiced this conversation in the mirror. While I usually crave her attention, right now, it's making me anxious. I look down at my lap before responding.

"Why do I have to go to the police station if I'm not in trouble?"

"They want to talk to you. Somebody told Rena that you've been having sex for money. Even if that's true, I want you to know you haven't done anything wrong. I'll be there with you."

I have that drowning feeling again. I wish I had a Valium. I rub the side of my face with the back of my hand, trying not to scratch it, and wait for her to say more. We both stay quiet. I wonder what the police will ask me, whether anybody else knows, and if I'll be arrested.

It's late afternoon when the taxi leaves my mother and me back at our apartment. It's too late for me to go anywhere without a good reason, which I don't have. Everybody's home: my mother, Walter, Chrissy, and Philip. We still don't have a phone, so I can't even call Dawn or Aunt Julie to ask them what I should do. I'm trapped.

AT THIRTEEN, I'M already well acquainted with the newer brick building that serves as Gloucester's police station and courthouse. This time though, I didn't get here in the back of a cruiser, and I don't have court or probation. I have no idea what to expect today.

My mother tells the man behind the counter that we have an appointment. A few minutes later, another man comes out to greet us. He opens the locked door and steps aside so we can enter.

"I'm Detective Adams," he says and motions with his head for us to follow behind him. He moves quickly through the familiar booking area and along a hallway filled with posters, notices, and closed doors. The detective is tall. His black polo shirt is tucked into khaki pants, which are topped with a gun belt and holster. His brown hair is cut so short it makes him look like a soldier, as does the freshly shaved line that runs straight across the back of his neck.

He stops at an open door on the right and again moves aside. I follow my mother through a door that opens into a small room. The door bumps against one of the two chairs in front of a paperwork-covered desk. Three tall filing cabinets take up the leftover wall space.

The detective introduces us to a man sitting behind the desk. They both look the same to me, except the new one isn't as neatly dressed as the other. He's wearing a t-shirt. When he stands, I notice he's also wearing jeans. His smile makes him seem friendly. "Hi, Jackie," he says and shakes her hand. He obviously knows my mother.

He turns his attention to me. "I'm Detective Kenney," he says as he puts his hand down.

"I'd shake your hand, but…."

"That's okay," I say, momentarily grateful for the poison ivy covering my face. The rash is so severe that my right eye is nearly swollen shut.

"Please, have a seat," he says, motioning to the chairs. I can tell he's the good cop.

For a moment after we sit, the two detectives stand shoulder to shoulder. I think they're doing it on purpose, to show this woman and her child who is in charge.

Good Cop sits and is the first to speak. "We'll get right to it. Do you know why you're here today, Gail?"

"I think so," I say quietly.

"We've gotten some information that you've been involved in a prostitution ring," says the one still standing. I almost laugh.

"Prostitution ring." The phrase sounds like some organized underground operation instead of a random group of old guys looking to get their rocks off. It's not like we walk the streets wearing tight leather pants and four-inch heels like the working girls on *T.J. Hooker*. This guy is definitely the bad cop.

I fidget in my seat, trying to relieve my itchy eye by rubbing it with the back of my hand. The lotion isn't helping. My mother takes in a loud, deep suck of breath.

Good Cop speaks again. "We'll be able to treat you as a victim, given your age, if you cooperate with this investigation. Tell us the names of the men you've been involved with and anybody else who participated.

Bad Cop chimes in, "But if you decide not to cooperate, then we will have no choice but to prosecute you along with the others."

The others? What others? They know something for sure. If they know about the others, then they should be here too. I'm thinking as fast as I can, but I'm sure they know more than me.

Good Cop speaks next. "Does your Aunt Julie bring you to meet men?"

I can hear my mother inhale as she turns to look at me. "My sister?" Her reaction is confirmation that she didn't know about Aunt Julie.

"Yes," I say, again looking down at my lap while giving them the expected answer. I feel bad for my mother, although I don't know how she's so surprised, especially when I've known for months about her making money. If she'd been doing her job as a mother, we wouldn't even be here. Good Cop hands her a tissue.

"When did Julie start introducing you to men?" Bad Cop asks. I hate him already.

I tell them about the first time Aunt Julie invited me for a ride in the truck with a guy, the pills she gave me, that she's introduced me to other men over the last few months, and that she's the one who arranges the meetings by phone. Following a call, we'll meet a man at a predetermined place or go by taxi to his apartment. I don't know any last names. We identify them by the car they drive, where they live, their first name, or an unusual characteristic; the old guy with the little silver car, the man in the second-floor apartment across from Richdale, Bobby, or the guy with the hole in his neck.

And I tell them about John. I give them his last name because I have to give them something. He's still the only paying guy I've let go all the way. I feel bad about telling on him, almost as bad as I do for my mother, but he's far from innocent, too.

Good Cop asks for specifics about the other men. "Paul had a blue car," I tell him. "He picked us up, we drove to a place in the woods, and I touched him." He's writing down my answers. "Where did he pick you up? Where did you go? Who is we? Where did you touch him? On his penis? Did he touch you?"

The single window behind Good Cop is so dirty it looks like dusk outside, even though it's barely noon. We've been here for more than two hours.

Bad Cop speaks. "Did you touch him with your hand? Did you perform oral sex on him?"

Each time, I answer with few words while searching the edges of my ragged fingernails for the slightest morsel of something to nibble.

The fluorescent lights are too bright. My back is aching. I need a cigarette, and my face burns with an itch I can't scratch. There's barely enough room to cross my legs between my chair and the desk, never mind stretch them. I'm well aware these men care as much for my well-being as the men they're looking to arrest.

Three hours have passed when Good Cop pushes his chair back from the desk and stands for the second time since we arrived. We are free to leave. Bad Cop assures us that they'll be in touch. Finally, I'm a spent resource.

Unlike the walk to the police station, I don't try to keep up with my mother. Even if I could match her speed, I wouldn't know what to say. Whatever comes next, I can't depend on her for help.

THE NEXT MORNING, I call Dawn from Little Nana's. Aunt Julie isn't home, and Little Nana is in the living room watching The Price is Right. I start talking as soon as I hear Dawn's voice on the line.

"They know, and I'm going to run."

"Who knows what?"

"The cops—they know about me making money."

"What the fuck are you talking about?" she asks.

I tell her about the social worker, the meeting, and what I said to the police. "I'm going to Texas to live with my father," I say.

"Then I'm going with you," she says. I know she means it. Dawn always has my back.

We meet at the arcade a few hours later to work out the details. I call John by pay phone; he's the only person I can think of who can help. He's also one of the only people with something to lose if I stay here. The police know his name, but they need me to confirm it. I'm sure of that much.

John picks us up in his truck and drives to his house. He paces while I tell him the story.

"We'll have to get to Boston," Dawn says. He agrees to drive us into the city.

"And we need money for plane tickets," I say. I'm starting to get excited about leaving Gloucester behind.

"How much?" he asks in his Italian accent.

"Two hundred and fifty dollars," I say. I have no idea how much we'll need, but that sounds like a lot. I feel guilty taking money from him. Although I've known him for barely six months, John is one of the closest people I have to a friend. But I don't have any choice.

The next night, long after everybody has gone to sleep, I creep past my mother and Walter on their mattress in the living room, through Philip's bedroom, and out the front door.

15

DETENTION

~1984~

D awn leaves me sitting near the airport door with our bags while she goes to buy the airline tickets. If everything goes as planned, we'll soon be on my father's doorstep. I would have called to let him know we're coming, but I only have an address.

I bite my nails and watch the doors open and close as travelers come and go. I'm worried the police will show up any minute and bring me back home. I've convinced myself that Philip woke up as I passed through his bedroom on my way out of the apartment. Maybe he awakened my mother, and she went to a neighbor's house to call the police. Or the police could be talking to John, who will surely crack to save himself by telling them he drove Dawn and me to Boston in the early morning hours.

Or, perhaps somebody thought two girls under sixteen traveling alone looked suspicious and alerted the authorities. Maybe the police were already on their way when we left the bus station, our first location. That's where we met a friendly security guard who showed me the lost and found, and I replaced my trash bag with a small suitcase. Of course, he could have just been pretending to be nice—buying time while waiting for the police to arrive. The cops can easily track our taxi from the Greyhound station to Logan Airport.

Dawn finally comes around the corner smiling, two plane tickets to Texas in her hand. I don't know how she did it with only our birth cer-tificates, but it doesn't matter. We're almost free. She grabs her bag and my hand and leads the way through security. On our way to the gate, we walk fast. Then we run.

We're the last to board. Once in my seat, I stay low, still expecting the police to run onto the plane, point at us, and yell: "That's them!"

The sun is starting to come up when the door finally closes. I'm seated next to the window, watching an empty luggage cart drive away. Before today, I'd never even seen an airplane in real life. Now, I'm inside one. Soon, we'll be up in the sky.

Holy shit—we'll be up in the sky.

I grip the arms of my seat when we start moving. If only I could smoke. They don't allow it until we're in the air. The loud noise from the engines drowns out the sounds of the people around me. When I close my eyes, it feels like I'm alone. I keep them closed until the wheels are off the ground. After a few minutes in the air, my stomach begins to settle, and I feel disconnected from the world. The separation makes me feel free in a way I've never known.

When I open my eyes, all I can see through our small window is the light blue sky above a blanket of fluffy, white clouds. It all feels perfect at first; until I feel a bump. There aren't any potholes in the sky. I listen for changes in the sound of the engines. I'm suddenly terrified all over again. Anything could go wrong, making the plane plummet to the ground in a fiery explosion. I almost laugh at the irony in my fear of dying when that's been my desire for as long as I can remember.

DAWN IS HER usual, cool-as-a-flirty-cucumber self. She's already convinced a middle-aged man seated near us to buy us each a rum and coke. As soon as the plastic cup is in my hand, I relax. Relief is on the way.

Now that I'm out of panic mode, I'm thinking about home. Maybe I'll miss my mother, maybe not. It seems like she's always been far away. I can't imagine this will feel any different. I'll definitely miss Chrissy and Philip. And Little Nana, of course. She loves me. I know she does. She's just too old to help any of us. Anyway, I'll be able to write letters and visit once the dust settles. I keep all my thoughts to myself.

AFTER LANDING, WE follow the carry-on-only crowd into the hot Texas air. We get on a bus that leaves us at a stop outside the airport. We'll hitchhike and ride for free as we have limited funds—less than fifty dollars now. Dawn sticks out her thumb while I sit on my bag. A few minutes later, as we're running to an eighteen-wheeler, Dawn tells me to keep my mouth shut and let her do all the talking. That's fine with me.

The driver is a heavy black man with an even heavier southern accent. He laughs when Dawn tells him where we're going. "Shit," he says, drawing out the I so much it sounds like she-it. "That's half a day away." When Dawn had asked for the earliest, cheapest flight to Texas, she didn't realize Texas was so damn big. He takes us outside of Houston and points us in the right direction.

Our next ride is a small blue pickup truck driven by an old white guy with silver hair. He can't take us to Fort Worth either but says he'll help. He talks into his CB radio. "I have a couple of girls looking for a ride." He turns his face toward the driver's side window and lowers his voice when he says, "They're young, so don't expect anything." I smile at his naivety. I think it's sweet how he's trying to shield us from the world.

I don't want to get into the next eighteen-wheeler that stops to give us a ride; the driver makes me feel uneasy. But we're in the middle of nowhere, and Dawn has decided. The guy's accent is so thick that it sounds like he's speaking a different language. His greasy hair falls over his shoulders in thick, loose black curls. His dingy tank top looks whiter than it is against the dark of his skin, and one of the straps of his faded dungaree overalls has fallen to his side.

Dawn climbs into the cab ahead of me. The man pulls the curtain aside while he motions for us to go into the truck's bed. Darkness surrounds us in the compartment when he lets the curtain fall.

The cabin is heavy with heat and the stench of his body odor, and Dawn lights a cigarette to mask the smell. She keeps the flame alive so we can see. She pinches the corner of a magazine sticking out from under the blanket—obviously kept within reach—and pulls it into full view. *Endless Load*, the cover reads. Below the title is a picture of a woman's face, her eyes wide and her mouth half open with semen dripping down her chin. Dawn tries to leaf through the pages, but they're stiff, and some are stuck together. She tosses the magazine aside and wipes her hands on her jeans. We stifle our laughter so he won't hear.

We've been on the road for less than an hour when the truck slows to a stop. With the engine still running, the driver pushes the curtain aside. We've been in the dark for so long, and the late afternoon light is so bright behind him that his face looks featureless, just a dark space outlined by curls. He gestures with his hand as he says, "Erp air."

At first, we don't understand him. Neither of us moves. He repeats it. A moment later—at the same time—Dawn and I realize he's saying "up here."

We both inch toward the opening. I'm halfway through when he starts to climb into the cabin, stopping Dawn with his arm. The man pulls the curtain closed again and leaves me alone in the passenger seat.

I wait. I don't know what else to do. A few minutes pass before my suitcase is pushed through the curtain, followed by Dawn's bag and then Dawn.

"Let's go," she says.

"What do you mean?"

"We're leaving."

"But…"

"Open the door!" she yells. I do as she says.

He leaves us on the side of the road and drives away. I wait until the truck is nearly out of view before asking. "What happened?"

"As soon as he got in the back, he started taking off his overalls," she says. "So, I said, what the fuck are you doing? He says, 'You want a ride, don't you?' I said, not that bad. And that's when I came out. No way in hell was I going to touch that!" Although it sucks to be sitting on the side of the road again, I can't blame her.

It's a sleepless night. Seems like there's nothing but dust and truck drivers in Texas. Each driver brings us as far as they can. We take turns— one of us puts her thumb out while the other sits. All I can see for miles are long, flat roads. I wish I were sitting in my chair at Little Nana's with a Fluffernutter sandwich, watching One Life to Live.

WE'VE FINALLY ARRIVED on the outskirts of Fort Worth. I count our money again while sipping a glass of sweet tea at a truck stop diner. We're down to thirty dollars. The trip from Houston took way more time and money than we thought it would. Good thing we're close.

I'd been so focused on getting here that I hadn't even thought to look for the small scrap of paper where Nana Raizin had written my father's address until now. It's about time we figure out exactly where we're going. The torn piece of notebook paper isn't in my suitcase. It's not in the jeans I'm wearing either. The pockets of my jean jacket are empty. I start taking clothes out, shaking them above the empty chair next to me.

"What are you doing?" Dawn asks.

"I can't find the address."

"What address?"

"My father's address."

"What do you mean you can't find it?" she asks impatiently.

"It's not here". I'm starting to panic. The contents of my bag are in a pile on the chair. "I don't have it."

"Did you check your back pockets?"

"Yes, I checked everywhere." My face is getting hot. I'm trying to remember if I grabbed it before we left. I filled a trash bag with my clothes, a couple of packs of cigarettes, and snacks and put it in Philip's closet. But the address was on the floor next to my makeshift bed. I must have left it behind in my rush to get out of the apartment. I can see it so clearly in my head. I can see the street name—Blandin. But, as hard as I try, I can't see the number.

"It's not here."

"Oh well," Dawn says. "We'll figure it out." I'm so glad she's with me. Nothing phases her. She's the exact opposite of me. I'm trying to follow her lead.

Outside in the parking lot, I look for my father's name in the telephone book hanging from the pay phone. He's not listed. I call the city hall, the fire department, and the police station. I tell them I'm a girl searching for her long-lost father—not a thirteen-year-old runaway. My father doesn't seem to be anywhere. He's as much a ghost as he's always been. I've made it all the way to Texas, and he's still out of my reach.

"It's on Blandin Street or Avenue," I say. "I know that much. We'll just have to knock on doors until we find him." I light a cigarette and repack my bag.

Once back on the road, we start walking in the direction the waitress pointed us. We don't notice the large green Cadillac creeping beside us until a voice comes from it. "Hey, y'all need a ride?" he asks, dragging the I the way they all do down here.

Dawn turns and starts walking toward the dirty old car. There are two men inside, in their twenties at least. I don't move. "We're going to Blandin," she says self-assuredly. We're in the back seat a few minutes later, and there's a joint in my hand. Tyrone is driving. Leroy is the passenger. I was right about their ages, and they're both from Fort Worth, born and raised.

"Y'all talk too fast," Leroy says while he takes a hit.

"You all talk too slow," Dawn says. Under other circumstances, I might've laughed, but I'm not in the mood. I can't help but think about how we don't fit in here.

Blandin is just a ten-minute drive from the Waffle House. I've never been so happy to see a street sign. But one of the first numbers I see is over a thousand, and Blandin doesn't go in a straight line like an ordinary street.

Tyrone drives slowly like he's stalking somebody. "Let me know when y'all want me to pull over." Dawn looks at me as though I have an answer. I shrug.

"Just keep driving," Dawn says.

At the end of the street, Tyrone turns right and left on Blandin. He drives to the end and then takes a left and another right back onto Blandin. Twelve hundred fifty-two…thirteen-twenty…fourteen seventy-five. There's no way we'll be able to find my father.

TYRONE AND LEROY offer to rent us a hotel room. Maybe they're just nice guys, but I don't wait to find out. I help myself to a fat bag of pot from the console of the Cadillac. We're long gone before they know it's missing. We stay on the move for the next week, hoping to figure something out. Selling some of the weed has helped us get a room for a couple of nights, but we're almost out of money, cigarettes, and pot.

At the end of our second week, we're completely broke. There's nowhere to go. While Dawn sleeps in the last room we can afford, I sneak out to the payphone in the parking lot and dial Little Nana's number. Her voice cracks when she hears mine, and I suddenly feel guilty about upsetting her. I was sure I wouldn't be missed. She promises to get a message to my mother, and she says to call back in an hour. I wait outside so Dawn can't talk me out of it.

I can tell my mother's been crying when I hear her voice. "Oh my God, Gail. We've been so worried about you."

"I'm sorry." I don't know what else to say. I'm surprised she's so upset.

"Where are you?"

"Texas."

She inhales deeply but doesn't say anything.

"I thought I could find my father."

"I don't know how I'll get you back here, but I'll see what I can do. Is there a number I can call you on?" She knows Dawn is with me.

I read her the number on the payphone.

"I love you more than I can say," she says before the call ends. She doesn't call me back. Instead, when I answer the ringing phone, it's a social worker on the line. A police cruiser will pick me up within the hour.

Dawn is awake when I get back to the room. I'm relieved she's not mad. She wants to go home too. She calls her mother before the police come. When the two cars arrive, I'm told to get in the back seat of one car, and Dawn gets into the other. I don't like that we're separated, but there's nothing I can do about it.

My car drives to an enormous brick building—a juvenile detention center—where I'm greeted by a tall, middle-aged woman with short dark hair. She leads me into an office with bare painted cement block walls and gives me a white t-shirt, a pair of jeans, and a list of the rules. She takes my bag before she calls a guard to bring me to my room, which I quickly realize is a cell consisting of a metal cot, a small desk, a sink, and a toilet.

When the door slams shut, I sit on the edge of the mattress and try to figure out my next move. I can't think of anything. I start to cry. I cry because Dawn left me and because I want to go home. I am alone. I cry until I feel like I can't breathe, but I have to get myself under control. I need to keep my head on straight. I'm on my own.

As my breathing steadies, anger begins to set in. I stand and move toward the door. *Why the hell am I locked up? I'm not a criminal. Who are they to keep me here?*

With my face covered in dry tears, I bang on the door with the side of my fist.

"Let me out!" I yell. I bang on it again. And then, I kick it.

"Let me out! I want to come out!" I'm screaming as loud as I can, but nobody comes.

I yell and bang until my throat is raw and my hands hurt. Still, nothing. Exhaustion finally pushes me into a restless sleep.

When the door opens again, it's morning. The woman from yesterday is standing in the hallway with another girl—my guide for the day.

Roselle is bigger than me. Rounder. Her thick, black, fuzzy hair grows out instead of down. Everything about her is dark. Her skin. Her eyes. Her humor.

"Y'all a Yankee, ain't ya?"

"I guess."

"Where y'all from?" She asks as we walk to the clothes closet to get me a clean uniform of jeans and a t-shirt.

"Massachusetts," I say, "near Boston."

She starts laughing, "Bawstun," she says, mocking me.

"I don't know what you're laughing at," I say. "You're the ones who talk funny."

"Yeah, well, you're the only one here who talks like that, so I'd keep my mouth shut if I was you." I know she's right. We've already passed a few girls in the halls—most of them dark-skinned, and none of them smiled at me.

I realize quickly that the constant fear of threat in this place isn't the hardest part of being here. I've always been afraid anyway. I can even deal with endless boredom. The worst thing about lockup is being confined to a small space. Roselle says you get used to it. I guess she'd know after being here for the better part of a year, but I never want to get used to somebody letting me in and out of a cage.

I've had a lot of time to think. I'm going to face this whole investigation thing when I get home. Whatever happens, happens. No more running away. I'll go back to school and maybe get back into the chorus. I'm definitely not going to do drugs. Most importantly, I won't sell myself anymore. The money isn't worth how bad it makes me feel.

16

DRAMATIC

~1984~

Two weeks after walking into the Texas detention center, a thin, serious-looking woman waits for me at the Logan Airport baggage claim. She's holding a sign with my name on it. Although a stranger to me, she doesn't need the sign; I can spot a social worker from a mile away. I don't have any baggage to claim, so she leads me out of the building.

I breathe in Boston's sweet ocean air while scanning the area for someone smoking a cigarette. The young guy I ask hands me a butt from his pack and lights it for me. It feels good to be back on the east coast.

The social worker waits for me to take a drag before she tells me she's bringing me to a foster home. Whatever. I knew there'd be consequences. I wish I could stay at Little Nana's apartment, but Aunt Julie is there unless she's in jail. I haven't forgotten why I ran in the first place. I close my eyes, take in a lungful of smoke, and remind myself of the decisions I made while locked up—to stay off drugs and go to school. It's time for a fresh start.

I wait until we get in the car before I ask any questions. "When can I go home?"

"I'm not sure," she says. "I don't know all of the circumstances since I'm not involved in your case."

"Who does know?"

"Your family worker. She'll call you at some point this week."

Forty-five minutes later, we're at an upscale housing complex in Beverly. The worker waits for me to get out of the car before she opens the trunk to get my bag. I don't mind making her wait. I fish a book of matches out of my pocket and light the remaining half of my airport-bummed cigarette.

When I'm done, I follow the woman through a door that leads directly into the living room of a sparkling-clean townhouse. It reminds me of John's house. For a moment, I imagine the skinny woman who has greeted us as John's wife—a woman oblivious to what her husband does in their bed when she's not home. But I quickly learn that this woman, Betty, doesn't have a husband. It's just she and her daughter, she says, after introducing herself. I'm happy about that.

After the introductions, Betty leads the way into the kitchen, where we sit at a glass table with brass chairs and cream-colored cushions. Betty puts the water on for tea.

They talk about the weather until Betty puts a steaming glass mug in front of each of us. She sits down and looks across the table at me. She's clearly done this before. I wonder if it's just as clear that I haven't. I wait to pick up the cup, so she won't see my hands shake. There are no fingernails left to bite, so I gnaw on a piece of skin on the thumb of my free hand.

"The rules are simple," Betty says. "Everybody has chores to do. You'll get an allowance if you do your chores and go to school. Do you smoke?"

"Yeah," I say, ready for a sermon.

"I'll also buy you a carton of cigarettes each week."

Wow, I think. Maybe this place won't be so bad.

When my escort leaves, Betty shows me to my room. Katie, another foster girl, is well-settled into her side of our room. Her walls are covered with posters of Van Halen and Motley Crue. The walls on my side are bare, except for some tack holes and a few stubborn pieces of tape, remnants of other girls who had nowhere else to go.

After unpacking and dinner, it's time for bed. As we lie in our twin beds, Katie tells me about the foster homes she's been in.

"Do you ever think about running away from here?" I ask.

"Why would I?" she asks.

"I don't know," I say, suddenly feeling stupid. "Maybe because being in a foster home sucks."

"Sucks even more having no place to sleep," she says. "And this is the best place I've been yet."

After Katie stops talking, I'm still staring at the dark ceiling. I feel cold even though it's warm in the room. I feel alone even though the other girl is only a few feet away. I have to pee, but I don't want to run into Betty in the hallway. I'm afraid she'll talk to me. Or worse, she'll think I'm sneaking around, looking for something to steal. Or worse still, that I'm going into the toy-stuffed bedroom of her seven-year-old daughter. That was the golden rule: stay out of the bedrooms.

I'VE ONLY MADE one friend in the two weeks I've been here. Michael lives in the same complex and is a foster kid. He also goes to the same school and doesn't fit in any better than I do, which is precisely why I trust him. All I've gotten from the girls at Beverly Middle School in the short time I've been a student here is grief. They don't like me. They call me names they can't know are true and make fun of how I cut my shirts to hang off one shoulder, and gather the bottom into a side knot to show my flat belly. I'm trying to bite my tongue, but I'm already itching to get out of this town. The good news is that we're finally meeting with my social worker. I'll get some answers about how long I'll have to stay here.

Rena sits at the kitchen table across from me—all business as usual. She's declined Betty's offer for a cup of tea and refuses to look at me. Something is wrong; I can feel it. After hanging her jacket on the back of her chair, Rena glances in my direction, at Betty, and then down at the table in front of her. She clears her throat before she speaks. "I wish I didn't have to tell you this."

I hold my breath.

"Your mother has had a relapse. Your sister is staying with a friend, and Philip is back in foster care." She looks up at me for a moment. She doesn't mention Walter. "I'm sorry," she says and looks at Betty, who is standing with her back to the kitchen sink, watching me.

"There was an eviction. Your mother doesn't have the apartment anymore." I'm not surprised. The last time I talked to my mother was when I called from the payphone in Texas. Still, the news makes me feel like I've just stepped in quicksand.

I can't speak. I have so many questions, but my voice is gone. I chew the skin around my fingernails and stare at the mug in front of me. My chest is heavy, and my eyes burn with the tears I can't hold back. It's my fault. If I hadn't run away... "Where's my mother?" I ask without looking up.

"I don't know," Rena says.

Water sloshes in the dishwasher. Betty and the social worker wait for me to say something.

"What about me?" I barely finish the question when the noise comes. The pain that has swollen within me rises despite my attempt to stop it. It hurts first in my stomach, then my chest and throat. When the wailing sound meets the room, it is deep and low. I hear the worker say I'll have to stay with Betty, but I'm already on my feet and moving toward the stairs.

I hear my mother's voice as I take them two at a time: "Oh, Gail, stop being so dramatic."

BETTY LET ME stay home from school yesterday—to recover from the bad news, I guess—but not today. Maybe I'd stay at Betty's forever if I didn't have to go to school. The name-calling is getting worse, and this one girl just won't let up. I hate this place.

"Slut," she spits when I walk past her, and her pack, in the cafeteria. Her friends snicker and whisper. It's hard to ignore them even though I have more important things to occupy my mind. I sit on a bench at one of the lunch tables with my back against the wall and open the small carton of chocolate milk that will be my lunch. All my attention is focused on the task in front of me—pushing the paper off the straw.

The girls got up shortly after I sat down and started moving in my direction. I stood when it became clear that I was their destination. I had planned to leave the room since I can't afford to get into trouble over a childish big mouth and her minions. It was the last thing I wanted, but she was looking for a fight.

Big Mouth—the ringleader—was out in front. I swung as soon as she got close enough for me to make contact.

Within minutes, I felt a hand pulling on the back of my shirt and noticed that Big Mouth's arms were swinging wildly in the air. Somebody was holding her, too. It was over almost as quickly as it began.

Instead of getting detention, we were brought to the guidance counselor's office for a "peer meeting."

Big Mouth, the principal, the guidance counselor, and I are seated in a circle. They let her speak first. She says it's my fault; that I started it. I cut her off. I'm not a rat, but this is bullshit.

"I was minding my own business," I say. "She's always calling me names and giving me a hard time. She doesn't even know me."

The counselor chimes in before Big Mouth has a chance to respond.

"Well," she says, "maybe if you stop wearing three-inch heels, the girls won't single you out." She's looking at me, her eyes narrow.

I wish I could slide off my chair, curl into a ball on the floor, and sob until I stop breathing. I stay quiet so they won't hear the pain in my voice. I pretend I'm somewhere else, like when John was on top of me or I had some old guy's dick in my hand.

Big Mouth is saying something, pointing in my direction. The sounds are muffled like we're underwater, but I hear an occasional word.

"Attention."

"Her."

The principal shifts his disinterested gaze from Big Mouth to the guidance counselor and then back to me. Fuck him. I bet he'd shell out fifty bucks for a blowjob.

"Inappropriate."

Fuck them all.

I leave through a side door and walk along the railroad tracks until I get to the station. The six quarters I didn't use for lunch are just enough to get a ticket to Gloucester.

I'm back at Little Nana's house before school lets out.

17

APE ARMS

~1984~

Turns out my mother is homeless too. She showed up at Little Nana's looking for a place to crash a few days after I did. That was a week ago. I thought it was Aunt Julie coming up the stairs, but my mother's face appeared in the doorway. It'd been close to two months since the last time we spoke.

"Hi," she said, smiling politely, moving past me through the living room with the grace of a dancer, so light on her feet she could be a ghost. She stopped only to pull a cigarette from Little Nana's pack on the coffee table and then disappeared around the corner into the kitchen before closing the bathroom door. Little Nana and I didn't speak or even look at each other. It happened so quickly; for a moment, I wasn't sure it happened at all.

I waited.

She didn't return to the living room after the bathroom door opened. The only sound in the apartment came from the TV. I hesitated before getting out of my chair—this was new territory.

She was lying on her back in the bedroom with her arms straight by her sides. Her eyes were closed, and her body still. I stood in the doorway and watched for the rise and fall of her chest. When she moved her hand, I released the breath I didn't realize I was holding.

I wanted to lie next to her, tell her how much I missed her and that I was sorry for running away. But she obviously hadn't come for me. My anger pushed me to hurl words at her instead.

"I thought you'd be in a program by now."

"Nope. Not this time." She didn't open her eyes.

"Why not?"

"Why bother?" Her answers were short, barbed.

"What about Chrissy and Philip?"

"They're better off where they are. I just can't do it anymore."

"What happened to Walter?"

"No idea."

"Where am I supposed to go?"

"I don't know, Gail; I'm doing the best I can. I'll get a place soon."

Bullshit. She won't get clean without the usual post-eviction detox or stay clean without a halfway house. I knew her last statement was my cue to leave, but instead, I kept my back pressed against the door frame, trying to figure out how to talk to her without sounding angry. I know my attitude pushes her away.

After a moment, she opened her eyes and craned her neck to look in my direction. I was nearly behind her.

"We'll talk later," she said. "I have a migraine. Will you shut off the light and close the door?"

As LITTLE NANA's oldest grandchild, my mother gets the bedroom. That means a shift in the sleeping arrangements. Aunt Julie takes the living room twin while I return to the cot. I don't mind giving up the bed. It doesn't matter where I sleep as long as I'm with my mother. Although I don't think she'll be here long.

From my seat at the kitchen table, I can see my mother sitting on the edge of the bed. There's a cigarette between the fingers of her right hand; her fingers barely grip the filter. I watch as her body slowly bends forward. Her eyes are closed. She keeps moving until her chest rests against her thighs, and the glowing head of the cigarette grazes the shaggy area rug next to the bed.

"Mom!" I yell.

She sits up immediately. Her eyes open wide.

"What?" she asks.

"You're going to burn the house down. You were nodding."

"Oh, stop being so dramatic. I was just resting my eyes." I think I see her roll them.

She stubs the cigarette out in the standing ashtray next to the bed. A few minutes later, she lights another one. I sit and watch. Somebody has to.

Again, she sits erect with her feet on the floor in front of her. Again, her head and shoulders fall slowly forward until her body is bent in half, the cigarette still in her hand at the end of a slack arm. The way she's positioned makes her arm seem longer than it is. It reminds me of an ape. I don't yell this time. Instead, I get up, go into the bedroom, and remove the butt from her hand.

"What the hell are you doing?"

"I'm putting your cigarette out. You keep nodding off with it in your hand," I say. And then slowly: "You're going to burn the house down."

"I'm not nodding off." Her voice rises, but it sounds as limp as her body. For a moment, I think about leaving her to care for herself. But then, if something does happen, we'll all be sleeping at the shelter.

I sit next to her on the bed. "This is what you look like." I hold my cigarette in my right hand and bend at the waist, letting my hands fall to the floor, and my head slump forward.

"Yeah, okay," she says, definitely rolling her eyes this time. She lights another cigarette and swings her legs over my head to lie back down. I wait for her breathing to deepen into a light snore before I take it out of her hand.

18

GULLS

~1984~

I really had been trying to do the right thing. The promises I made to myself while I was in Texas meant something to me. But I don't even know where to start to get the things I need. I have a few pieces of clothing, a couple of shirts, and a pair of shorts I left here before running away. I also have two pairs of underwear; I wash one in the kitchen sink and hang it on Little Nana's indoor clothesline to dry while I wear the other. The clothes I took to Texas might still be at Betty's, but as a runaway, I can't call for them. Whatever I didn't bring to Texas was probably hauled out to the curb with the rest of our post-eviction belongings. That's what usually happens.

I don't even know who to ask for help. My mother is gone again. Not that she was helpful when she was here. I talk to Dawn on the phone but don't see her. Same with Chrissy. I've been lying low in Little Nana's apartment. The only two people I see daily are Little Nana and Aunt Julie.

I can't get a job—I don't know of any real work for a thirteen-year-old runaway. Of course, Little Nana can't help. Her social security check is barely enough to cover food and bills. Social services are certainly not trying to track me down with an offer of support. In fact, I'm sure they already know where I am—Little Nana has lived here my whole life. Clearly, the police aren't all that concerned about me either. They made a big show of hauling me down to the station, and they still haven't done anything about the big "prostitution ring." If they ever questioned Aunt

Julie, she hasn't mentioned it.

The bottom line is that I need money. That's why when Aunt Julie said she "knows a guy" the other day, I agreed to meet him. I don't see any other way. And as bad as making money that way feels, it is an option, and at least it's quick.

The next day, Aunt Julie and I walked to Main Street. She stopped in front of a gate I wouldn't have noticed otherwise. I paused for a moment before following her through it. We were just a few houses from where I had collected the twenty dollars for my mother five years before. I was struck with a sudden understanding of how she'd earned the money. In my head, I could hear the voices of the men who, over the last few years, have said: "You are the spitting image of your mother." I was sure they knew her the same way they knew me. The thought of those men putting their hands on my mother made my stomach so tight it ached. I wondered if she felt the same when she imagined their hands on me.

On the other side of the gate, an outside staircase brought us to the door of a third-floor apartment. Aunt Julie knocked twice and let herself in. The door opened into a bedroom. A thick stink of body odor hit me in the face as I stepped into the room. The king-sized bed was unmade. Pieces of clothing were piled on the dresser and scattered around on the floor. Dark stains spotted the wall-to-wall carpeting. To my left, I caught a glimpse of a refrigerator but turned right to follow Aunt Julie toward the front of the building.

In the living room, a man sat in a black recliner, the chair worn from years of supporting his heavy body. He muted the television as we made our way into the room. The air was stagnant with the smell of stale cigar smoke, although a fresh one smoldered between his thick fingers. His dingy white t-shirt, a few inches too short to meet his plaid boxers, was taut over his ugly, fat belly. He smirked when he saw me. I fantasized about the queasy feeling in my stomach rising up and erupting like a volcano, a spray of vomit directed toward the man, sure to wipe that disgusting look right off his stubbly, fat face.

I smiled back.

"This is my niece, Gail," Aunt Julie said, glancing in my direction. She had a look of satisfaction, her expression a lot like his. "This is Archie

Babe," she said as she sat on the worn black, faux leather couch adjacent to his chair.

I walked to the window. From there, up on the third floor, I could see much of Main Street and a slightly obstructed view of the harbor where there's always a frenzy of activity: fishing boats coming and going, fishermen unloading their hauls on the docks while seagulls vet the scene, screeching and whining, swooping in to scavenge whatever they can. I thought about Archie Babe standing there, watching the fishing boats come in, the fishermen his bread and butter. That's when it registered—he's just like the gulls.

Aunt Julie and Archie Babe started to talk. From where I stood at the window, I could hear everything they said. I realized quickly that this wasn't their first conversation about me. Many of the details had already been negotiated. Aunt Julie will get ten percent of everything I make. Archie Babe will get fifteen and an occasional freebie. For Aunt Julie, the money is an ongoing bonus for the introduction. For Archie Babe, it's a standard fee for his service as the connector and translator between the nameless, horny, Italian-speaking-fishermen and me.

The visit lasted less than thirty minutes.

As we walked down the stairs, Aunt Julie turned to me.

"You're lucky," she said. "You'll make a shitload of money because you're so young. Guys like that."

19

DEAD TIME

~1984~

I'm sitting on Little Nana's porch smoking a cigarette when I see Aunt Julie jump down from the passenger side of a large, black van. She glances at me with bloodshot eyes as she rushes up the stairs past me. "We're going to Dogtown to party. Wanna come?"

"Who's we?" I flick my butt and follow her into the house.

"There's a bunch of us in Jimmy's van."

"Who's Jimmy?" She doesn't answer, but it doesn't matter. I'm already in. It's not like I have anything else to do on a Saturday morning.

The van is taller than most but unremarkable otherwise. That is until I step up through the side door and into what looks exactly like, a small apartment. Blue shag rug covers the floor and walls. In front of me, behind the driver's seat, there's a small refrigerator with a cabinet above it. I'm amazed at how clean and put-together the place is. It's the coolest thing I've ever seen.

I'm standing before the open door, taking it all in, when Aunt Julie speaks to the group. "This is my niece, Gail," she says from the front seat. She introduces the people in the back—a twenty-something guy and a girl who share a bench at the dining booth to my left. "And this is Jimmy," she says, pointing at the guy behind the wheel.

I say hello toward the booth and then look at the driver. I mean to say hi and sit at the table, but I'm caught off guard. I expected him to be old and creepy, like most people Aunt Julie hangs out with. Jimmy's far from that. He's clean and good-looking, older than me for sure; of course, he has to be to have his license. But behind a neatly trimmed beard, I'm guessing he's not over twenty. I feel the same way about him as I do his van.

He sees me just as I see him, and if his silence is any indication, I think he's surprised too. I nod toward him with my chin. He smiles and nods back.

I close the door, sit on the booth's empty side, and lean against the back door with my legs stretched along the bench, crossing them at the ankles. I'm careful to keep my gaze on the joint the girl's rolling and not on Jimmy. I'm happy I wore shorts today, jean cutoffs, with my favorite blue t-shirt that matches my eyes as perfectly as it molds to the shape of my body. I hope he's happy about it, too.

As THE VAN pulls away from the curb, I feel Jimmy looking at me. After a couple of hits, I finally gather the courage to look in his direction. Our eyes meet in the rearview mirror. He shifts his gaze between the road and me for the rest of the drive. Every time we connect, he smiles at me like I'm a present he can't wait to open. I love how it feels to be wanted this way.

Jimmy stops at a liquor store and speaks to me through the mirror. "What do you like to drink?"

"Rum and Coke," I answer quickly as though it's a coolness quiz. He doesn't need to know I don't like the taste of alcohol.

We all hold on to the table as Jimmy tries to dodge potholes and boulders on the dirt road leading to Dogtown Common, an old settlement and the best place to party in Gloucester.

When the van stops in a clearing, everybody gets out and finds a place to sit. I wait for him. Jimmy slides the greatest hits of Credence Clearwater Revival into the cassette deck and mixes drinks in the van. I wait until he hands me one before I get out and join the others. We sit for hours drinking, getting high, telling stories, and laughing at everything and nothing.

It's late afternoon when Jimmy decides to get steak tips to cook on the hibachi.

"Do you want to ride shotgun?" he asks me. I look at Aunt Julie before responding. I think she might like him, but she hasn't said anything. So, I go.

"How old are you anyway?" Jimmy asks when we're alone. "Or don't

I want to know?"

"Maybe you don't, but it's no secret. I'm thirteen. Almost fourteen."

"Jailbait," he says. We laugh.

"How old are you?" I smile. "Or don't I want to know?"

"Well, that's a secret. My license says I'm twenty-one, but I'm not."

"So, how old are you then?"

"Maybe I'll tell you someday." He reaches for my hand, and I don't ask again. All that matters right now is that when Jimmy looks at me, I feel like I'm the only girl in the world.

When we return to Dogtown, Jimmy grills the steak while the other guy builds a fire. After we eat, Jimmy takes my hand and leads me to a boulder imprinted with the words Spiritual Power. It makes me think about God and how, until this very moment, I was sure that if there was a God, he didn't care about me. Maybe I was wrong.

Jimmy climbs to the top and then helps me up. It's just the two of us in the dark, quiet, sitting so close our bodies touch. The others are far enough away that we can barely hear them. He reaches into his pocket and holds out his hand. A red capsule sits in his palm.

"Have you ever tried Seconal?" he asks.

"Not yet," I say as I take the pill, put it on my tongue, and wash it down with the warm drink I've been nursing. I smile, feeling connected to the world—a feeling I'd only ever experienced with a buzz until now. With Jimmy's full attention on me, I finally feel like I belong here—that there is a reason I exist. When his hand reaches to touch my face, I know I will be his.

JIMMY AND I had been together nearly every day for two months but not so much for the last couple of weeks. I can't shake the feeling that he's been cheating on me. I don't know why I'm not enough for him. Maybe it's because of the things I do for money, although he wasn't surprised by the information. He knew all about Aunt Julie. He also knows Kathy and my mother. I still haven't told him that I've had intercourse with some of the men. Jimmy thinks I save that for him, which is far from the truth. Especially since Aunt Julie was right about Archie Babe, he's got connections.

I've been cleaning Archie Babe's apartment when I spend time there. I do it because the place disgusts me, and it's a compromise to avoid having to touch him. This new agreement seems to be working. He sets up the meetings and takes his cut before I even see the guys. He could be over-charging them and taking more than he should, but it doesn't matter to me as long as I get my share. Aunt Julie was also right about them liking that I'm young. They ask for me, and as far as I know, I make more money than anybody else.

Aunt Julie usually takes Archie Babe's calls, but she's out today, and Little Nana is napping. He skips past hello and starts talking as soon as he hears my voice.

"I set up a meeting for today at the Wingaersheek Motel." His breath is as thick and heavy as he is. "The room's paid for. It's in my name. Just go to the reservation desk and ask for the key. There's three guys." I cut him off.

"Three guys?" My mind is racing.

"Yeah, it's all set for two o'clock."

I look at the clock. It's eleven thirty.

"I don't know. I don't think I can do that."

"Don't worry about it," he snorts like a pig. "Not all at once."

I don't respond.

"Five hundred dollars in your pocket," he says before he hangs up.

I sit at the kitchen table. I feel like I've been punched in the stomach. I wish Aunt Julie were here. Of course, I can't talk to Jimmy—not about this. He's not home anyway. I called a little while ago.

I have to go. It's not that I'm afraid that Archie Babe will hurt me; I'm worried he'll stop doing business with me if I don't show, and I need the money.

At one fifteen, I call for a taxi and arrive at the motel with twenty minutes to spare. The room is outdated but clean. It smells like Pine Sol. Aside from a dresser and television, a nightstand separates two queen beds. The shade is rolled up over the single window, and the curtains are pulled to the sides. Daylight pours into the room. I close them and sit on the end of the bed closest to the door. This will be the bed we use. Dealer's choice. I smile wryly. If nothing else, I have my mother's wit.

The waiting is the hardest part. Dead time. After they arrive, the countdown to the end begins.

I get up to make sure the door is locked. Sit back on the bed. Go to the bathroom. Sit back down. Wait. It's so quiet; all I can hear are my thoughts. I consider turning on the TV for background noise, but it might be more of a distraction. I don't want this to take any longer than it has to.

Finally, there's a knock on the door. Number One smiles when he sees me. He looks me up and down. We've never met. At least, I don't think we have. He's short, not much taller than me, maybe five-and-a-half feet, with dark hair slicked back. I'm grateful he smells good until it occurs to me that he probably uses so much cologne to cover up the smell of fish.

He closes the door behind him and follows me into the room. He's not fluent in English. Perfect, we don't have to talk.

I move to the left side of the bed closest to the door. I undress from the waist down and get under the covers. He takes everything off except his socks and a thick Figaro gold chain that reminds me of a collar. He puts a condom on the nightstand and gets into bed.

Archie Babe must've said something because he brought protection. I won't have sex with any of them without it. I'm not worried about getting pregnant. Jimmy and I never use anything, and I haven't gotten pregnant yet. My concern is that I'll catch something; I don't know where these guys have been. Also, if our skin doesn't touch, I can pretend the whole thing never happened.

When he tries to touch me, I stop him. There's no foreplay. I don't allow it. No kissing. I don't want their mouths on me. Instead, I begin to rub him with my hand, even though he's probably been hard since I opened the door. A few minutes later, he reaches for the condom, rolls it on, and moves over me. He rubs himself against me to get inside, but it doesn't work.

"Wait," I say, holding up a finger as I reach for the lubricant in my purse on the floor next to the bed.

It's done in less than ten minutes. As soon as he's off me, I go into the bathroom to clean up, but I don't get dressed. When I come back out, he's got his clothes on. There's no need to count the wad of money he hands me. I've never had a problem getting paid. I understand his limited English when he says thank you and maybe something about next time. All I want is for him to leave.

Number Two knocks almost right away. He looks the same as the other one, a little taller, maybe. Sounds the same. Smells the same. His name is Salvatore or Joseph, or Angelo. He doesn't seem to mind that he's second. The scenario is identical.

A few minutes after he leaves, Number Three is at the door. I wonder if they all rode together and whether they're tagging each other in and out. This one speaks the most English, which gives him courage. He tries harder than the others to touch me. He lifts my shirt while he's lying next to me. He says please. I have to push his hand away a few times before he gives up. Eventually, he does. When we do what he came here for, his body shudders, and he finishes like the others.

When the door closes, it's quiet again. The smell of Giorgio clings to me. I take off the rest of my clothes to shower.

I sit on the end of the unused bed with a towel on my head and another wrapped around my body. I notice I'm holding my breath. My stomach is clenched. I let the air out and breathe deep, but my belly stays tight. In my head, I see their faces above mine, indistinguishable from each other. Like a movie playing on a loop, they arrive, and then they're on me and in me. I'm holding my breath again. I try to relax, but it hurts. There's an ache crawling up my back, neck, and left shoulder. Always the left.

I don't realize I'm sad until I begin sobbing. Even then, I'm not exactly sure why. I hear Walter's voice telling my brother, "Stop crying before I give you something to cry about." *You have nothing to cry about. It's over,* I tell myself. *Five hundred dollars.* But I can't catch my breath. There's a phone in the room, but there's nobody to call. I can't tell Aunt Julie where I am, she'll want money, and it's not like she did anything to earn it. Jimmy can't find out—he won't want to touch me if he does. I wouldn't blame him. Nobody would.

Three cigarettes later, I take another shower. The room is mine for the night if I want it. I don't, so I call a cab.

20

THE SCRIPT

~ 1984 ~

Jimmy and I are on our way to the Hilltop Steakhouse. I called and invited him for dinner after I got back from the Wingaersheek Motel. It's time to tell him the truth about everything. He might never want to talk to me again, but at least I won't be lying anymore.

We're about halfway there when he asks me where I got the money. Hilltop isn't cheap. Instead of waiting to get to the restaurant as planned, I start talking. I tell him about the motel, although in my Jimmy version, there's only one Italian instead of three. I confess to him that it wasn't the first time. I tell him about John and how I had to stop seeing him because of the police. And about Archie Babe. Turns out Jimmy knows Archie Babe too.

He pulls the van over to the side of the road. His face is crimson. I've never seen him so angry. "How the hell could you let those guys fuck you?" It's the same question I keep asking myself. He won't look at me. I can see the veins in his neck. "I can't fucking believe you would do this to me."

"What's the difference?" I ask. My bottom lip is trembling, but I'm trying not to cry. I have a hard time believing he didn't already know, but even if he didn't, he certainly knows about the other things I do with men—things most guys wouldn't let their girlfriends do. And he's always right there to help me spend the money.

Jimmy slides out of his seat and kneels beside me. My silence must've caught his attention. He reaches for me, and I let him take my hand as he wipes the tears away from my cheek.

"I'm sorry I got so upset," he says, his voice calm again. "It's just that I love you so much that the thought of another man inside you makes me sick to my stomach." Of course, he's upset. It's understandable. I wouldn't want him to be with another girl for any reason. "I don't like it either," I say. "I just close my eyes and pretend it's you." He smiles then, and everything is okay. If he didn't love me as much as he does, he'd leave me instead of giving me his blessing.

JIMMY IS AN entrepreneur. A businessman. A money-maker. And he's shown me that there are so many ways to make money—selling drugs, buying booze for underaged kids (even with a fake ID), stealing things, and selling contraband. He likes to have a whole bunch of money. Like a squirrel, he hides it in various places: under a floorboard in his bedroom, inside the van's mattress, and in a hollow book in his mother's living room. He saves it for later, although later rarely comes since he hates to spend it. Jimmy also likes to get high, and as good as he is at making money, he's even better at finding ways to get stuff without paying for it.

This afternoon, Jimmy and I are lying in the bed of an apartment left vacant by a couple we know. They moved a week ago, and we get to pretend we live together before the owner comes to throw away everything they left behind. Jimmy turns onto his side and faces me. He props his head up with one hand and runs the pointer finger of the other lightly up and down my arm, giving me goosebumps.

"There's this guy Hal," he says.

"Yeah?" I'm half listening.

"He gets a shitload of pills. Scripts. Perc's, Valiums."

"And?"

"And he's got a fetish," he says.

"What kind of fetish?"

"He likes to watch. All we have to do is go into a room where he works, and he'll find us. It's the best of both worlds—we get to make love and get paid for it." I love that he calls it making love.

"Where does he work?" I ask. I've never been able to tell Jimmy no.

"You'll see." He's smiling when he leans in to kiss me. Just like that, we have a regular Saturday night gig.

There's a light on in the foyer for us, illuminating a small portion of the walkway through the double glass doors. There's a desk to the left where Hal, the security guard, sits, but he's already standing by the time we get inside.

With a shaky hand, Hal pulls a small plastic baggie from the front pocket of his pants and passes it to Jimmy. He looks at Jimmy and then through the glass behind him several times while discussing the weather. Jimmy hands me two Valium, takes out something for himself, and puts what's left in a hidden compartment inside the lining of his jacket. The blue pills in my hand have a V-shaped cutout in the middle. Hal gets the good stuff, none of the generic bullshit. I put one on my tongue and swallow hard. Relief sets in immediately because I know what I'll feel in a little while.

Jimmy and I move farther inside, down one of the long corridors to the right of the entrance. This hallway looks like all the others; long and wide, with white walls and flat gray carpeting. Jimmy is opening and closing doors on either side of the corridor. He's shopping. I don't care about the room, so I leave the search to him.

Aside from our footsteps, it's quiet. I don't know what the place is like during the day, but I'm sure it's filled with people talking and laughing. I wonder what it would be like to work in a place like this. It makes me think about the dead-end jobs I'll be able to get if I don't finish high school. Maybe I'll go back someday. I think I'm as smart as any other ninth-grader.

When Jimmy stops and turns to grin at me, I know he's made his choice. He pushes the door open and follows me into the corner office. As part of the unwritten script, he leaves the door ajar. I watch Jimmy as he moves to the large dark wooden desk and pulls the short gold chain of a lamp next to a framed photo. In the picture, a middle-aged man wearing a polo shirt has his arm around a woman with blond hair and white teeth. A plant hangs in the corner of the room where Jimmy has gone to close the blinds. I don't know what kind of plant it is, because I don't know about that kind of thing, but I'm taken with how green it is. It's so green; I need to touch it to see if it's real. It is.

Jimmy is looking around the room, deciding where we'll set up. He's sizing up the two identical gray and chrome chairs angled in front of the desk. They're small, maybe a foot and a half across. They won't do, so he moves to the black leather wingback chair behind the desk. I follow him because I can see this is our only option aside from standing, which I think we did last time.

As soon as I'm beside him, Jimmy puts his hand beneath my chin and gently turns my face toward his before he kisses me. When he pushes my hair back to kiss my neck, I shiver. His hands are working the buttons on my shirt—a prop I wore for this particular occasion—and he only stops touching me long enough for us to undress. Soon, we're both naked. I kiss his bare chest as he guides me onto the chair. I feel on fire when he pulls me on top of him, my legs straddling his. All I can think about is being with him.

When I hear the quiet creak of the door, my eyes open instinctively. I don't turn to the noise because I recognize the jingle of keys on Hal's belt, and I know he has found us. I can picture him standing in the hallway, with his white hair and wrinkled face, ogling us through the partially open door.

Suddenly, I'm aware of the gold rivets surrounding the back of the chair. There's one missing near the top. I look to the bookcase behind the desk where important-looking books and manuals are arranged by size.

I'm trying to focus on Jimmy and how good being here felt just a few minutes ago. But now, all I can think about is Hal, his khakis pooled around his ankles and his old thing in his hand, watching us.

21

FLASH

~1985~

I t's early afternoon when the taxi leaves Aunt Julie and me in front of the east Gloucester motel. According to her, there's money to be made. As much as I try to avoid her these days, the proposition is hard to pass up. I'm broke, and at the very least, I'll have a place to stay for the night. Finding somewhere to sleep is getting more difficult with the cold November weather.

My mother had a place for a while, or more accurately, she met a guy who had a place. They met at the beginning of summer, and we all—except for Chrissy—moved into his three-bedroom apartment. Chrissy was the smart one because when my mother left the guy in early fall, she didn't have to scramble for a place to lay her head at night.

I stayed in Jimmy's van for a month, even after finding out he has another girlfriend. Now, it's too cold. My only other option is to stay at Little Nana's, which is my last resort. Aunt Julie is way too unpredictable. A couple of weeks ago, I thought she would hit me. She started on me as soon as I walked into Little Nana's living room.

"What the fuck did you do with my jeans?" she asked with her fists clenched as she rushed toward me.

I took a step back. "What are you talking about?"

"My jeans," she said again, moving closer until her red face was inches from mine. "What the fuck did you do with them?"

"Julie, I have no idea what you're talking about. What the hell would I want with your pants? You're three sizes bigger than me."

"I know you took them. You wanted them, so you took them."

She took a deep breath and spoke slowly: "Where. The. Fuck. Are. They?" She enunciated each syllable as though I must not understand the question.

"Julie, I have no idea where your pants are. Did you check in your laundry basket?"

"Fine. You don't want to tell me? Payback's a bitch." Then she smiled the kind of smile that gives me nightmares and said: "That's okay, you took my clothes, so I took yours."

She wasn't joking. The two trash bags containing every piece of clothing I owned were gone from the bedroom.

I looked everywhere: in the kitchen closet, the shower, the hall closet where Little Nana keeps the dishes, and under the sink. I looked in the back hall—on all three landings—the front entrance, under the porch, and in the backyard. I checked the trash barrels that belong to our building and then the barrels belonging to the apartment building next door.

Every day for a week, I asked her what she did with my things. The last time I asked, she smiled, looked me in the eye, and said: "Maybe they disappeared." At this point, I'm sure they're gone for good. I haven't forgiven her, but I have to make allowances. She's definitely got some issues.

I can handle Aunt Julie in small doses, and other people will be around tonight. She's always better with a buffer.

We walk up a flight of outside steps to the second floor. I'm glad this is a motel; the room has an entrance from the outside, so I won't have to face anybody at the front desk or in an elevator. The door is unlocked.

The large room is set up like an apartment—a small kitchenette, dining table, two beds, a dresser, and a TV stand. Kathy, my mother's friend, and her boyfriend Artie sit on one of the beds. Another guy, a stranger to me, sits at the round table next to the room's only window. In front of him, there's a small, oakwood-framed mirror. I sit in the chair opposite the man and watch as he chops at a white rock of cocaine with a razor blade until it becomes a pile of fine powder.

He doesn't speak as he stretches some of the powder out into a line and hands me a short straw. I take the straw, let my breath out away from the mirror, and snort the line in one fluid motion. It's not my first time.

The drug's effect on me is instantaneous. My heartbeat quickens, and my scalp feels numb. Everything in the room becomes clearer. The orange bedspreads glow. The music on the radio sounds so beautiful; it makes me want to dance. Somebody hands me a sombrero.

The pile of coke never seems to shrink. I'm snorting lines in between touching and pleasing the guy who first handed me the straw. I don't know how or when my clothes came off, but I'm naked. Some people come and go, but I lose track of who's present at any time.

At some point during the night, as I walk toward the bathroom, I see a flash come from somewhere in the room. Maybe it's from a camera. It flashes a couple more times before I close the bathroom door behind me. I have a moment of concern that somebody has taken pictures of my naked body, but it passes quickly. Doesn't matter. My body has never been all that important.

The room is dark when I wake up. Thankfully, I'm alone. I feel like I'm moving in slow motion. My body feels heavier than its one hundred and ten pounds. Although there's still some cocaine on the mirror, I know better than to start that ball rolling again. There's a pile of twenty-dollar bills next to it—enough to stay another night or two.

22

CARBON COPIES

~1985~

My mother has a new apartment. She takes me on the tour shortly after Christmas. "This will be my room," she says, waving her hand in front of the glass-paned door like Vanna White on the Wheel of Fortune. "It's supposed to be the dining room, but I'll just throw a curtain over the door." My heels click on the clean hardwood floor in the living room. The sound muffles as I move across the kitchen linoleum. "There are three bedrooms upstairs, one for each of you." The way she says "upstairs" makes it sound like having two floors means we're moving up in the world.

"Philip's coming home at the end of the month, and Chrissy should be here next week." She's smiling, hopeful. It makes me think of the possibilities—a fresh start for all of us.

"It's just what we need to come back together as a family," she says as if reading my thoughts. She's trying to convince me to stay, and she also knows I don't trust her even though she's fresh out of detox and her eyes are clear. She also knows I'm making my own decisions these days.

Since I didn't have anything to move in, I just stayed. Tony, my new boyfriend, is staying with me. We share a donated double mattress on the floor in my bedroom. I bought a rectangular area rug, painted the walls, and hung shelves to compensate for the lack of a closet. It's already starting to feel like home.

I'm seriously considering returning to school now that I have a stable place to live. I'll be fifteen in six months, closer to having the option to quit and get my GED, but I want to go back. I'd give anything to be sitting in a classroom. I miss the smell of carbon copies and how it feels to feather the pages of a textbook with my thumb. I miss learning and having someplace to be. I want to know what it feels like to be in high school—to go to football games and prom—and graduate. I just want to be like other kids my age, but as has always been the problem, I don't know where to start.

I'm sitting at the kitchen table. It's early Monday morning, and my mother is standing in front of the stove, waiting for her coffee water to boil. She's dressed, so I know she's getting ready to leave. We've been here for less than two months, and she's already started to disappear for long periods.

"I'm thinking about going back to school," I say.

"I think that's a great idea—you're way too smart to waste it."

"I don't know," I say.

She turns to go into her bedroom. I follow her.

"I'm so far behind. I don't even know what grade I'm in."

"You really should finish high school and go to college. I wish I'd gone to college," she says as she brushes her hair in the small mirror that hangs above her dresser. I wish she'd look at me.

"I have to go. I have an appointment," she says, already moving toward the door.

I want her to stay, but I don't say that. Instead, I question her. "What appointment?

"Nothing that concerns you," she says, glancing back at me over her shoulder. My mother doesn't break her stride.

"Are you getting high again?" We both know I'm talking about dope since we smoke pot together now.

"No, I'm not getting high. I told you I have an appointment. Stop giving me the third degree." Before I have the chance to say anything else, she's gone.

By the end of February, the apartment is like every other place we've lived—a layover for Gloucester's homeless, the unemployed, and the mentally ill. My mother attracts them. Even on her worst days, she greets the outcasts with a smile. "Hi, beautiful," she'll say to a middle-aged woman at the food pantry who hasn't bathed for a long time and then accepts a hug from the woman who cries in gratitude. "Well don't you look handsome," she'll say to a wrinkled old man with thin, graying hair, who responds with a grin that exposes his few remaining teeth.

Some drifters come to our apartment for a day to escape the cold; others stay for a night or weekend. One of them moved into the bedroom meant for Chrissy, who never ended up coming to live with us. I don't blame her. I wouldn't stay either if I had another option.

That's what I was thinking when I was struck with the idea of going to live with my father. Although I haven't seen him in the year and a half since I ran away, now I know where he is. We've talked on the phone. I'll start over down there. I'll stay clean and get a job. I'm sure there's more for me in Texas than in Gloucester. Here, I don't have anything. Tony left after he found out I hooked up with Jimmy behind his back, I don't have a job, and I'm not in school. There isn't one single reason for me to stay.

"Of course, you can stay here," my father says when I ask him during a scheduled call at Nana Raizin's. "I'm livin' in Frank Pearson's house," he says. "The house ain't finished. There ain't no inside walls yet, no air. Just plywood on the floor," he says. "And, you'll have to use the bathroom in the trailer where Frank's livin', but sure, come on down."

At the end of May, my mother, Chrissy, and I crowd into my mother's friend's rusty old two-door car for the drive to Logan airport. Chrissy and I hug and promise to write. She's crying. We haven't lived together since I ran away, but I'll still miss her the most. She's the one person I know I can count on. The goodbyes are quick and, for me, tearless. I hug my mother last.

My father is waiting for me at the baggage claim. I worried I might not recognize him after not seeing him for three years, but besides weight gain and hair loss, he looks the same. As I walk toward him, I wonder what I'll call him—Dad? Daddy? Al? None of the names feel right. And how should I greet him? With a hug? No, we don't hug. Shake his hand? That's just weird. My head hurts from thinking so much.

When I'm within reach, my father steps forward with his arms out. I think he's trying to hug me. I try to do the same, but we end up bumping awkwardly into each other because we don't know how to embrace.

"Hell, Gail, you sure have growed up," he says.

"Yeah, that's what happens," I say. I want to tell him it wouldn't be such a surprise if he'd visited once in a while, but I don't want to start us off on a negative note.

By the time we get my bag and get to his car, I've decided to call him Dad.

I start singing along with the first song I hear on his chosen radio station. It makes me happy that we like the same music. The conversation comes easily, most of which is him talking about himself. There isn't much I want to tell him about me. He's still racing homing pigeons, his lifelong passion and hobby. He can't keep them where he's living, but he says he'll take me to see the coops. He's also still playing pool. Since all the action happens at night, he stays out late and sleeps during the day. We become quiet when we run out of things to talk about.

He breaks the silence. "Did I ever tell you why I left your mother?" he asks.

"No," I say, surprised by the question. Aside from the fact that we barely see each other, we've never had any deep conversations.

"Well, she was cheatin' on me," he says, in the thick southern drawl he's adopted through a decade of living down south. "You see, your mother was kind of a mess when I met her. She was alone with your sister." Chrissy was just one then. "We both loved to dance. We started spending time together, and then we had you, so we got married." He chuckles at that. "We got an apartment, and she started hangin' around with that ole boy Phil and then she started actin' funny. Now I like to smoke me some weed but I ain't never been into them other drugs. That's what he was doin'—that heroin shit. I had a feelin' she was doin' somethin', but I wanted to help her with you and your sister."

The way he's telling the story reminds me of Arlo Guthrie in the song Alice's Restaurant.

"One day, I was down the Bee Hive shootin' some pool. Well, Phil was there, and he asked me to drive his car somewhere, so I did, but I had a bad feelin' that somethin' wasn't right. It was snowin' that night, and when

I got back to the apartment, there were his footprints in the snow. He was shackin' up with your mother right under my nose. That's when I knew I had to get the hell out of there."

"Why didn't you take me with you?" I ask, after years of wondering why he left me behind.

"Well, I told your mother she better straighten her shit out, or I was gonna take you girls away from her," he says, finishing with a nod like he's adding a period at the end of a long overdue sentence.

That's obviously bullshit. We both know my mother has yet to "straighten her shit out," but I leave it alone. Nothing can change the past. I still wonder why he moved so far away and didn't call for months at a time. Or why he's never, at the very least, sent a Christmas or birthday gift. Or even a card. But I don't ask him. I don't want to ruin this time we have together.

The story was enough of an opening for me to tell him about my drug problem. "I just need to stay away from them," I say.

"Does that mean you don't want to smoke a joint?" he asks as he pulls a fatty out of his shirt pocket.

"Uh, no. I'm always up for a joint. Pot's fine," I tell him. "The other stuff is what gets me in trouble."

ON MY FIRST night in Texas, my father drives us from barroom to pool hall to tavern while he searches for other pool players to hustle. This is his job. After assembling his two-piece custom pool cue, my father looks for his mark. Having a nice stick seems like a good indication that he knows how to play, but somebody in the room will always take the bait. After a coin toss for the break, the game begins. He doesn't run the table even if he wins the break and a ball goes in. Not yet. He's a master hustler.

He looks thoughtful and contemplative as he lines up the next shot. He acts out the play with the stick in his hand. First, he closes one eye, sighs, and chalks the tip of his stick. He moves to the other side of the table, sizing up his options. Sometimes he'll do this for five minutes before finally taking a shot, only to miss the pocket. The other player, my father's unsuspecting prey, smiles and, thinking he's doing the hustling, suggests they up the ante. What began as a five-dollar wager becomes a twenty or fifty-dollar game.

With the bigger jackpot, my father transforms. He no longer holds back. He lines up each shot and the ones that will follow with the precision of an archer aiming at a bull's eye. His playing reminds me of a dance. As I watch him and see the admiration in the faces of the other onlookers, I'm proud to be his daughter.

Within a week, I've established a whole new life here. I go out with my father at night and work during the day. I've got a job cleaning the high school nearby, getting it ready for the new school year. The work keeps me busy and is an honest way to make money.

I still don't have my license at fourteen, but my father lets me take his car to work in the morning. Before I got here, my only experience with driving had been when Jimmy let me steer his van from my milk-crate seat beside him. I love the freedom of having a car to drive, especially in Texas, where I get to navigate my father's Chevy Impala over the long, straight roads of Alvarado and Cleburne.

When I first got here a couple of weeks ago, I loved how it felt to be in a bar—the noise, loud music, and meeting new people. I even laughed at the stupid things my father's friends would say: "There's no way that's your daughter; she's way too pretty," or "Hell, Al, you make good-looking kids." I drink Coke, Sprite, then Coke again, and chain-smoke Newports while I wait for him to finish taking everybody's money. Sometimes I practice my pool game on an empty table or ask my father for quarters for video poker or the jukebox. But now, I'm tired of just sitting, watching, and waiting.

My only other option is to stay at the house when my father goes out at night, and I'd rather not since there's no kitchen which means there's no food. We eat at the local diner or Waffle House. And, of course, there's no air conditioning in the house. It's always sweltering in my bedroom. If Frank is out, I'll go inside his trailer and soak up the cool air while looking for his stash of weed. If there's enough, I'll help myself to whatever won't be missed.

Living in Texas isn't anything like I thought it would be. For one thing, I'm sure I'll kill somebody if I have to hear "Baby's Got Her Blue Jeans On" one more time. I'm sick and tired of people asking me to say, "park the car in Harvard Yard" so they can laugh at my accent, and it sucks that I have to leave the house to go to the bathroom. Worst of all, I hate having to depend on my father, especially when it comes to getting weed. He doesn't need it like I do. My mind never stops; I have to have something to take the edge off.

I've been here just over a month, and I'm already thinking about returning to the northeast. The more I think about it, the better the idea sounds. I miss my mother, Chrissy, Philip, and Little Nana. I miss the ocean. Maybe the issue was never the place; perhaps I'm the problem. If that's true, then I can fix it. If I can work in Alvarado, there's no reason I can't get a job in Gloucester. That way, I won't have to make money with guys. And now that the pills are out of my system, I just won't start up again. As long as I stay clean, I won't need much money anyway. If I don't get back into school, I'll get my GED. Everything will be different because I'll be different.

While celebrating my fifteenth birthday with one of his friends at the Waffle House, I tell my father I'm going home. If he's upset about my decision, he keeps that to himself. I'm sure it's just how he is, as Nana Raizin says, but I wish he'd ask me to stay. I can imagine it would feel good to be missed. On the upside, I'm sure he'll do a better job of keeping in touch now that we've made a stronger connection.

My father offers to pitch in for my ticket, and by the end of August, I have enough money for a one-way trip back to Boston.

EVEN THOUGH JIMMY'S not my boyfriend anymore, he picks me up at Logan Airport. As soon as I close the passenger door, he fishes two Valium out of the van's unused ashtray.

"A welcome home present," he says, smiling.

"I don't want them," I say. I mean it.

"Are you sure?" he asks.

"Well, maybe I'll keep them for later," I say, taking them. I put them in the front pocket of my jeans—just in case.

I swallow the pills dry before we make it back to Gloucester.

23

FOUNDATION

~1986~

Not much changed during my absence, aside from Philip living with my mother full-time. I've been back for over a month, and like most nights since my return, my mother is out. I'm in my bedroom reading a book when Philip passes by my open door. Tonight, it's just the two of us in the apartment.

"Where are you going?" I ask.

"I'm going out," he says over his shoulder.

"Where?" I ask, getting up.

"Out," he says.

"You're not going out, Phil. It's nine o'clock at night."

"Fuck you," he says. "You're not my mother." He's right, of course, but there's nobody else here to stop him.

"There's no reason for a nine-year-old to be out at this time of night," I say as I move toward him.

He's at the top of the stairs when I grab his shirt, pull him into his bedroom, and onto his bed. He struggles to free himself from my grip. I sit on him, pinning his arms down with my knees. His face is red, and he's crying. We're both sweating.

"I'll let you up if you promise you won't go anywhere," I say.

His body relaxes. "I promise," he says.

When I move aside, he jumps up and runs for the door. He pulls it closed behind him to give him a head start, but I don't follow. I'm done.

"Whatever, Phil. Do whatever the hell you want," I yell.

A few seconds later, he screams my name from the bottom of the stairs. I leap from his bed, but he's already on his way back up to the second floor when I get the door open. He's holding his right wrist—the hand is covered in blood, gushing from where his dangling fingernail had been. He must've caught it in the door's latch.

I meet him on the steps and guide him down to the kitchen sink. He starts screaming again when I try to put his hand near the water, so I lay it on a dish towel instead. I don't know what to do. We don't have a phone.

"Stay here," I say. "I'm going to get help."

"No, please don't leave," he says, his voice high. I know he's afraid, but I have to go.

"I'll be right back," I say and run down the stairs to the street below.

"Help. My brother is hurt!" I yell from the middle of the street. All I can hear is the echo of my voice. "I need help!" I yell. The road is quiet. I pound on the door of the house next to ours, no answer. I dash to the next house, the pavement tearing at my bare feet. Nobody is home, but I keep trying.

I'm about five houses down from ours, near the end of the small street, when I see the red flashing lights of an ambulance rounding the corner. Somebody must have heard me. Philip has seen them too. He's on his way down the outside stairs, still holding the towel under his mangled fingertip.

An EMT helps my brother into the back of the ambulance while another asks me questions. "Is this your brother? Does he have any allergies to medications? Where's your mother? Who did this to him? Are you babysitting? Why weren't you with him?"

"Yes. No. I don't know. He did it himself. No, I'm not babysitting. We don't have a phone," I say. "Listen, I don't know where my mother is, and at this point, I don't care. My brother needs help." With that, the interrogation ends, and we leave for the hospital.

A doctor examines Philip as soon as we get into a room. He then stitches his finger. As he wraps the wound, a woman asks me to step out of the room with her. She asks the same questions as the EMT. I answer as best I can.

Once back in the room, the doctor hands me an antibiotic prescription. I thank him, help Philip to his feet, grab hold of his good hand, and head for the exit. In the hallway, a nurse steps in front of us, blocking our path.

"You can't take him," she says. "He needs to be signed out by an adult."

"Try and stop me," I say as I pull Philip around her and out the door.

SOCIAL SERVICES SHOWED up at our apartment with the police this morning. The social worker kept her coat on as she stood in the kitchen. The policeman stayed next to the door.

"There was a report that your brother was hurt last night," she said. "And that there was nobody to care for him—for both of you."

"Bullshit, I took care of him," I said. "And I'm old enough to take care of myself.

"I know you did the best you could."

"I did what anybody would have done; I got him to the hospital." I could feel the lump pushing its way up my throat. My eyes stung.

"Yes, you did. But, it's not your responsibility," she said.

My bottom lip trembled. I hoped she couldn't see it. I didn't speak because I was sure I'd cry.

"We're going to have to place you both in foster homes," she said.

"Hell, you are." I pulled out a kitchen chair and sat with my arms folded across my chest.

I stood again when she moved to the bottom of the stairs for my brother. The cop took a step forward in keeping with mine. There was nothing I could do. She agreed to let me stay but took Philip away with her.

I MEET MY mother at the door when she finally comes home late in the afternoon. She's with her friend Kathy, evidence that she's getting high—if I needed any.

"They took Philip," I say. She knows who "they" are. "He needed stitches, so I got him to the hospital," I say, emphasizing the word "I" so she knows I'm pissed.

"What the fuck, Gail," she says. She's not mad about the bill—the state of Massachusetts will take care of that—she's angry because it's my fault Philip was taken away again.

I want to yell at her, but I suddenly feel exhausted. In my mind, I can say all the things I need her to hear. You're getting high again; I know it. You're doing the same thing you always do. This is your fault, not mine. How can you keep doing this to us? Why don't you care about me? But all I can do is cry. My family is as broken as every single one of her promises.

I retreat to the living room, leaving her and Kathy in the kitchen. I sit on the arm of the couch, fish half of a joint out of my cigarette pack, and look out the window to the street as I light it. I'm just starting to settle into the peace of the high when my mother comes into the room. She sits on the couch, and I hand her the joint. She's the first to speak.

"I'm sorry," she says. She's crying. "You did the right thing. It was my fault, not yours. I should've been here. I'm screwed up again, and I can't stop. I'm going back into detox."

THAT WAS A week ago. My mother left a few days later. Now it's time for me to clean up my own act. Earlier today, when I called Gloucester's Addison Gilbert Hospital and told them I needed help, they told me to come right in.

I thought I was ready for the kind of fresh start my mother is always talking about, but we haven't even finished the intake process, and I'm already having doubts. A staff member is going through my bag, shaking things, making sure I don't have any drugs.

"There's nothing in there," I say, trying to move the process along so I can go smoke.

"It's protocol," she says without looking up.

"It wouldn't make much sense for me to bring drugs to detox."

"You'd be surprised." Again, she speaks without looking in my direction.

She takes my cigarettes, lighter, and razor. I'll have to ask for them whenever I want to smoke or shave.

When she's done, I ask to go outside for a cigarette.

"We have a room for that," she says, pointing behind me with her chin. "You can't go outside." This statement makes my stomach clench. Maybe my mother likes to be cooped up like a prisoner, but not me. I ask for a cigarette and go into the room where I can light up. The more I think about it, the more I realize I can't stay here. After just three hours, the walls are already closing in.

That's it. I decide it's time to go.

The woman who checked my bag is hunched over paperwork inside an enclosure. I lay my crossed arms on the high counter and rest my chin on them.

"I'm going to leave," I say.

"Sorry," she says. "That's not an option." This time, she looks at me.

"Bullshit, it's not." I'm ready for a fight if she wants one.

"You signed yourself in," she says, her voice flat. "You agreed to four days." She puts her head back down.

"I didn't know that," I say. My heart is beating fast. She doesn't respond.

I turn toward the exit and walk as fast as I can without running. I don't look to see if she's watching. I reach for the door handle. It doesn't move. It takes a moment for me to realize it's locked. I'm stuck.

I return to my room and sit on my bed, keeping my hospital-bootie-clad feet on the floor. Only five of us are in the unit, so I have the two-person room to myself. That's good because I'm coming undone. My head won't shut off. I have the chills, yet I'm sweating, and it feels like things are moving under my skin.

Suddenly, it occurs to me—I feel like shit because I haven't gotten high today. Now, I know what to do. I go back to the counter and tell the woman about my symptoms. She looks at a chart, takes my blood pressure, and hands me a small cup of Methadone magic. Fifteen minutes later, everything is okay.

AFTER THREE DAYS in captivity, I'm starting to understand why my mother doesn't mind detox so much. There's an unexpected feeling of safety in confinement. Between recovery-focused meetings, I spend my time smoking and eating. I've also started weaving a potholder. Occasionally, there's even something interesting on TV.

This morning, there's a group of us in the common room. We are an eclectic bunch. A balding middle-aged man sits at a table with playing cards in front of him. Another guy, a younger one, is making a cup of decaf coffee in the kitchen area. I'm in one of the armchairs eating saltines and reading a worn copy of Stephen King's *Carrie*. A lady, my mother's age, is watching television on the couch across from me. "The space shuttle is about to launch," she says.

One of the clinicians comes into the room. Somebody turns up the volume on the small TV set. The screen is split. There's a reporter on one side and the docked shuttle on the other. The reporter says the Challenger holds the first teacher to ever go into space. I've never seen a launch before. Hell, I wouldn't even be watching this one if I wasn't being held hostage. But the excitement of the live audience is infectious, at least until seventy-three seconds after take-off, when there is an explosion. At first, we all sit in silence, looking for the shuttle. Nothing happens. It takes a few minutes for it to sink in. Christa McAuliffe, the teacher, has vanished. All those on board are gone in a puff of smoke.

The camera pans to show the reaction of the Florida audience. They look confused. When the reality of the situation sets in, they start to cry. I feel like joining them. I'm sad for the people who died, but my emotion comes from the sudden realization that, for the first time in a long time, I want to live.

Throughout the rest of my time at Addison Gilbert, each one of my visitors has tried to hand me illegal drugs: Aunt Julie, my boyfriend, and Jimmy, who wants me back. I refuse all of them. I can do this.

I'VE BEEN OUT of the hospital for a month. I lasted two weeks without getting high before I hooked up with Jimmy one night; he had a gram of cocaine. Now, I'm right back where I started. I'm at Little Nana's, where I've been crashing most nights. There are too many people staying at my mother's apartment. She's on the phone, calling from her latest recovery program.

"Hi, beautiful," she says. She sounds clear. "How are you doing?"

"I'm okay, I guess."

"Did you get anything out of the detox?" she asks. I don't know who told her I spent time in the hospital.

"Yeah, but I didn't stay clean," I say.

"That's okay. Just keep trying. Don't give up. I won't either." I don't think she'll ever stay clean, but I don't tell her that.

"I won't," I say.

"I'm going into a six-month halfway house when I leave here. I have a little over a month now."

"What about the apartment?" I ask. I can feel the familiar pressure on my chest, and my throat is tight. Without an apartment, there's no possibility of us being together.

"Well, hopefully, I'll be able to keep it. If I go back there now, I'll just get screwed up again." I know she's right. "I have to build a foundation if I'm going to stay clean," she says. "It's like building a house—you have to start from the bottom. This will be the best move I've ever made. I can feel it. I want, more than anything, to be a good mother to you, Chrissy and Philip. I love you more than I can say."

I want to tell her that I don't know what to do. I'm fifteen, and I have nowhere to go. I can't even get a real job yet. But I don't want to say anything that'll get in her way. I don't want to ruin this for her—for all of us. Instead, I say the only thing I know she wants to hear.

"I love you too."

24

PLACEMENT

~1986~

I'm sitting on Little Nana's porch, waiting for Rena while replaying the telephone conversation we had yesterday. Jimmy always said I analyze everything to death. Anyway, a few days ago, I finally sucked it up and called for Rena to find me a foster home. I had to do something. I rarely sleep anyplace for more than two nights in a row, and the last time I went to my mother's apartment, it was filled with people—some of whom I didn't even know.

Of course, I can't stay here either. Aunt Julie is scarier than ever. She's been hospitalized a couple of times during the last year for schizophrenia, according to the nanas. It's good to know why she acts the way she does, but the diagnosis doesn't make her any easier to be around. That's why I was excited when Rena said she had good news.

"There's a new placement," she said. "A married couple with three young boys in west Gloucester. I think the family will be a good fit for you."

Now that I've had a chance to think, I'm more worried than anything. First off, the word family alone is enough to make me feel sick with anxiety. It's not a word I'd use to describe the group of people I've grown up around. I can't recall being in the vicinity of an actual family for any extended period, never mind live with one. I don't even know anybody whose parents live together—relatives or friends.

I stop biting my thumbnail long enough to take a puff of my cigarette. What if they don't like me? How could they? I can't imagine they'll want me around their kids once they know everything about me. I doubt it'll work out anyway. Foster homes aren't my thing; I didn't last much longer at the second one than I did at Betty's. I'm not very good at following rules.

I'll also be this family's first foster kid. Maybe that'll be a good thing since they won't know how screwed-up I am without anybody to compare me to. On the other hand, I wouldn't say I'm ideal first-foster-kid material. I'm not sure I classify as a kid at all. I haven't been to school in over a year, and I can't remember the last time I hung out with somebody my age.

Rena pulls up in front of Little Nana's at ten o'clock on the dot. It's just like her to be on time. I glide down the banister, skip down the rest of the stairs, and slip into her sensible sedan. I'm actually relieved she's here. It's ironic, I used to think she was my enemy, and today she's my only hope. I hated her when I thought we'd be fine if people would just mind their business. Now, I know things wouldn't have been half as bad if somebody had intervened.

"How are you feeling?" Rena asks.

"Okay, I guess," I say, even though I feel like throwing up.

"I think this is going to work out," she says, glancing at me before pulling onto the street. I stay quiet.

At the rotary, Rena keeps to the right and pulls onto the highway, Route 128, south. I suddenly question whether I can trust this woman and whether she's taking me away from Gloucester.

"Do you have any questions?" she asks, glancing at me.

A million thoughts are swimming around in my head, but I can't think of one thing to say out loud.

"Are you nervous?"

"No," I answer too quickly. She doesn't push.

Rena takes the second exit off the highway—Exit Thirteen. We drive past the small hidden road where Aunt Julie held my hair back just a few years before while I vomited in the weeds. We're headed toward Wingaersheek beach and the small boat launch, where a high-as-a-kite Jimmy nearly drove us off the dirt pier and into the ocean.

Instead of taking a right toward the beach, Rena turns left onto a small street. Despite being just a fifteen-minute ride from Little Nana's apartment, the neighborhood is far from where I belong. This part of town has no apartment rentals. There aren't any cable wires snaked along the front of buildings, disappearing into the top and first-floor windows for illegal service sharing. We've passed three or four single-family houses with doorbells and well-manicured lawns when Rena pulls into the driveway of a white split-level.

She cuts the engine and waits for me to reach for my door handle before she gets out of the car. I let her lead the way to the front of the house. The squeak of the screen door triggers the deep, steady bark of a dog inside. A woman's voice yells above the noise, "Shush, Cassie. Stop it."

The door opens before Rena has a chance to knock. A short, young-looking blond woman stands in the opening, holding a dog who looks like Lassie by the collar with both hands. "Don't worry about her," she says. "She's just excited. She won't bite you, but she might try to lick you to death."

When the woman laughs, the skin around her eyes crinkles, and she shows big white teeth. The cheerful sound fills the entire space and puts me at ease.

"I'm Becky, this is Cassie, and that's Greg," she says, turning and pointing her chin toward a man at the top of the stairs.

"Hi," he says, reaching to shake my hand even though we're still on the landing. Becky again uses her chin to motion for us to go up ahead of her. Rena shakes Greg's outstretched hand first. After we shake, the three of us stand together in a brief awkward silence.

"Let's sit in the kitchen," Becky says as she closes the gate at the top of the stairs. "I run a daycare during the day," she says, pushing down the latch. When she lets go of the dog, Cassie runs to me, tail whipping back and forth. Her wet nose is sniffing my shoes and my legs. She licks my hands. "Cassie leave her alone," Greg says. His smile is as broad and joyful as Becky's.

"Do you want a cup of tea?" Becky asks as she fills the kettle. I nod and sit on one of the wooden chairs around the oval table. They're tea drinkers, like me.

"Hi, Timmy," Becky says to a young, small-framed boy who pokes his head into the kitchen. "Meet Gail. She might be coming to live here with us. That is if she wants to." She looks at me and smiles again.

"Hi," Timmy says with a flash of blue eyes before he turns and runs back down the hallway. Timmy is six, the oldest of the boys, who are all two years apart. Anthony comes out to say hello a few minutes later, a light-haired version of his brother. Ricky, the youngest, is taking a nap.

"It'll be nice to have another female in the house," Becky says. "Somebody else who won't leave the seat up." We all laugh this time.

Becky gets up to pour steaming water into mugs for the three of us. Rena declined the offer of a cup. When Becky returns to the table, she brings a pack of Marlboros and an ashtray.

"Is it okay if I smoke?" I ask.

"Sure," she says, sliding the pack my way.

"Oh, I have my own, but thank you." I'm surprised at how comfortable I feel in this home—in this family.

"Greg quit a couple of years ago, but I'm not ready to give them up yet. It's enough that I've been sober for two years," Becky says. She looks at Greg and smiles again. "Everybody's grateful for that. Right, Greg?"

"Ha. That's right, Becky," he says, smiling back at her.

Becky shows me the house when we're done with our tea. She and Greg have a bedroom and bathroom on the lower level. The boys share one of the rooms at the back of the house on the main floor. The one that will be mine is across the hall from them. It's already been outfitted with matching furniture, a colorful bulky comforter, and coordinating sheets. The third bedroom is empty. All the kids share the bathroom upstairs. The tour ends outside, where there's a pool and a grill on the deck.

"We don't want to put you on the spot," Greg says.

"We'd love to have you," Becky says, as though she's completing Greg's sentence.

For me, it's an easy decision. It's the best offer I've ever had.

A FEW DAYS after settling into my new bedroom, Becky took me shopping for school clothes. She spent much more than the one hundred fifty dollars foster-kid-clothing allowance. I've been around the system long enough to know what social services dole out. The money must've come out of her own pocket. Normally, I'd think there was a motive, people don't do things without looking for something in return, but Becky and Greg are different from anybody I know. They seem to genuinely want to help.

I'm starting school tomorrow. I'm nervous for so many reasons. First, it's March, so all the clicks are already formed. It's also been nearly two years since I stepped foot in a mainstream classroom, although I spent some time at the alternative school. And while I know a lot of the kids from when I was younger, I haven't seen them for a long time. I'm not even sure I'll recognize the kids from middle school and junior high.

At my age, I should be at the beginning of my junior year, but since I never even completed the eighth grade, I don't have any credits. I'll be starting from scratch. Even though the rest of my class will graduate way before me, I want to do this. Now that I have a place to live, I just might be able to pull it off.

TONIGHT, I'M at a twelve-step meeting with Becky. She didn't force me to come, which is why I agreed to check it out. I'm sure it's a waste of time, but I don't have anything better to do. My mother went to meetings sometimes. She'd come home afterward and tell me how great it was while we smoked a joint. Maybe they work for some people, but certainly not for her, and probably not for me.

Becky leads the way into the smoky meeting room. It's crowded with men and women twice my age. Folding tables form a large rectangle in the center of the room, and the outer walls are lined with chairs. I'm surprised to see familiar faces—friends and acquaintances of my mother. Walter's father is also here; he's sober now, too. He says Walter is still drinking and living in Gloucester. I wonder when I'll run into him.

Becky chooses two seats for us at one of the tables and hands me a foil ashtray.

The speaker, a stocky, balding man in his forties, sits at the front of the room. He introduces himself as an alcoholic and then launches into a sermon on the misfortunes of his life. He sounds so much like a sad country song that, in my head, I start singing his story: "My wife left me, I lost my job, my kids wouldn't talk to me, and my dog died." I almost laugh out loud. Boo-fucking-hoo, I think. You wouldn't know the first thing about how much life can suck.

But then, as though sensing he's losing me, the guy changes tracks. "Even worse than losing all those things, I could be in a room with a hundred people and still feel like I was by myself. That, folks, is the loneliness of the alcoholic." It's the first time I've heard anybody describe so perfectly how I've felt my whole life. It makes me feel a sudden and deep connection to this stranger. "Here," he says before closing, "I know I'm not alone." As soon as the words come out of his mouth, I realize I want to belong here too.

IT'S THE END of spring, and I've been going to meetings regularly. I've got a job now too. I'm working in the kitchen at the hospital. It feels good to earn money without feeling bad about myself. I also opened a checking account, and I'm starting to save. The day my checks came, I couldn't stop looking at my name in the upper left-hand corner: Gail Brenner. I feel like I'm starting to become a regular person.

High school has been as new an experience as everything else. Now that I'm able to focus, I'm reminded of how much I love to learn. I'm studying geography, algebra, and the human body. I've been reading Shakespeare in literature, studying the Holocaust in history, and learning how to make clothes in home economics.

Maybe things were going too well. I can't say why for sure, but I let my guard down. After almost two months of clean time, somebody handed me a joint out at the canal during the school lunch period, and I took a hit. I don't know why I took the thing; I didn't even want it, and I felt terrible right away. I knew I'd have to start over at day one.

I was in my head, barely feeling the weed when undercover police suddenly surrounded the small group of us. Unbeknownst to me, they'd been keeping an eye on the canal.

The bell rang right as they surprised us, and nobody went inside. Half the school watched while the police conducted their search. The one who took my purse upended it, and as he dumped the contents onto the ground, he asked: "How's your mother?"

"I don't know," I said as the tears came. It was all too much; I had no idea how my mother was, I'd disappointed Becky, Greg, and myself, and I'd probably never change.

I think the police pitied me because I couldn't stop crying. They didn't arrest me. Instead, they brought me to the principal's office, where I was suspended for three days. The principal called Becky to pick me up.

Now that I'm in the car, I'm not high at all, and I can't stop crying. Becky keeps telling me everything is okay, but still, I can't stop.

I go directly to my room when we get home. All I can think about is how I'll have to face Greg when he gets out of work.

When I first met Greg, I worried he might be a problem. He didn't seem like the kind of guy who would pay for sex with a thirteen-year-old girl, but then again, most of them didn't. Like cockroaches, for everyone you can see, there are a thousand more in the shadows, waiting for the lights to go out. But unlike cockroaches, they're not so easy to identify. They are fathers, grandfathers, brothers, and uncles with regular-looking faces who have everyday jobs like the corner store clerk and the ice cream man.

Greg is not like those men. I learned quickly that he is mild-mannered, patient, and kind. Even though I wear loose-fitting clothes, I don't have to. He doesn't look at me the way most men look at me—the way men look at women. I don't feel his eyes on me when I walk out of the room.

It's almost dinnertime when I hear the squeak and bang of the screen door. Greg is home. Soon after, I hear his footsteps sound in the hall. They stop at my door, and he knocks.

"Come in," I say. I'm sitting on my bed with my feet on the floor.

Greg is smiling when he opens the door and steps inside. Becky hasn't told him.

"I just wanted to tell you that I'm really proud of you. You've done a great job of turning your life around, and you deserve recognition for that," he says. He pulls a dozen red roses and baby's breath from behind his back. The gesture sets me off crying all over again. Nobody's ever given me flowers.

"Thank you," I say, looking at the floor. "But I don't deserve them. I got high today. And suspended."

"Thank you for telling me, and you do deserve them. More than anybody," he says.

He comes into the room far enough to hand me the bouquet. "One mistake doesn't take away all of your progress." On his way out the door, Greg turns back and says: "By the way, Becky told me everything before I bought the flowers."

25

RULES

~1986~

Even though the black town car sent by WCVB-TV is idling out front, I still can't believe what's about to happen—that I will be a guest on daytime television. I check myself in the mirror once more before leaving for my debut. My bangs won't feather, my earrings are too big, and I look fat, but it's too late to change now; my ride awaits.

I'd been back in school for a week after summer break when Mr. Simonds, the high school principal, called me to the main office. He waited for me to take my seat on the other side of his desk before he started talking.

"You've been doing so well," he said. "It shows a lot of guts to return to school after all you've been through." At first, I was surprised he knew anything about me, but then I realized he must know I'm in a foster home at least. "Would you be interested in being a guest on the *Good Day!* show?" he asked. "They're looking for somebody like you who's overcome problems with drugs." Oh yeah, he knows about that too. He was also the one who called Becky the day I got caught getting high at school.

"Really?" I asked. "Me?" All I knew about *Good Day!*—all I still know—is that it's a morning TV show.

"Yes, you," he said, smiling.

Why me? I wanted to ask, but I didn't. Why not me? I said to myself instead, trying the phrase on for size.

"I guess," I said finally. Why not?

THE STUDIO IS outside of Boston, nearly an hour away, which gives me plenty of time to overthink what I'm going to say. I'll just tell it like it is. Well, everything except for anything about making money, or prostitution, whatever you call it. There's no way I can talk about that. It was hard enough to tell Becky and Greg. The truth about Aunt Julie, the men, and the money spilled out of me one night as we sat around the kitchen table. Their responses were not what I expected.

"You were taken advantage of," Becky said.

"There are some really sick people out there," Greg said.

They also want to see the best in me. They need to believe I was a victim, but I'm too smart for that. No number of excuses made on my behalf will convince me otherwise. As much as I wanted to accept their version of who I was, I knew what I was doing. As far as I've always believed, the real truth is that I'm not a very good person.

Although, now I am starting to wonder whether Becky and Greg know something I don't.

Still, I don't need to share all of my past with the whole country. There are plenty of good things to talk about. For one thing, I've been able to stay clean all summer—a little more than three months. It helps that I don't have to worry about where I'll sleep or whether I'll have something to eat. I also get to see Chrissy nearly every day since her foster home is just a five-minute ride from mine. And Philip moved in with us in July. He'd been staying with his father, and although I don't know the details, I'm not surprised it didn't last long. Phil is no better at parenting than my mother.

When we arrive at the studio, I'm guided through the side door of a large, brick building where a woman with a headset greets and ushers me along to the "green room." The other guests are already waiting. We're running late.

"Gail, meet Mark—Mark, Gail." The woman introduces me to the tall, eighteen-year-old boy with whom I'll share the spotlight. He has a long, curly mullet and a pointy chin.

"You two will be the first on stage," she says, glancing at me and then at Mark. After your twelve-minute segment, we'll seat you in the audience during a commercial break." She keeps talking as she leads us onto the set.

"Remember," she says, "this is a live show."

"Holy shit," I whisper. "I didn't know that."

"Yeah, me neither," Mark says.

Mark and I are seated on a dusty-rose-colored couch facing the audience, which is full. Mark is to my right. The host, Dr. Tom Cottle, will sit on a matching loveseat to my left. There's a bouquet of flowers on a glass table in front of us.

We've only been in our places for a few minutes when the music starts, and the countdown begins. I look down at my shaky hands. I've bitten my fingernails so aggressively that they're now little, bloody stumps. I put them under my thighs.

After a short introduction with his co-host, Janet Langhart, the doctor moves to the loveseat and begins the interview.

"Gail, if I may start with you as I welcome you to *Good Day!* Why? How did it begin? What was going on? Give us the story." I'm frozen for a few seconds. I didn't know he'd start with me or ask so many questions at once.

"Well," I say, "I never expected to end up here or expected to stop doing drugs, but I don't know how I really felt. But I know my mother was an addict, and she tried to be with me as much as possible, and she tried to give me as much love as I needed, but I don't think she could give it to herself, so it was kind of hard to give it to me too."

"You started finding those kids in school that at age ten or eleven were taking drugs? How does it start? Maybe you were prone or ripe for it, but how did it begin, Gail?"

"I always hung around with people that were older than me, never people my age, so it wasn't the people that were eleven and twelve that had the drugs. They were getting it from the older kids." It's not a lie; it's just not the whole truth.

"No problem getting it," he says as a statement more than a question.

"No."

"Started with what? Alcohol? Cigarettes? What?"

"Pot," I say.

"Pot. And then moved on to?"

"Pills. That's when it started getting uncool—when I started doing pills."

"Spending how much a week, may I ask?"

"I never really paid for any of them."

"You just got them?" He's being pushy. I think about punishing him with the truth. *Well, you see, Tom, I became involved with prostitution when I was twelve at the urging of my aunt. Yes, I'm an addict, but that's not all. There are two kinds of people, Tom, good ones and bad ones. And I'm one of the bad ones. I was just born that way.*

"Yeah," I say instead. He can't handle hearing the truth any more than I can handle telling it. I say what he wants to hear. I'm a kid who got wrapped up in some bad stuff, but I'm better now.

"Did your parents know what you were doing?" Tom asks. "Your mother was taking drugs, Gail, so she knew you were taking drugs."

"Well, most of the time, she did, but there wasn't really much she could say about it because she was too."

"She's not a heck of a role model for you?" Tom says but doesn't wait for an answer.

"Gail, really quickly, what turned you around?"

This time, I don't hesitate. "Well, for me, I really didn't have a lot of places to live for a long time, since I was thirteen, I think, to fifteen. And in March, they put me in a foster home, and everything just turned around. I got all the care I needed. I liked it there. I like my foster parents. I like their kids. Everything got better, so I figured I ought to get better too." At least that much is true.

Near the end of the hour-long show, the people watching from home are invited to call in.

"Good morning, you're on *Good Day!* and I'd love to get your first name, please, if I could," Tom says to the second caller.

"Hello, my name's Jackie." I know my mother's voice as well as I know my own.

"Jackie?"

"Yes."

"Hi, what's on your mind?"

"I'd like to respond to Gail, my daughter."

I haven't heard her voice for months. Last I knew, she'd gone into another detox—the second since I've been with Becky and Greg—and that she planned to go through aftercare treatment. It was all in a letter I received from her shortly before my sixteenth birthday. I knew the letter was coming because Chrissy got a similar one for her eighteenth birthday the week before.

The camera is trained on Tom, whose expression shifts from composed to surprised. Mark, now seated next to me in the front row of the audience, nudges me with his elbow. My mother doesn't miss a beat.

"I'd like to say that I think it's beautiful that she can understand her mother was sick and was unable to help her, and I give her a lot of credit. She's a power of example to me. I'm in a halfway house at this time, trying to deal with my own addiction."

The audience claps as Tom moves toward me. The closer he gets, the more I want to crawl under my seat. I don't like being caught off-guard like this, exposed for all to see.

"Stand up," he says, reaching for my hand.

"Hold on, Jackie. We'll let Gail speak to you."

What can I say to the mother I haven't seen for more than eight months? My mind is racing, but I can't think. Finally, I say the only thing that comes to mind: "I love you, Mom."

"I love you too," she says.

"Thank you for the call, Jackie. Touching moment. Very nice."

There's a black stretch limousine waiting to take me home after the show, compliments of the network. I have the driver stop at the high school before bringing me home. For today, I'm a celebrity.

A FEW DAYS after my appearance on TV, my mother called to tell me that one of the women in her halfway house had been flipping through the television channels when she saw my face—a face that looked nearly identical to my mother's. She then yelled for my mother, who dialed a telephone number as it scrolled across the bottom of the screen. When she told the network who she was, they patched her through.

"What are the odds that somebody in the house would be channel surfing, that the woman would know your face, or that I would get through to the station for a live call?" she asked.

"I know. It's crazy."

"This was definitely meant to be," she said. "We have important things to do. Every experience teaches us more about how to help others."

I'm still not convinced I'm all that important, but maybe she's right—it was a pretty big coincidence. The thought gives me goosebumps and makes me think that perhaps I am meant to do something worthwhile.

BECKY AND GREG sent Philip away at the beginning of February. I don't even know where he is now. I wish I didn't feel so angry, but I don't think they tried hard enough to help him. I'm trying to keep in mind that they were worried about how Philip's behavior would affect their kids, but it's not easy. They must've known he had problems. Of course, he did. He was nine when he got here, and the kid has been through more in his short life than most adults. Becky and Greg will never understand how much it messes with your head growing up the way we have. It's one thing to hear about it and another to know what it's really like.

I also feel guilty. When Philip first moved into the bedroom next to mine, I was happy enough that we were together again. But before long, I started to worry that his behavior would compromise my home here. I began parenting him. "Did you brush your teeth?" I'd ask. "That shirt doesn't look clean," I'd say. Becky told me that she and Greg could handle taking care of Philip, to focus on being a teenager. But he had been my responsibility for so much of my life that I couldn't help myself. Now there's nothing I can do for him. And I feel like it's all my fault.

A new foster girl, Sandy, has moved into the vacant spot left by my brother. Although a stranger to Becky and Greg, I already knew Sandy from school. She's blond, skinny, and she's trouble. Just a week after moving in, she started climbing in and out of her bedroom window at night to ride around and get high with her boyfriend, Danny. Turns out, it was the same Danny who tried to have sex with me when I was eleven. She introduced us one afternoon when he picked her up in his car. Of course, he didn't recognize me; I'm not a little girl anymore.

Sandy confides in me. She tells me things I don't want to know about getting high and the things she does with Danny. I won't say anything to

Becky and Greg; secrecy is the value I cherish most. But I resent that they don't notice the burden I'm carrying. They treat me differently now, as though they need to lay down the law to establish whatever authority they didn't when I got here nearly a year ago. Gone are the days when we sat around the kitchen table with hot tea, the three of us talking like friends. I feel like I don't matter to them anymore.

In the middle of the night, less than two months after Sandy's arrival, I pack as much as I can carry and leave through my bedroom window.

26

PARENTAL CONSENT

~1987~

"You're pregnant," the nurse practitioner says as solemnly as if she's just told me I have a terminal illness. I can understand her lack of excitement. As my doctor's right hand, Alice has known me for much of my life, and she's well aware that I've yet to turn seventeen and, as always, my housing situation is unstable. I've been living in Lynn for the last couple of months with my mother and Philip. He's been back with her for as long as I've been there. After leaving Becky and Greg's house, I stayed with Chrissy and her foster family for a short time. That's where I met Mark.

"Do you want me to get your boyfriend?" Alice asks. Mark is in the waiting room.

"No, I'll tell him when I leave." I'm sitting on the table with a paper blanket covering me from the waist down.

"Okay, she says as she moves toward the door. I'm going to write you a prescription for some prenatal vitamins. I'll need to see you again in a month." I won't need to see her since I'll no longer be pregnant in a month, but I keep that to myself.

I light a Newport as soon as we step outside. Mark gets into his Blazer to wait for me to finish. The fact that he hates the smell of cigarette smoke is just one of the many differences between us. He looks like my type—tall, dark, good-looking—but unlike any of my other boyfriends. For one thing, he's never even tried smoking pot. He's only been drunk a handful of times, and he hated it. He knows I used to do drugs, but I can't bring myself to tell him everything about my past. I make money legitimately now, working three jobs, so he doesn't need to know.

I smoke the cigarette down to its filter and flick the butt into the parking lot. I'm sweating when I pull myself up and into the Blazer's passenger seat. Even with the windows down, the July heat is stifling. Once settled, I tuck my hair behind my ear and clear my throat.

"I'm pregnant," I say.

Mark is quiet. I already know what he's thinking. Neither one of us is ready for this. He's a few years older than me and doesn't have his shit together any better than I do. He's been renting a room near my mother's apartment with some other guys. Before that, he'd been living in an apartment he shared with his ex-girlfriend. He had to move out because he couldn't afford it on his own. Maybe we'll get a place together in the future, but after knowing each other for just three months, that's another thing we're not ready for.

"You're not keeping it, right?" Mark asks.

"Of course not. We need to at least get an apartment before thinking about having a baby."

"I don't want kids," he says. He's already told me that. I can't say I never want kids, but I definitely don't want one right now.

Mark and I speak little during the ride back to Lynn from my Gloucester doctor's office. It's strange knowing a baby is growing inside of me. I wasn't sure I could get pregnant after all the drugs I've done, but I'm not surprised. Mark is always coming at me, and even though I'm on the pill, I hardly ever remember to take it.

It's early afternoon when Mark drops me off at home. My mother is in her bedroom, standing in front of her dresser. I speak to her from the doorway.

"I'm pregnant," I say. Again, the words make me cry.

"Oh, Gail," she says as she moves toward me with open arms. "Having a child is an awesome responsibility." Under different circumstances, I'm sure I'd say something sarcastic, but today I just let her hug me. We sit side by side on her perfectly made double bed. I wipe my eyes with the back of my hand.

"I'll support you in whatever decision you make," she says. When I look at her, I notice that her pupils are pinned—specks of black in a sea of foggy blue. She's high. How did I miss this when I came in? I wasn't paying attention. I almost laugh at her offer of support. She won't even be able to hang on to this apartment for long. I think about confronting her, but that's not a priority right now.

"I'm going to have an abortion," I say without looking at her. She hugs me again before she stands and changes into the long-sleeved shirt that had been folded next to her on the bed.

"I'll be back later, and we can talk about this some more," she says. I love you more than I can say." She splashes rose water on her face, and she's gone.

I GOT A quick appointment at an abortion clinic in Boston. My state insurance will cover the cost. Thankfully, it'll all be over soon, and Mark and I can get a place as planned. I doubt I'll return to high school; I'm so far behind. At this point, it makes more sense for me to get my GED. Maybe I'll go to college. Either way, the sooner this is done, the better.

I avoid meeting the accusatory stares of the people on the clinic steps. The handful of protesters hold pictures of babies and signs with the word "abortion" circled in red with a line crossed through it. They speak directly to me.

"Please reconsider. There are people who can help you." I want to respond, but I don't. *Bullshit*, I want to say. *Do you mean the same people who helped my mother with her kids?* One of them touches me on the arm as though this human contact is enough to make me change my mind. It isn't.

Once inside, the receptionist hands me a clipboard. I sit next to Mark on one of the stained, worn fabric chairs in the waiting area, along with another couple and a man sitting alone. I fill out the paperwork quickly and slide it through a hole in the glass to the woman who greeted me.

I'm surprised—but grateful—when my name is called a few minutes later.

"I'll be back," I say to Mark as I stand.

At the window, the woman pushes a sheet of paper toward me. "You need to have parental consent," she says.

"What do you mean?"

"You're a minor, and a parent or guardian needs to sign the form."

My stomach dips like it does whenever it's time to move again. I feel powerless. "But you don't understand," I say. My voice sounds high and thin, like I'm speaking from inside a tin can.

"I've been on my own for years. I take care of myself. My mother is fresh out of her most recent halfway house, and she's getting high again." I know I'm rambling, but I feel like I'm fighting for my life. "My father lives in Texas, and I don't even know if I could reach him if I wanted to—which I don't." Everybody in the room is watching. The desk lady looks sympathetic, but nothing has changed.

"I'm sorry," she says. "I don't make the rules."

I can't talk to Mark on the way home. I'm thinking about my options. The most logical thing to do is to get my mother's signature and make another appointment. Maybe I'll forge it—they don't know her handwriting.

Mark is quiet too. I know he's as frustrated as I am, but there's probably more to it. I'm sure he's worried I'll change my mind now that I have time to think.

Maybe I will change my mind.

The idea comes out of nowhere. I hadn't even considered the possibility. But why not? I mean, how hard can it be to have a baby? You love it, change its diapers, feed it. I know how to do those things; I've been babysitting since I was ten. This little human being will need all the love and caring I wish my mother had given me. It'll give me something meaningful and important to focus on.

By the time Mark leaves me at my mother's apartment, I've decided to keep the baby.

I'D BEEN WAITING for a good time to tell Mark that I'm not going to have an abortion. I wanted to be one hundred percent sure. It's been a few days, and now, I'm positive.

After picking me up at my mother's, Mark drives to a playground nearby. In the lot, he parks in the shade of a maple tree. The sun is still hot even though it's late afternoon. I feel like I might burst with the news that I hurl at him.

"What if we keep the baby?" I say without looking at him. "We love each other, and we're both working."

"No," he says without hesitation.

"Why not?"

"Please don't do this," he says.

"Why are you being so stubborn?" I ask, turning to him.

"I told you I don't want any kids." I know he means it when he flashes his angry eyes at me.

"Well, it's not like we planned this, but it happened. I'll stay with my mother until we can get a place and—"

"What the fuck Gail. I already told you I don't want any kids. Not now—not ever."

There's no changing his mind, but there's no changing mine either. "I'm keeping the baby," I say.

I can feel the air shift in the car as it fills with his anger. There's no point in saying anything else. When he opens the door, I glance in his direction one more time. Just as I start to turn away from him, he slams the door with such force that the tempered glass of the window shatters and sprays chunks of sparkling light onto the driver's seat, the floor, and me. I see it just in time to shield my face. When the noise stops and everything has settled, I look up again to see him walking away without looking back.

Fuck him, I think. I don't need him; I don't need anybody.

27

OVERDRAWN

~1987~

I'm due in April. The way it breaks down, I must have gotten pregnant sometime in late June, about six weeks before my seventeenth birthday. Not the birthday present I had in mind, but maybe it's exactly what I needed.

Mark is still coming around, although I'm sure it's only a matter of time before we break up. It's simple: he doesn't want kids and I'm having one. And he likes skinny girls. Pretty soon, I won't be that either.

I can't be bothered with that right now. I have to think about where I'm going to live. If my mother is back on heroin, and I'm sure she is, she won't be able to hang onto this place for long. In addition to her appearance, there are other tell-tale signs that she's headed back down that road. She won't look me in the eye, which is always a dead giveaway. She's also been going out a lot. In fact, she's out more than she's home. And, although it might not seem like a big deal to anybody else, she hasn't been cooking dinner like she had when I first got here. I just hope she can hold it together for a few more months so I can save some money.

It's nearly impossible to save anything while working for crappy wages. I can't find a job that pays more than the three dollar and sixty-five-cent minimum wage. Unskilled teenage girls aren't in high demand. Even with the three jobs I juggle, my take-home pay is only a few hundred dollars a week. As hard as it is, making money illegally is unthinkable to me now. I want to set a good example for my baby. If I can stay honest and clean,

I'll have already given him or her more than my mother has given me.

Right now, my most significant expense is a solid nicotine habit, which I've been trying to quit. I'm down to less than a pack a day, but they're so damn hard to stop. I love the way the filter rolls between my fingers and the rush of thick, white, minty smoke as it fills my lungs. There's also nothing I can rely on more than a fresh pack of Newports.

After smokes, the rest of the money I make goes directly into the bank. In the month since I found out I'm pregnant, I've been able to save a few hundred dollars. I should be able to get an apartment well before the baby comes.

I keep meticulous records of my bank account, which is why I was so surprised to receive a letter on Friday saying I was overdrawn. The bank has also added fees, bringing my account to a whopping negative seventy-five dollars. Without a phone at home, I had to wait all weekend to resolve the issue. Now that I'm at work and my store manager is in the storage room, I finally have an opportunity to reach out to the bank. The woman who answers my call listens as I explain the bank's mistake before she puts me on hold.

"I don't see an error," she says flatly upon returning to the phone. Her we-can-fix-this-problem tone is gone.

"That doesn't make any sense," I say. I'm starting to panic. "I can't be overdrawn. My balance should be three-hundred-and-forty dollars."

When she responds, she sounds angry. "Well, if you'd stop writing checks when you don't have the money in your account to cover them, then you wouldn't be overdrawn."

I think about telling her to go to hell. Who is she to judge me after all the hard work I've put into saving that money? And I'm staying clean, and—all at once, I realize there hasn't been a mistake. The revelation slams into me, hitting me so hard I can't speak. My mother is responsible. She has somehow stolen my money.

The bank lady is still talking when I hang up. I'm rooted in place behind the counter. I don't want to cry, but I'm powerless to stop it. Gratefully, there aren't any customers in the store. A few minutes later—five, maybe ten—the manager comes in from the back.

"I have to go home," I say. Instead of waiting for a response, I pull my purse from underneath the counter and leave. Wearing flats, the fifteen-minute walk takes me less than ten.

By the time I get to the front steps of the apartment, I'm sweating so heavily from the August heat that my button-down shirt and black dress pants are sticking to my body.

Once inside, I go to my bedroom and open the sock drawer where I keep my box of checks. I drop the cover to the floor and pull out the first book. I thumb through it before holding the pages sideways to look for empty spaces. It's full. I do the same with the second book. As soon as the third book is in my shaky hand, I know it has been tampered with. It's lighter than the others. I don't need to feather the pages. When I hold it up to the light, I can see a thin sliver in the middle of the pad where the checks used to be.

Aside from the sound of my heartbeat throbbing in my ears, the apartment is quiet. I don't think anybody else is home. If my mother is here, she's sleeping.

I move quickly through the rooms, looking for her. Philip's room is next to mine. His unmade bed is empty. He's at school. Though I came in through the living room, I check it again since I wasn't paying attention when I got here. It's empty except for the few pieces of Goodwill furniture my mother has collected.

I don't even know what I'll say when I find her. Though there's nobody else to blame, my mother will deny taking the checks, which is why the proof is still clutched in my hand. I go back through the dining room to the empty kitchen, where I can see that her bedroom door is ajar. I pause next to the refrigerator and admire a small heart-shaped picture of her and Philip, taken when she was still in the halfway house a few months ago. They're smiling like we all do when she's not getting high.

When I feel ready, I step forward and push the door open. The room is empty.

I go back into my bedroom and sit on the bed with my feet on the floor. I feel like I can't catch my breath, but I have to move.

Again, I check the living room and the kitchen and look into my mother's empty bedroom as though I might have missed her the first time. The bed is still perfectly made, as always. The ends of the sheer scarf that hangs over her dresser fall evenly on either side. Everything has been placed on top with intention: her hairbrush, a blue bottle of rose water, a scented candle, and a large white shell. She told me before about how she tries to keep everything organized on the outside, so nobody will know how messed up she is on the inside. I feel sorry for her for a moment. But can I forgive her? Can I continue to stay here?

If I leave, I won't be able to keep an eye out for my brother, who, I'm pretty sure, is already smoking pot and is on the same path as his parents. But if I go now, I won't have to wait for the inevitable eviction.

I'm torn.

Back in the living room, I sit perched on the edge of the couch, trying to decide what to do next. If I stay, I'll have to keep everything under lock and key. I can't trust my mother. And the baby. I have somebody else to consider now.

As soon I hear a door slam outside, I'm up and swinging the front door open. My mother hasn't even made it onto the porch. She hesitates on the last step when she sees me, and says hello before her eyes move to the checkbook in my outstretched hand.

Silently, I turn around and move toward the kitchen, away from her and the idling car she'd come from. I can hear her walking behind me, but she doesn't speak. She must be waiting for us to sit down. I settle on one of the unmatched chairs at the kitchen table, but she doesn't stop in the kitchen. Instead, she goes into her bedroom and closes the door.

I light a cigarette and wait.

A few minutes pass before she comes out of her room. She doesn't sit at the table. She walks out of the kitchen and into the dining room. She's heading for the door.

"Wait," I say, getting up to follow her. "Where are you going?

"I'll be back shortly, and we'll talk about this," she says without stopping.

"I need to talk to you now," I say.

"I know. I'm sorry, but I have to be somewhere," she says.

I'm in the living room when my mother closes the door behind her. She's always been faster than me. It's quiet when I'm alone again. Standing in the middle of the room, I open the checkbook, tear the remaining checks in half, and drop them on the floor. She can have them now. We don't even need to talk. She could apologize and promise she'll never steal from me again, but I can't trust her. I can't stay here.

Now that I've decided to leave, I can't get away quickly enough. I take whatever clothes I can stuff into a canvas bag and head toward the train station—a twenty-minute walk, at least. I'll call Mark at his mechanic job when I get to Gloucester unless I come across a pay phone before then.

I'm nearly jogging despite the heat, and I don't slow down until I'm halfway to the station. I move my bag from one shoulder to the other and push my soggy bangs behind my ear. Of course, I'm not showing yet, but I can already feel my body changing. I'm panting, and my hamstrings burn. I don't know whether I want to scream or cry. My eyes sting. I need a drink of water. And a cigarette.

Suddenly, I hear my mother's voice. "Gail," she says from the passenger seat of a car, moving slowly along to match my pace.

I turn my head slightly but then back to the ground, keeping my eyes focused. I don't answer.

"Just wait," she says.

When I don't respond, she continues. "I'll pay you back. I promise. You don't have to leave. Just get in the car so that we can talk."

I don't say anything. I can't. I'm afraid she'll convince me to stay if I give her a chance.

"I relapsed. I'm sorry. I love you."

I can only respond in my head. *Go to hell. You took money away from my baby to feed your baby heroin. How could you? Don't worry; the one thing I learned growing up is that you don't rat. You're in the clear. You can have the money, but I'm not coming back. I love you too.* I hold myself together until the car pulls away and out of my sight. When she's gone, I sit on the stone steps of an apartment building and allow myself to break down for a few minutes. That's all I need, just a moment to feel sorry for myself before I catch the train.

As always, landing back in Gloucester feels like coming home, even though I don't have a home here. Little Nana's place is only five minutes from the train station, so that's where I go first. She's on the couch watching

General Hospital. Her warm, dark living room embraces me when I step inside. For the time being, there's nowhere else I'd rather be. Thankfully, Aunt Julie isn't home. These days, she tends to ramble about how there are people "looking to kill her—mobsters and politicians—very powerful people." She refuses to take her medication because the pills make her gain weight.

I call Mark at work to tell him that I'm in Gloucester and I won't be returning to Lynn. The conversation is brief; the pregnancy has driven us so far apart. But I can't worry about that right now. My main concern is how badly I want to get high. The only thing I can think to do is go to a twelve-step meeting.

THERE ARE PROBABLY fifty people in the church gathering room, which can seat seventy-five. I haven't been here for a few months, at least. Even before I moved to Lynn, I'd been getting away from meetings. I could say I didn't go because it was hard to get to them without a car, but the truth is, I was spending all of my time with Mark. It feels good to be here tonight. I feel safe. I usually sit in the back and whisper to whoever is next to me, but tonight I sit quietly in the second row.

When the main speaker is finished, he opens the floor for discussion. My hand is the first one up. I tell the story in between sobs. My only worry about giving so much away is that many people in the room know my mother, and I don't want them to view her in a negative light. But I'm pregnant, and I have nowhere to go. Right now, my need to share this predicament is more significant than my need to protect my mother.

As I talk, the person sitting behind me puts a hand on my shoulder. When I finish, I take a deep breath and wipe my eyes before turning to see who has extended their hand. It's Greg. Becky is sitting next to him. Their sad eyes make me start crying again. I want to tell them about all that's happened in the seven months since I ran from their house, but another person is talking, so it'll have to wait.

Greg leans forward and whispers, "You can stay with us for as long as you need to."

Becky says: "You always have a home with us."

28

EXPECTING

~1987~

It's early on a Saturday afternoon as I watch Mark from my new empty living room. He backs a borrowed pick-up truck into the open space in front of my car, an old four-door Ford from his father's junkyard. Until today, aside from getting me the car, Mark hadn't been much help. I can't blame him, I guess. He doesn't want any kids, and I'm having his baby against his wishes.

But things may be different now that I have my own place. It's been a long time since Mark and I have been alone. After leaving Lynn, I went to Becky and Greg's and Wellspring House, a local shelter. Here, we'll have the space to focus on our relationship and the family we're going to have. He'll fall back in love with me and his baby; how could he not?

I WAIT UNTIL Mark and his friend are out of the truck before I step outside into the October cold. From my vantage point above them on the front stoop, I have a full view of the truck's bed. It's packed with pieces they'll have to lug up the four stone steps and carry along the short pathway to the front door of my apartment. I also have a full view of Gloucester's once-dilapidated Alper Road. It's had a face-lift and is now home to thirty or so low-income families.

Mark looks up at me as he pulls the straps off the load. "There's a ton of stuff there. I couldn't fit it all in one trip," he says. He sounds annoyed, but I'm excited. It's the first time I've seen the furniture—a donation from a family whose mother recently passed away.

My furniture. Before Mark arrived with the truck, my possessions were limited to a couple of trash bags filled with clothes, books, journals, and thrift-store finds. Now, the place will look like a home.

"There's more?" I ask.

"Yeah, the rest of the bedroom stuff."

They carry the couch up the stairs first. Mark is on one end, and his redheaded, chubby buddy is on the other. The sofa is an ugly plaid, but I can imagine what it will look like with some modifications. After learning to sew in home economics while I lived with Becky and Greg, I doubt I'll have a problem learning how to reupholster.

The guys bring in two, what I now know to be, Adirondack chairs. Their low, deep wooden frames, flat arms, and foam cushions remind me of the ones where I'd find sleeping strangers when I was a kid. I tell them to place the chairs on the wall opposite the couch. Those, too, will undergo changes. All I need for the living room is a coffee table. In the kitchen, there's a small alcove that perfectly fits the round oak table and four matching chairs.

They leave to get the rest and return with the bed frame, side tables, and dresser.

"I have to bring Hadley back to Ipswich," Mark says after he carries the last piece into the bedroom.

"Are you coming over after?" I ask, wishing for his company, although I don't expect that he will.

"I don't know. It'll probably be too late. I have to work early tomorrow."

I reflexively suck in my belly. At nearly seventeen weeks, it's starting to swell, and I know that's why Mark isn't attracted to me anymore. I just hope he changes his mind about the baby and me soon; I don't want to be alone.

After they leave, it's still early enough in the day to do some shopping. Between working part-time, delivering meals to the elderly, and collecting welfare, I was able to save some money and food stamps while at Wellspring. Ames, Gloucester's only department store, has everything I need for the apartment: bedsheets, a mop, a broom, plates, cups, silverware, a dish strainer, a can opener, curtains, and a candle. The sheets are white with tiny red, and blue flowers like my mother used to have. The candle reminds me of her, too. I splurge on a gold-framed, three-piece picture set of a lake with mountains behind it that I hope will class up the place and a puzzle in case I get bored.

The supermarket is right next to Ames. I quickly realize I should have made a list. Of course, I've been food shopping, but I've never been responsible for getting all of the essentials. There's so much to choose from. I have no idea what to get. It might help if I knew how to cook. As tension begins to creep up my back, I think about what my mother would buy: bread, milk, butter, and eggs. I find them and put them in the cart. Salt and pepper. Shit. I don't have any of that stuff, either. I decide to come back another day with a list.

IT TAKES THREE trips to get all the bags from my car and into the apartment. Although hot and tired, I slide a cassette tape into my hand-me-down boombox and begin to sing along with a "Whiter Shade of Pale" as I get to work setting up my new home. The song reminds me of the best parts of my mother. I can't help but wonder if this is how she felt as she prepared each new apartment for us.

It's after midnight by the time I finish. Nothing is left undone. I tour the rooms as though I'm a guest who's just arrived. Starting in the living room, I stand at the front door and take it all in. Although it's a basement unit, it doesn't feel that way. The house is on a hill, so there are full-sized windows on the front walls.

While on my way to the kitchen, I bend to pick a piece of lint from the thin industrial carpet. Everything is in its place. The chairs are tucked neatly into the table, and the pink placemats rival those of John the john. In my bathroom, a blue curtain hangs along the bathtub, and a small matching rug covers the linoleum in front of it. Two blue towels, as many as I could afford, hang neatly folded over the single silver towel rod.

And the bedroom—my bedroom—is perfect. The foundation's ledge, which wraps around the room on its two outside walls, is mostly empty, except for the books I've arranged near the corner, largest to smallest. Even with all the furniture in here, there's still enough space to spin around with my arms outstretched, so that's what I do.

Though exhausted by the time I crawl between my crisp new sheets, I lie awake. My body aches from all the day's activity. I'm overwhelmed with the newness of everything, and I'm lying in a bed that belongs to me for the first time in my life. The nightstand, the digital alarm clock, the candle—everything here is mine and mine alone. Now that I don't have to depend on anybody else for a place to live, I know I'll never be homeless again.

29

MERRY CHRISTMAS

~1987~

My first major purchase is a Sears Kenmore sewing machine that costs more than half of my biweekly welfare check. Now that I'm back in school, Mrs. Donoghue, my home economics teacher, will teach me how to reupholster. With such a skill, I'll be able to take on paid sewing projects for other people, and the machine will pay for itself.

More importantly, sewing keeps my mind busy. Even if there were no chance it could earn me money, I would've spent everything I had on the machine. There's also the bonus of having something of value that Aunt Julie can't steal and that my mother can't pawn.

In early November, I arrive at Mrs. Donoghue's Home Ec classroom—couch cushion in hand—shortly after the last bell rings. With the door open, I can see her cleaning inside. She's wearing what seems to be her uniform: a dark below-the-knee wool skirt, a button-up shirt, a button-down sweater, and rubber-soled loafers. Her short brown hair is as serious as she is—perfect for the important job of teaching teens the how-to of household chores.

When she sees me, Mrs. Donoghue waves me in and offers me a chocolate chip cookie, compliments of her last-period class. The room feels different with just the two of us—empty but peaceful.

We get to work right away. My teacher shows me how to lay the fabric over the cushion and cut along the edge. What I like most about Mrs.

Donoghue is that, unlike other adults, she sticks to what she knows. She teaches me how to sew without trying to tell me how to live a life in which she has no experience.

I begin cutting the rest of the pieces as soon as I get home. I know I should go to a meeting, I haven't been for over a month, but instead, I sew. My justification is simple—the meeting people can't understand what I'm going through, as none of them are seventeen and pregnant. It's been hard enough going to school looking the way I do; my belly too big to hide. So, I work until I can't keep my eyes open. By the time I triumphantly squeeze the first cushion into its new case, it's past midnight. For the rest of the week, I spend my afternoons and nights cutting fabric for the other four cushions, and then I sew some more.

Mrs. Donoghue then shows me how to insert a zipper into the back of the cover. After three weeks of working on the project, I've finished one cushion, zipper, and all. The remaining five cushions need only zippers, but the bigger I get, the harder it is to work the sewing machine. My belly is in the way. Until last week, I was able to wear jeans with a string tied between the button and buttonhole. Now, even pants with elastic bands around the waist are too tight at twenty-four weeks. As much as I hated to spend money on something I'll only use for a few months, I finally broke down and bought a maternity outfit.

It also hurts me to sit for too long. My back aches and a random sharp pain shoots down the back of my leg. Pregnancy doesn't agree with me. I don't regret the baby growing inside my belly, but I hate the changes in my body. A new dark line runs from my belly button to my pubic hair, flanked by wide, vertical purple marks—my body's response to the rapid stretching of my formerly twenty-seven-inch waist to whatever ungodly number it is now. Add that to the painful swelling of my already too-large breasts.

There's no way I'll be able to finish the furniture by the holiday. When I explain to Mrs. Donoghue that the work of the couch reupholstery is too much for me, she offers to teach me how to knit. "It'll give you something to do over break," she says. I don't know if she spends much time alone, but Mrs. Donoghue seems to sense my need for something to occupy my mind.

After my first lesson, I purchased a pattern for a cropped sweater with long, raglan sleeves and the yarn I'll need to make it. When I got home, I set myself up on the couch with brand-new knitting needles and a skein of yarn and began. Knit one, pearl one. Ten minutes later, I had the first row of stitches on the needle. An hour later, I was still curled in the corner of the couch, knitting row after row.

The more effortless knitting becomes, the less it occupies my mind. I think about how lonely I am and all the people I miss. Mark hasn't been around much the last couple of weeks; I'm pretty sure he's seeing somebody else. I haven't heard from my mother since I left her Lynn apartment three months ago. She could be dead, and I wouldn't even know it. My father is doing his own thing, as usual. I haven't heard from him for months either. And Philip. If only I could have him with me. Chrissy's living her own life, and I can't remember the last time I saw Little Nana. That's my fault. I can't deal with Aunt Julie and Big Nana.

Sometimes, I go out to Friday night sober dances with my friend Melissa, but I feel as awkward on the dance floor as I do in a meeting. I blame the pregnancy, but the truth is, I've always felt this way. Unlike Melissa, I'm not sure of myself.

Melissa lives in one of the other buildings in our small neighborhood. We have a lot in common: we're the same age, she'd also been a homeless child, and she's got a baby. We spend a lot of time together, but I'd rather be at my apartment, surrounded by my own things, and she has to stay home with her little girl.

Most nights, I sit on the couch alone and knit until I need to eat, stretch, or go to the bathroom. Occasionally, I move to the living room floor, where I've started putting together the puzzle I bought when I moved in.

By Christmas vacation, I've finished the right front side of the sweater with just a couple of mistakes, but the instructions are too complicated for me to move on to the next stage without help. Since I can't ask Mrs. Donoghue until after the holidays, I pack the finished panel, yarn, and needles in a box and push it to the back of my bedroom closet.

WITH CHRISTMAS JUST a week away, I'm in overdrive trying to get everything ready. As the first in my apartment, I'm determined to make it a perfect holiday. The traditions start today. In my mind, the family

I can't quite imagine joins me in celebration. Maybe Chrissy will come by, or my mother and Philip. Other than that, I'm not sure. Either way, when whoever arrives, we'll listen to festive holiday songs and drink hot chocolate while we take turns opening presents. I don't have it all figured out, but whatever is to come, I'm sure it starts with a tree.

I've never been tree shopping. If we had a Christmas tree when I was a kid, either my mother came home with it, or it was there when I woke up in the morning. Mark said he didn't have time to shop with me, so I'm at the lot by myself. It's a Saturday afternoon, and the place is packed. Families weave in and out of the trees stuffed in the supermarket parking lot. Some trees are stacked horizontally, wrapped in netting, while others are on display, open, and full. I take a deep breath before getting out of the car. From what I can see, I'm the only person here alone.

Once on the lot, I start imagining what the other people must think of me—a lonely, pregnant teenage girl. They're judging me for sure. I suddenly feel as out of place here as I do everywhere else. All I want is to get what I came for so I can go home. I choose a display tree, one closest to my parked car. The salesman throws in the stand for an extra five dollars; I forgot to buy one. I skip the two-dollar netting wrap and sit in the car while a twenty-something guy ties the tree to my roof.

When he's done, I crack the window and take a deep, relieving drag from a freshly lit Newport. Tree shopping was not at all what I expected.

On the other hand, getting the tree into the house is easier than I thought it would be. I stand in my tiny front yard, at the edge of the stone retaining wall, and slide the tree directly from the roof of my car, bypassing the stairs altogether. I drag it into the apartment and set the stand in the far corner of the living room. I want the tree to be the first thing anybody sees when they enter, although I'm not sure who will see it other than me.

I lean the tree upright against the wall before moving it into the stand. My arms aren't quite long enough to get a hold of the trunk, and when I try, a branch pokes me in the eye. This is, most certainly, a two-person job. I turn my face to the side, close my eyes, wrap my arms around the tree as though we're in a slow dance, and lift it as high as I can while blindly moving it to where I'm sure the hole must be.

I miss my mark the first couple of times but finally land it in the center.

Now I'm stuck. I can't bend down to tighten the screws into the trunk while holding the tree. And I'm sweating. I pull the whole setup closer to the wall and lean it again so I can move to the floor. I grab the trunk, ignoring the branches pressed against my face, and turn the screws to lock it in place. Finally, when the tree stands nearly straight, I pull it away from the wall.

As exhausted as I am from the effort, I want to finish decorating. I start at the bottom and run a string of small blinking lights deep in the branches, criss-crossing them to the top. I don't have enough lights to wrap them around, but nobody will see the back anyway. I tack the other strand of lights around the window and door and cover them with silver garland.

After I hang the last glass bulb on the tree and make myself a cup of hot chocolate, I admire the room. Sitting on the couch, with the doorway to my left and the tree to my right, colorful, blinking lights surround me. Red, green, blue, and yellow flicker and reflect off the bulbs and the cup I'm holding. The tree could use more decorations—maybe some tinsel— and I don't have anything for the top yet, but I must admit, it looks pretty damn good. It looks like Christmas.

ON CHRISTMAS MORNING, I wake feeling queasy. The morning sickness is mostly gone, but not today. In my t-shirt and underwear, I make my way to the bathroom. I don't need to put on pants; I'm alone.

I splash water on my face and brush my teeth before looking my reflection in the eye. Today, I don't say, "What the fuck is wrong with you?" Today, I force a smile and pretend that the person in the mirror is a stranger. "Merry Christmas," I tell her.

I know better than to think there will be a present under the tree, but a part of me still wants to believe in fairy tales, so I look anyway. Of course, it's empty, aside from some fallen needles.

I put a cassette of classic holiday songs in the player and sit on the couch while I wait for company that never comes.

By noon, although it's still December twenty-fifth, Christmas is over for me. I start to undecorate the tree. I wrap each bulb in newspaper before adding it to a cardboard box I've labeled "Christmas." As I remove the lights, I wrap the strands around my hand and secure them with trash bag twist ties. Now that the tree is dry, I'm able to easily lift it out of the stand and toss it outside my door, near the trash. Halfway through the day, after sweeping every needle from the rug, all signs of Christmas are gone.

THE DAY AFTER Christmas, I sit cross-legged on the floor in the living room, puzzle pieces in front of me, my pregnant belly bulging. I'm searching for pieces of a kitten's face, but my mind is elsewhere. All I can think about is how alone I am in the world. Nobody cares about me. It wouldn't matter if I died tomorrow. Maybe I will. I could swallow a bottle of pills. No, I have this baby to think about. I feel trapped in this city, this apartment, this body, this head. I don't want to live. I just need some relief, even for a short time. It's been a year and a half since the last time I got high—the day I got suspended, and Greg brought me flowers.

"Fuck it," I say out loud. I pick up the cordless phone from the floor next to me. I'll do it this once and then go back to meetings.

Half an hour later, after a short ride, I'm again sitting in front of the puzzle, now with two Valium in my hand. I'm not thinking about dying, being clean, or even my baby when I put the pills on my tongue and wash them down with a loud gulp of iced tea. The only thing I'm thinking about is how much better I'll feel in twenty minutes.

30

SOLIDARITY IN ANIMOSITY

~1988~

A sudden rapping on the window pane makes me jump, although I can't move quickly with my big baby belly. The sound repeats—ratta-tatta-tat-tat—like the secret knock of a friend on the door of a kid's clubhouse.

I'm startled by the noise because everything about having a visitor right now is strange. Although I've been in this apartment for over four months, only a handful of people know where I live. I'd also be at school if I'd returned after Christmas break instead of getting my GED in January.

I could ignore the intrusion, but I'm curious, and whoever it is might have a joint to smoke. With the blind down, I can't see who's on the other side of the door. I use the chair next to me to haul myself up off the floor and away from my puzzle.

At the door, I bend one of the slats to see a man standing on the front stoop. He has shoulder-length hair and a full beard which makes him hard to place. I crack the door to get a better look. Without the glass between us, I see eyes I'd recognize anywhere—it's Walter.

The last time I saw Walter was four years ago when I snuck past him and my mother on my way to meet my runaway-to-Texas ride. I was just a kid then and at the mercy of the adults around me. I'm still not eighteen, but I'm an adult in every way that matters.

"Hey, stranger," he says, breaking the silence.

"Holy shit," I say. "What hole did you crawl out of?"

"Oh, I've been around," he says. "A little time in the shit-can, but other than that, living large." He looks at my belly and points with his chin. "I see you've been busy."

"Haha. That was nothing."

"You gonna let me in, or what? It's fucking freezing out here." I open the door all the way so he can step inside. His leather jacket is hardly a match for the barely-above-freezing, late-February day.

We both take a seat, me on the couch, him in a chair across from me.

"Nice place," he says. "It looks like you're doing pretty well for yourself."

"Yeah, I'm trying. It's been a couple of rough years."

"Know what you're having?" he asks.

"A girl."

"Uh oh, you're in trouble," he laughs. "The father around?"

"Sometimes. He didn't want kids."

"Shitbag should've thought of that before he started screwing around," he says, his voice rising in anger. I like that he sounds protective.

"Why were you in jail?" I ask.

"Stupid drunken bullshit," he says. "Nothing worth talking about. How's your mother doing?"

"I don't know. I haven't heard from her since fall, just before I moved here. The last time I saw her didn't go so well." I light a cigarette in preparation for the story.

"Hey, you got an extra smoke?"

I hand Walter a Newport and slide the ashtray across the floor for us to share; I haven't yet gotten a coffee table. Walter lights the cigarette and takes a drag.

"How can you smoke this shit?" he asks, coughing. "It's like smoking a fucking piece of spearmint gum."

"Beggars can't be choosers," I say. We laugh before I launch into the story of my mother. He stays quiet until I stop talking.

"What about Phildrip?" he asks. I smile at hearing my brother's old nickname.

"I think he's still with mom. I hope he is, anyway. He's had it pretty rough too."

Our conversation is easy. It's been a long time since I last talked with somebody who knows my history and the people in it.

After an hour of catching up, Walter stands and stretches his arms above his head.

"Got any coffee?"

"No, but I have tea."

"Want a cup?" he asks.

"Sure."

"How about cards?" he asks.

"How about Yahtzee?"

"Break it out," he says. "I'll put the water on."

It's been over a week since Walter came knocking. He's been crashing on my couch. I'm glad he's here. I like the sound of him talking to Alex Trebek on the television in the next room, telling him the correct answer to nearly every Jeopardy question.

Things are different between Walter and me. He's no longer my quasi-stepfather, so now we can be friends. It helps that he's not drinking. We smoke pot and laugh at each other's jokes. We've played so many games of Yahtzee that we ran out of score sheets and had to make up our own. We drink tea and talk about the books we're reading. We've also developed, what we call, a mutual shit list. We each hate all those who earn a place on the list. We call it solidarity in animosity because even in animosity, solidarity feels good.

31

SCABS

~1988~

The pain in my back is especially severe tonight. It feels like something hard is pressing just below my belly button. I can't get comfortable. I've tried lying on my back and my side. Moving around seems to help, but there's little room to do that in my tiny apartment. With my due date just two days away, I know labor can start anytime.

I wish Walter were here; he's all I've got. I think he's with Melissa. I'm pretty sure they started hooking up while I was in Texas, where I had originally planned to give birth. I got the airline ticket before Walter came back into my life. I was going to stay with my father, find a family to adopt my baby, and then return to Massachusetts. I felt like a failure because I'd been getting high since my post-Christmas relapse. I'd ask myself: What kind of mother gets high while pregnant? The answer: A bad one, for sure. I was convinced the baby would be better off with somebody else.

After Walter showed up at my door, I started to rethink the whole adoption thing. I got clean before; I could do it again. Shit, all I'd have to do is show up for my child, and I'd be a better mother than mine had been. And with Walter around, I wouldn't have to care for the baby alone. I decided to take the trip to Texas anyway. At the very least, it would give me a minute to get my head together. It certainly couldn't hurt to have a little time away from obsessing about Mark and his new girlfriend.

During the trip, I spent most days in my bedroom at Chuck and Estelle's, long-time friends of my father, writing lists: Things to Do, Things I Need,

Things I Want to Accomplish, and Things I'm Grateful For. At night—like when I was fourteen—I sat in barrooms, smoking cigarettes and watching my father play pool. Of course, at eight months pregnant, I had no more business being in a bar than when I was a kid.

I quickly realized how ridiculous the Texas-adoption idea had been. Although perhaps a fine establishment, Rusty's Tavern was probably not the best place to find a good, quality family to take care of my baby girl.

As though responding to my thoughts, another pain seizes my abdomen.

"Hang on, Alita," I say out loud. "This is not a good time. It's the middle of the night, and I'm alone."

Again, as if in response, my lower abdomen tightens like a fist. The feeling recedes as quickly as it came on, like an ocean wave after the crash. That was definitely a contraction—I think, but don't say out loud—just in case she can hear me.

Deep breaths. Maybe if I try to think about something else, I can hold this whole thing off till morning. I need some ice. That's what I crave the most. I could call Mark, but since he's living at his girlfriend's apartment, there's a good chance she'll answer. I can't handle that right now. The pant breathing, as described in my book, isn't helping either. It's just making me dizzy and thirsty. Another wave hits while I make a cup of tea. The next one comes just as I get to the couch. Fuck it. I can't have this baby by myself, here in the living room.

I have my shoes on in two minutes, and I'm at Melissa's door in five. I let myself into the dark apartment. None of us on Alper Road lock our doors. I tiptoe through the living room so I don't wake Cassandra, Melissa's one-year-old. Thankfully, there's enough illumination from the bathroom for me to avoid banging into the kitchen table. I go around it to Melissa's bedroom. The door is ajar, and my knocking pushes it open further.

"Hello," Melissa says, which I take as an invitation to step into the room, so I do. With help from the thin sliver of light spilling through the doorway, I can see Melissa and Walter lying under the covers on her double bed. Their smiles remind me of that saying about the cat who ate the canary.

"It's that time," I say.

"Oh my God," Melissa says.

"Are you sure?" Walter asks.

"I'd place a bet on it."

"You've got to be fucking kidding me," Walter says, still smiling.

"Would I joke about such a thing?" I ask.

"Nope," Melissa says. "She wouldn't."

"Jesus, Gail, can't you see I'm busy?"

"Yeah, well, sorry to have a baby while you're busy getting busy."

"Ha ha. All right, I'm coming. Give me five minutes."

"Good luck," Melissa says. "Call and let me know what's going on."

WALTER WALKED ME into the emergency room before leaving. He promised to return after getting some sleep. I hope he called Mark as I asked. Now, I'm alone in a delivery room, wearing nothing but a hospital gown. With the monitor strapped across my belly, I can hear the quick, steady whoosh, whoosh, whoosh of Alita's heartbeat.

I've been here for an hour, maybe less, when the nurse comes in to check on me. Her hair is pulled back into a low ponytail. The eyeglasses hanging around her neck rest against my belly as she tightens the monitor strap. "That hurts," I say. The hard plastic is digging into my skin. She ignores my complaint.

"Well," she says as she pulls off her gloves, "get ready for a long haul. You're just a couple of centimeters dilated."

"I'm waiting for the baby's father," I say. "Will he know where I am?"

"I'm sure he'll find you," she says and leaves the room.

The contractions seem to be coming closer together, but it's hard for me to tell. It hurts too much to keep count. Instead of breathing through them as the book said, I keep holding my breath. I'm watching the printer to my right, the needle moving up and down on a piece of paper, drawing a mountain landscape with black ink. Every stroke corresponds with the monitor attached to my belly. The peaks grow along with the contractions, starting slowly at first. As they build, the electronic pen goes wild, and the jagged mountains get taller and taller. When my belly relaxes again, the drawing slows, and the strokes become shorter. These are the valleys.

Half an hour later, the nurse is back. She's looking down, writing something on a clipboard, when I notice the sudden change in my body.

The feeling is overwhelming. It's as though something has taken over, and I am just an observer.

"I think the baby's coming," I whisper to the nurse.

"The baby's not coming," she snaps. "With a first-time delivery, you won't dilate that fast."

I don't know how to tell her she's wrong. I can feel it. The baby's lower now, even more than a few minutes ago. There's a noise—a pop that sounds through the monitor and briefly interferes with the sound of the baby's heartbeat. It's warm and wet beneath me.

"My water just broke." This much I know for sure.

"Listen, there's no way. You were only two centimeters an hour ago." I can tell she's getting annoyed, but it is her job. She lifts the front of my johnny and looks between my legs. "Oh my God," she says. "The baby's coming; don't push." She rushes out of the room, leaving me uncovered.

All I want to do is push. It's too much pressure for me to hold the baby in. Yet, I do as I'm told. A few minutes later, when the nurse returns with the doctor, I'm relieved to see Mark behind them.

The nurse stands next to the monitor to the right of the bed. "Breathe," she says softly. Her tone is entirely different now. I hope she realized she'd been harsh with me and wants to put me at ease, but I'm sure her attitude has only changed because we're no longer alone.

The doctor takes his place on a stool at the end of the bed. Mark stands to my left, his face pale against his yellow paper robe. I want to tell him it'll be okay, but I'm not convinced of that myself.

"Take a deep breath, and push," the doctor says. He's just a few feet away, but he sounds like he could be in the next room.

I push.

"Okay, wait for the next contraction before you push again," he says. "You're doing great." When I look at him, I notice that the curtain and the door are open behind him. People are walking past the room, and all I can think is that if I can see them, they can see me.

When I push the last time, I feel her body slide out of me. I glance over at Mark, who looks stricken like he's going to pass out. He's pressed against the wall with his arms outstretched. The doctor hands the baby to me and cuts the cord.

Everything happened so fast that I barely had a chance to look at her before the nurse took her away.

"We're not done yet," the doctor says, pushing on my stomach. "We have to deliver the placenta." I have no idea what he's talking about. Apparently, I didn't get that far in the book. I have to push all over again, and it hurts more than it did having the baby.

The nurse returns a few minutes after the doctor leaves. "Here she is, mom and dad," she says. I can tell she's judging us by her sicky-sweet tone. "Say hello before I bring her to the nursery so you can get some rest." She hands Alita to me. She's clean now and wrapped in a thin blanket. Her eyes are open but unfocused. Her hands are so small, and her features are perfect. It's hard to imagine I had any part in creating this new life. Mark leans over to examine her with me. For a few minutes, I pretend we're a family. But after the nurse takes the baby, Mark is ready to go home to his girlfriend. I wish he'd stay because I'll be alone again when he leaves.

It's early morning by the time they move me into a room. Although there are four beds, I have the space to myself. I'm hungry, and I want a cigarette. My head is spinning. I haven't slept in over twenty-four hours, yet my eyes won't stay closed. I hate it here, and I don't think the nurses like me. My body feels empty. Under my johnny, I'm wearing a pair of fishnet briefs and a thick pad that needs to be changed every hour.

A nurse wheels Alita's bassinet into my room every couple of hours. The first time, the woman asks if I'm planning to breastfeed.

"No," I answer quickly.

"You know it's much better for the baby," she says. She continues when I fail to respond. "Studies have shown that breastfed babies develop a deeper bond with their mothers. They're also healthier. In my opinion, it's selfish to bottle feed unless there's a problem with breastfeeding."

I didn't ask her opinion, and I don't want it. "How soon can I go home?" I ask.

"The doctor will come by in a little while. You can ask him."

The nurse is all business as she shows me how to feed Alita with a small glass bottle. Two ounces of formula every three hours. She demonstrates how to burp her by holding Alita's tiny body against her chest and patting her back with what seems to be way too much force. The tutorial continues with a diaper change. She cleans Alita with a baby wipe and then sprinkles her with a bit of powder before folding down the front of the diaper and closing it with a sticky tab on each side. "It's important to fold the front over so it doesn't rub against the baby's belly button," she says. I've yet to see Alita's belly button, as it's still covered with gauze.

Finally, the nurse shows me how to wrap Alita in a thin receiving blanket, like a burrito. "Lay her on her belly like this," she says as she puts Alita in the bassinet. "That way, she doesn't choke while she's sleeping."

When the nurse leaves the room, I try to close my eyes for some much-needed sleep, but it's impossible. There's too much to think about. How will I remember everything? This isn't how it should be. I shouldn't be alone in a hospital bed with a brand-new baby, scared shitless that I'll screw this whole thing up. I wish my mother were here. She should be here, showing me how to be a mother. But she's not, and I don't know how to reach her. I'll call my father when I go home, but it's not like he'll make the trip up from Texas. I haven't seen Becky and Greg for the last few months. They don't know I'm getting high—one look in my eyes, and that'll change. It'll be easier to talk to them once I'm clean again. I'll call Little Nana later. She'll tell Big Nana and Aunt Julie. There's no rush; they won't come to the hospital anyway. None of them have even been to my apartment.

I've had several visits throughout the day—an obviously buzzed Walter arrived in the afternoon, followed by Mark, Chrissy, Melissa, and a couple of friends. I wanted to leave with each of them, but the doctor said I should stay for a night. "It'll give you a chance to heal a little," he said. "And I'm sure you could use the help." I couldn't argue with that.

I'VE BEEN DRESSED since sunrise. Walter is here with my car. I have a hospital-gifted canvas tote filled with glass bottles, formula, pacifiers, diapers, coupons, and samples of all things baby-related, and the small suitcase I brought. Everything is ready to go. All I need now is my baby, and we'll be on our way.

Again, a nurse wheels in the bassinet. "Where's your car seat?" she asks.

"What car seat?" I ask and hold my breath.

"You need to have a car seat. We can't let you take the baby without one."

"I don't have a car seat," I say, letting my breath out in a loud, exasperated sigh. Another thing I didn't know about.

She must see the panic on my face because she responds right away. "We can rent you one for fifteen dollars, but you'll need to bring it back in a week. It's for emergencies." If there ever was an emergency, this is it. We can't stay here forever.

I GET TO KNOW Alita quickly at home. Mostly, I handle her with ease. I'm surprised that being a mother and loving another person so entirely seems to come naturally to me. I recognize my baby's sounds and know whether she's hungry, tired, or needs to be burped or changed. I'm getting to know her moods and sleep patterns. I sleep while she sleeps, and if I get too tired, I bring her to Walter in the living room.

Sometimes, I wake up, afraid she's not breathing, and watch for the rise and fall of her chest. But so far, the hardest part of caring for Alita has been the umbilical cord wound. Every time she needs a diaper change, I check the site. The scab is still there; it's loose and bleeding around the edge a little bit. I'm terrified it'll come off too soon, and I won't be able to stop the bleeding. I put the ointment on, cover it with a light piece of gauze, and fold the diaper, so it doesn't rub. The pregnancy book says the scab can stay on for up to two months, and it's only been a couple of weeks. I don't think I can take the stress of it much longer.

As though my mother knows I need her, she surprises me with a visit. I'm sure she's high, and I'm still pissed about her taking my money, but I'm glad she's here. Now that I'm a mother myself, I have questions. I want to know what it was like to be twenty and have a new baby with a two-year-old. And whether or not I was as easy a baby as Alita. Most importantly, at the moment, I need to know what to do about this scab that won't let go.

We talk about other things first. She's still living in Lynn, and Philip is still with her. "He's okay," she says. "As much as he can be after all he's been through." She holds Alita while I snap their picture in my front yard. Then, just a couple of hours into the visit, she stands to leave. I haven't even had a chance to ask her anything about mothering.

"I'm so happy you have Walter here to help you," she says. "I love you more than I can say."

We hug in the doorway. Her hugs are full-bodied and deep, as though each one contains everything she has to give. I don't want to let her go, but I have no choice. As I watch her walk down the stairs and around the corner, I wonder when I'll see her again.

The day after my mother's visit, when I pull the covering from Alita's belly, the scab comes with it. I hold my breath; I'm afraid to look. I smile when I see what's been hidden there all along—a perfect little belly button.

32

EXPOSURE

~1988~

The line to purchase textbooks stretches at least thirty feet down a narrow hallway. Either the air conditioning isn't on, or it's not working, and the August heat is worse than outside in this crowded space. My purse hangs over my left shoulder, and I hold Alita against my right hip. I didn't bring her carrier since I hadn't planned on being here long. Despite the heat and the ache in my arm, I'm glad she's here with me. It feels like we're in this together—this exposure to the world of higher education.

Nobody ever asked me what I wanted to be when I grew up. It never occurred to me that I would get to choose. Now, here I am, ready to start college in the fall, right on time with the rest of Gloucester High School's graduating class of 1988. I'm officially enrolled at the Essex Agricultural & Technical Institute, also known as "Essex Aggie," which is just a twenty-minute drive from Gloucester. The small school's proximity to home made it an easy choice. My decision to major in fashion merchandising was easy, too, because it sounds like fun.

"Oh my God, she's adorable!" one of the girls standing directly in front of me says, pushing her blonde bangs away from her eyes. She's smiling as she reaches for Alita's hand.

The girl standing next to her, her friend, I assume, turns around. They look the same to me. Both girls have their hair pulled back with a scrunchie in a low ponytail. Each of them wears shorts, a short-sleeved tee, and sandals.

"She is so cute," the second girl says. Alita smiles when she notices the girls' attention.

The one who saw Alita first asks, "Is she yours?"

"Yeah." I look at Alita, not the girl, when I answer. I didn't plan on meeting anybody today, and I don't feel ready for this.

"How old is she?" she asks.

"A little over four months." I'm sure she's trying to figure out how old I am and how old I was when I had Alita. I don't tell her I turned eighteen earlier this month.

"Wow," she says, "I can't even imagine having a baby and going to college—if it's anything like high school, anyway. I'm lucky to get myself out of the house in the morning. My mother has to wake me up like three times before I finally roll out of bed."

"Me too," the other girl says.

I guess it's my turn to talk, but I don't know what to say. I know little about high school, mothers, or being mothered, for that matter. I'm sweating, and my arm is starting to cramp. As though she can feel my rising anxiety, Alita is beginning to whine. It's past noon and her nap time.

I let my pocketbook slide to my left elbow before switching Alita to that side and my bag to the right. When I reach for the strap, I notice how gross my stubby fingernails look. I tuck them into my fist so the girls won't see, making it even harder to move her from one side to the other. For a moment, with the change of scenery, Alita is quiet again.

"Are you in fashion merchandising?" the first girl asks. She's got a lot of questions.

"Yeah," I say. I'm relieved the topic of conversation has shifted, although I wish the girl would stop talking. She doesn't.

"I'm Kelly," she says.

"Oh, I'm Gail. And this is Alita."

"Can I hold her?" Kelly asks.

"Sure," I say as I hand my little girl over, grateful to give my arm a rest.

"I love babies," she says. The other girl has already lost interest.

"Yeah," I say, "She's great." I want to tell her how hard it is, that being a mother is nothing like babysitting, but I don't. I doubt it'll be this hard for her with a mother who will be there to help. Good for her, I think.

She'll probably never know what it's like to be really alone.

Not that I've been spending much time by myself lately. In fact, it's a miracle I was able to pull everything together for school, with the constant flow of company all summer. My apartment has become much like my mother's apartments, where people drop in unexpectedly throughout the day. I'm not complaining; there's still something I like about not knowing who will appear at the door. It reminds me of when I was a kid making a guessing game out of who was coming up the stairs.

Besides Walter, and his new girlfriend Cheryl, Walter's sister Beth, who lives just a few houses over from mine, has been a regular. The same goes for Walter's only living brother, Rich. Some of Phil's kids too: Linda, Terry with her baby, Zachery—just two months older than Alita—and Dawn with her little boy.

Even Aunt Julie surprised me with a visit one day. I was sitting in the living room at a table farthest from the front entrance when I saw a woman's shadow as she moved past the window to my door. It took a few moments for me to recognize Aunt Julie through the glass. I hadn't seen her for months.

"Come in," I said, loud enough for her to hear but not so loud as to wake Alita.

A gust of warm, fresh June air brushed against my face when she opened the door.

"Hey," I said and pointed my chin toward the door: "You can leave that open."

"Hey, Gail. How are you doing?" she asked as she walked into the room, stopping behind the chair to my left. Her appearance was shocking. Her perfectly parted and combed shiny hair was her only identifiable feature. Her face was so swollen it looked as though she was squinting through the slits where her brown eyes used to be, and her body was double the size it had been the last time I saw her. Gone were the tube tops and cutoffs. In their place, even though it had to be seventy-five degrees outside, she wore an oversized t-shirt and long sweatpants.

"I know I'm getting fat," she said, as though she could hear my thoughts. "It's a side-effect from the medication."

"That sucks, but it's good you're taking it," I said. Her grin made me wonder if she had, in fact, been taking her medication.

"How's Little Nana?" I asked. Even though she lives less than ten minutes away, I still don't see much of her. I did bring Alita to her apartment once before, but I'm afraid to unwittingly bring a pregnant cockroach home with me after a visit. I've never seen one in my apartment, but that doesn't stop me from waiting in the doorway after I turn on the kitchen light to make sure it's all clear. I'm also worried about running into Big Nana, who goes to Little Nana's every time she fights with her husband. Whenever I see her, she's drinking, and I wouldn't want her to scare Alita the way she's always scared me.

Aunt Julie didn't answer. She kept looking at me, grinning. Instead of pressing her, I turned my attention to the gallon milk jug she was holding in her hand, the contents of which were most certainly not milk. The nasty grayish liquid had pieces of something floating in it.

"Julie, what the hell is that?" I asked, keeping my eyes on the container.

"It's my cancer," she said. "Dusty cancer. See all those pieces in there? I've been picking it out of my skin."

"That's disgusting," I said, deciding she was definitely not taking her medication.

I almost told her it wasn't cancer but decided against it. We'd been around that cul-de-sac before. She could have her cancer. I looked her in the eye and said, "You need to put that thing outside before I throw up."

"I can't let it out of my sight," she said as she put the container on the floor next to her. "The doctors keep telling me that I don't have cancer, but I have the proof right here. I've gone to see at least five lawyers, and none of them will take my case, but I promise you I'll find somebody, and then the doctors will be sorry because when I win my lawsuit for malpractice, they'll have to pay millions of dollars. I'll buy you, Chrissy, and Philip all your own houses wherever you want to live, and I'll take you on a trip to Florida or Bermuda. Or even Hawaii," she said, her eyes as wide as they could be and a smile so broad that I thought she might start laughing. "Where's the baby? she asked. I want to see her. How old is she now? She must be getting big."

"She's two months, and she's taking a nap," I said, still unable to ignore the jug. "You can hang out for a while and wait for her to wake up, but you have to put that thing outside."

"No, I can't do that," she said. "This is the only evidence I have, and I can't take any chances. I'm going to go now, but I'll come back tomorrow. Give the baby a kiss and a hug from me."

"Okay, I will."

"You're so beautiful," she said.

"Thank you," I said. I'm sure I rolled my eyes as I responded.

She looked me right in the eye and said, "I love you, Gail." For a moment, she seemed almost normal.

"I love you too," I said, surprised by how much I felt the rare glimpse of her heart beneath the sickness. People can say what they will about Aunt Julie, but at least she shows up. That's more than I can say for the rest of my family.

I barely see Chrissy these days, although I can't blame her. She's just graduated from college, and she has a boyfriend. I'm happy for her. Although we don't talk about it, I know that even though she stayed in one place after we were separated, her life has been hard too.

Nana Raizin comes for a short visit every couple of weeks. She always brings a small gift for Alita, just as she did for Chrissy and me when we were kids. Sometimes she takes us to Charlie's restaurant for lunch and slips a ten-dollar bill into my hand before I get out of her car.

Just as I predicted, Mark has returned along with my flat belly. He's not always around, which is good because now that he wants me again, I don't think I want him. He still doesn't want to be a father. He doesn't change Alita's diapers or take care of her alone. He won't even put a car seat in his truck because he's worried about what people will think. It makes me worry that, like me, Alita will grow up thinking there's something wrong with her instead of him. Of course, that's ridiculous. Alita is perfect, and he's far from it.

As for my mother's other four siblings, my other aunt is the only one I see. Although in defense of an uncle, he's been in a state hospital for most of my life—he's got schizophrenia, too. Mental illness runs rampant in my family. I think the other two just wanted to get away. I can't blame them either; normal is hard to accomplish from the middle of this herd. I'm not even sure how many cousins I have at this point. At one time, I wished to have the kind of family that gets together for holidays. Now, I hardly think of them at all.

These days, Walter and Cheryl are the closest people I have to family. It's no big surprise that things didn't work out between Walter and Melissa. He's a lot older than her, and truth be told, he's not the most stable guy around. However, unlike Walter, Cheryl seems to have her shit together. She's got a car that's registered and insured. Her clothes are always clean, and she cares enough about herself to put on earrings every day. Cheryl's not as pretty as my mother, but as Walter would say, she's a keeper. She's also tough, which is good. To be in a relationship with Walter for any length of time, a woman has to have pretty thick skin.

One of the best things about Cheryl is that she can cook. On one of her first Friday mornings at my apartment, she showed me how to prepare meatballs for dinner. She mixed egg, spices, Italian bread crumbs, and ground beef in a large bowl with her hands. I helped her roll the mixture into balls that we oven-baked until brown. She added them to a tomato sauce as it simmered over a low flame. It was the first time anybody had shown me how to cook something.

Cheryl also has an uncanny ability to get things done, and she makes it look so easy. Not only does she help keep my apartment clean, but she's also able to have Alita fed, burped, bathed, and dressed for the day in half an hour. She says she hasn't always known how to care for a baby; she learned by caring for her six-year-old daughter, who now lives with Cheryl's mother. I don't ask why she doesn't live with Cheryl; I just watch closely and hope that someday, I'll be able to manage things as well as she does.

I'D BEEN SO caught up in my head that I didn't notice Kelly was next in line until she turned to hand Alita to me. With my baby back in my arms, I pretend to look for something in my purse so Kelly won't try to talk to me again. I just want to get my books and go home. It's not that I don't like the girl; I don't even know her. She doesn't know me either, and if she did, she probably wouldn't have turned around in the first place. My biggest fear is that all the students here will be as normal as these two—nothing like me. And if they are, this will be just another place where I don't belong.

33

MAGIC MAN

~1988~

When my tire blows, I'm going seventy in the fast lane heading north on Route 128, belting out "Magic Man" along with Heart. The steering wheel pulls so hard to the right that it nearly slips out of my grip. With a pounding heart, I wrangle the car into the breakdown lane, shift into park, and light a cigarette with shaky hands.

Shit. Shit. Shit. I'm still at least five miles from Gloucester. So much for being on time to get Alita from daycare. This is the last thing I need. Of course, this has to happen today instead of two weeks from now, when the school semester will be over.

I can't afford a new tire. If this one can't be fixed, I'll have to figure out how to get to school every day, on top of having to shop, do laundry, study for finals, and take care of Alita. I can't even depend on Walter and Cheryl for help these days. They lived with me all summer, and now, when I need them most, they're nowhere to be found.

I'm still behind the wheel, thinking about hitchhiking home, when a mid-sized blue car pulls into the breakdown lane half a mile ahead of me. It backs up and slowly closes the gap between us. As it gets closer, I can see the backs of two heads, the driver and a passenger. The car stops ten feet in front of mine, and both doors swing open. A man steps out of each side. I hold my breath until I see the familiar face of the passenger, CJ, a friend from high school. I step out of my car and into the cold.

"Hey," CJ says, smiling. "Long time no see."

"No kidding," I say. "Am I glad to see you. I was trying to decide whether I should stick out my thumb."

The driver is walking toward me. "Gimme your keys," he says.

"Okay." I look at CJ and back at the driver.

"That's Jack," CJ says as I drop the keys into Jack's palm.

"Time us," Jack says while he opens the trunk.

I like him already.

I stand nearby while they work with my hands in my jacket pockets where they're warm. CJ and I talk about the last few years. We haven't seen each other since high school. Apparently, he left shortly after I did. Like me, he's spent much of his life on his own.

Jack is quietly engrossed in his task at hand. I can't stop looking at him. He's so damn cute. I'd say he's older than me by a couple of years. He's tall, too, got to be close to six feet. Dark hair, dark eyes—my type, for sure. Perfect. But, of course, I have a boyfriend. I always have a boyfriend. Jack isn't looking at me anyway.

Ten minutes later, the blown tire has been replaced with the spare I didn't know I had. I follow behind Jack as he rolls the mangled tire to the back of my car, puts it in the trunk, and steps aside to allow me to close it.

"How long?" Jack asks.

"Sorry, I was busy talking," I say. I hope he can tell I'm flirting.

"Definitely less than fifteen minutes," he says, smiling.

"Thank you," I say, as I feel around in my purse for my keys. Jack is sure he gave them back to me.

"Shit," I say. "I must have dropped them in the trunk. I'm having that kind of day."

"Want me to bring you somewhere?" Jack asks. I want you to bring me everywhere, I think.

"That would be great," I say. "I have to get my daughter. Do you mind stopping to pick her up?"

"Not at all," he says.

WHEN I COME out of the house with Alita, Jack is standing next to the open driver's side door, and his seat is pulled forward. He smiles and puts his arms out.

"Want me to take her?" he asks.

I hand Alita to him as easily as I handed him my keys and go around to the passenger side to sit behind CJ.

Jack talks to Alita while he buckles her into her car seat. During the ride to my place, he makes faces at her in the rearview mirror. I've never seen a guy take so much interest in an eight-month-old baby.

When we get to my apartment, before I can even get out of the back seat, Jack has already taken care of getting Alita, and her car seat, out of the car. He's not only adorable, he's thoughtful too.

As I stand in my apartment doorway, watching Jack back up to pull out of the dead-end street, I reach into my pockets and feel a bulge under the lining. I move my fingers around inside until I find a hole where my keys have slipped through. It sucks that I'll have to get a ride to get my car, but I'm glad I didn't find them sooner. Maybe it's wishful thinking, but I think Jack might be happy about that too. I swear he watched me in his rearview mirror as he drove away.

I HAVEN'T STOPPED thinking about Jack in the week since we met. At least finals are done. Another distraction from school was the last thing I needed. Not that I tried really hard to achieve my whopping D-plus average. I'm sure I would've done better if I wasn't getting high every day and trying to study with a dozen people partying around me in my cramped living room. It appears I'm not as good at multitasking as I thought.

Tonight, I had good intentions. I'd been sitting on the couch thinking about getting a Christmas tree when my boyfriend John, his sister Nancy, and a small group of people showed up with a case of Budweiser and some weed. Now, with that plan shot to hell, I'm smoking a joint with Dawn and a guy she brought over with her.

We're sitting at the table. "Kashmir" is playing on the boom box. The music is low so as not to wake Alita, who is asleep in the bedroom. Nancy and the others are gathered around the coffee table playing quarters, a game where they bounce a quarter off the table and into a small cup filled with beer. The winner drinks. They all drink.

I'm holding in a hit when somebody knocks on the door. The Xanax I took earlier keeps me from getting anxious that it might be the police. I often worry someone will call because of the noise, but they never do.

Somebody opens the door, and CJ walks in with a six-pack under his arm. He's never been here before. Jack walks in behind him. The group around the coffee table cheers for the new company, the beer, or both and returns to their game as I breathe out a puff of smoke. CJ sits on the couch, but Jack stays standing after closing the door. While he surveys the room, I take him in. He seems taller than I remember, even better looking. His hair is freshly cut, and his face is smooth like he's got a date.

Jack smiles at me and steps into the room, shakes hands with his friend—my boyfriend, John—and sits on the arm of the couch to watch the game.

With Jack here, I can't think about anything else. He's just ten feet from me, and all I want is to be near him. I wish everybody else would leave.

An hour after Jack's arrival, I sneak away to the bedroom and call Melissa. She knows all about Jack and the flat tire. I whisper that he's in the next room. "I'm going to tell him to stop at your apartment when he leaves," I say. "Tell him to come back when everybody is gone." She sounds as excited about the plan as I am.

It's past midnight when the door closes for the last time. Less than ten minutes later, there's a soft knock on the door. I've had just enough time to run a brush through my hair and dab perfume behind my ears.

Jack is smiling when I open the door. "Hi," he says.

"Hi yourself," I say. I can't stop grinning. "I'm glad you came."

"Me too," he says and steps into the room.

We've just sat down on the couch when he speaks.

"These guys are slobs," he says, looking at the cans and sticky mess of beer around the empty cup on the coffee table.

"Yeah, it's disgusting," I say. "Especially since I don't even drink."

"You got a sponge?" he asks.

Jack is already moving the chairs against the wall where they belong when I return from the kitchen with Windex, a rag, and the trash barrel. I put my favorite tape in the cassette player, and we begin tossing empty cans into the trash to the beat of "Dear Mr. Fantasy."

"I love Traffic," he says.

"Way underrated," I say.

Once the living room is in order, we sit together on the couch. I'm facing him with my back against the arm, and my knees are bent. He's at my feet with his arm slung across the back of the couch. All I can think about is him touching me. I wish he'd let his arm fall and rest against my knee.

"Thank you," I say. "This could've waited until tomorrow, but it'll be nice to wake up to a clean house."

"No problem," he says.

"And thank you again for the tire change, the ride, and picking up Alita. There aren't many people who would've done that."

"Just in the right place at the right time," he says. "So," he continues, laughing, "when you told me to go to Melissa's, I thought she wanted to hook up."

I laugh too. "I didn't know how else to tell you."

"Yeah, well, I'm psyched to be here. You're the reason I came tonight. And your daughter is adorable, just like her mother." He's still talking as he reaches for my hand and pulls me closer to him. "I haven't stopped thinking about you since that day," he says.

The feeling is mutual," I say. John crosses my mind for a moment, but we've only been dating for a few months, nothing serious. He barely notices Alita exists, never mind showing her any affection. I don't owe John anything, I think, right before Jack kisses me.

WHEN I OPEN my eyes the next morning, Jack's not beside me, and the bedroom is quiet. Strange that I was able to sleep so late without Alita waking me; she's always up by seven. Her crib is empty, and my bedroom door is closed. I get out of bed quickly, worried something terrible has happened.

When I round the corner to the living room, I can see Alita standing in her playpen, holding onto the side. Jack is crouched behind one of the living room chairs. "Peek-a-boo," he says as he pops his head up. Alita laughs from deep in her belly. She's so engaged in their game that she doesn't even notice I've entered the room.

He smiles at me. "Good morning. I figured I'd let you sleep since we were up so late."

"Early," I say, smiling back. "John is going to be pissed."

"You got that right. I'm sure he'll want to fight me," he says before turning his attention back to Alita.

"Peek-a-boo," he says, popping his head up and making Alita laugh again. "It's worth it." He looks at me and smiles. "You're worth it."

WE WERE ABLE to keep our new relationship a secret all weekend, but as of Monday night, just three days in, we've been outed. Nancy knows. John knows. The pending confrontation with John makes me feel sick, but at least Jack and I can be a couple in public.

Now that we're official, Jack brings me to meet his parents. They live in the same community, the duplex, where Jack grew up. John lives just a few houses over. Two of Jack's six sisters are still living with their parents. I meet them too. Francine, the oldest of the siblings, lives in the apartment next door. After meeting his parents, we go to her place and smoke a joint in the kitchen before Francine gives me a tour. Her children's bedrooms are decorated to perfection—every inch of space has received meticulous attention. Most of the bedding and curtains have been handmade by this family, who knows how to create beautiful things. In each room, everything is in its place.

All of the family are warm and welcoming. Before we leave Francine's, she invites us over for Christmas Eve pie. By the night's end, we've also accepted an invitation to Dottie's place, another sister, on Christmas day.

On the fifth night of our relationship, Jack comes through my apartment door, dragging a tree behind him. I pull the Christmas box from my closet, and we decorate while Alita rolls around in her walker.

Later, after she's gone to sleep, we lie together on the couch, our legs intertwined, my head resting on his chest. It's been the best week of my life, and as much as I want to believe I can have a future with Jack, he still doesn't know about my past. Not yet. With his family being so big and Gloucester being so small, it won't be long before he hears something. I can't help but think he'll leave when that day comes.

34

PARTNERS

~1988~

Christmas is two days away, and I can't wait to celebrate. I'm hell-bent on getting this holiday right. Alita is napping while Jack and I clean the apartment to seventies classic rock. I'm scrubbing the bathtub; he's sweeping the living room rug. When the phone rings, he answers.

"Gail," Jack says, his voice just loud enough for me to hear him over the radio. "Your mother is on the phone."

"My mother?" I stand quickly, knocking a bottle of shampoo into the tub.

"What's wrong?" Jack asks from the bathroom doorway, squinting his eyes.

"I'm just surprised, that's all." He hands me the phone and follows me into the living room.

"Hello," I say, taking a seat on the couch.

"Hi," she says as though we just talked yesterday. "How are you?" she asks.

"I'm okay. Just cleaning, getting ready for Christmas."

"Was that your boyfriend?" she asks.

"Yes, Jack."

"I'd like to meet him," she says.

"Well, I'm still in the same place," I say, thinking back to her one visit to my apartment. I pull my knees up and wrap my free arm around them.

Jack is pacing. He knows I haven't seen my mother since May. I motion to him for a smoke.

"I was thinking about coming for Christmas," my mother says. "Maybe

195

staying over tomorrow night. I know I have so much to make up for, and it'll probably take me a lifetime, but I have to start somewhere."

Jack hands me a lit Newport. "Okay," I say. "We have plans, but we'll be back around seven." I take a deep drag from the cigarette and watch the white smoke mingle with the dust in a streak of afternoon sunlight.

"Okay. I love you more than I can say," she says.

"I love you too," I say before ending the call.

Jack sits next to me on the couch.

"My mother's coming tomorrow. At least, that's what she says."

"Wow," he says, "I know you haven't seen her, but when was the last time you guys talked?" Jack is sitting close enough for me to feel the warmth of his body.

"It's been a few months at least."

"That's crazy," he says.

When I notice I'm biting my fingernail, I lay my hand on the couch next to me, put my feet on the floor, and lean forward to reach the ashtray. "I don't know how I'll do with this," I say. "I'm pretty angry. What if I can't pretend everything's okay?"

"You don't have to pretend, Gail. She's your mother, and she loves you. She's just messed up." I don't know how he knows so much about it, but he's right. Even so, my stomach is already starting to hurt.

"Sometimes I wonder if she does," I say. As soon as the words are out, I wish I could take them back. I've never said them aloud. When my eyes fill with tears, I look away. Jack puts his arms around me and pulls me into him. I'm glad my head is on his chest where he can't see me cry.

AFTER NINE, ON Christmas Eve, when the glare from headlights passes through the living room window, Jack and I look at each other. I assume it's my mother since she hasn't canceled, and there's hardly ever traffic on this dead-end street, especially not on a holiday. Jack kisses my cheek before getting up from the couch.

I'm anxious and tired. I didn't sleep very well last night. I'm worried Jack will see who I become when my mother is nearby. He hasn't met bitter, resentful Gail, the little girl who surfaces when either my mother or father is in the room. I'm afraid that, like them, when he sees me that way, he'll run too.

I'm also excited for them to meet—Jack and Jackie—the man I love, and my mother, the two most important adults in my life. They share so many qualities. Both are likable, funny, quick-witted, and enjoy the same dry humor.

"Yup, it's a taxi. It's got to be her," Jack says, looking out the window. I swing my feet onto the floor so my back is straight, as though I'm sitting in the waiting room of my doctor's office. My heart is racing. I need something to do with my hands. Jack turns and looks at me. "Are you okay?" he asks.

"I'm okay. I just need a cigarette," I say as I reach for my pack on the table. I pull a butt from the box but don't light it. The feel of it between my fingers is enough to calm me. A minute later, Jack opens the door.

"Hi Jackie," he says, as though they've known each other for years.

"Hi, Jack," my mother hugs him in the doorway. "It's nice to meet you." I love seeing them next to each other.

When my mother steps into the room, I see a man behind her. She looks from me to Jack and then at the man. With her body half turned toward him, she says: "This is my boyfriend, Larry."

"Hi, Larry," Jack says and reaches to shake the man's hand. "Nice to meet you."

When I stand to hug my mother, my body is stiff. Of course, she didn't mention having, never mind bringing, a boyfriend.

She smells like roses.

"Hey, Larry," I say over her shoulder. I hate him already, and it takes everything I have to sound friendly.

When Jack offers to take their coats, my mother hands him a shopping bag. "Will you put these under the tree?" she asks.

Jack takes the bag, removes three neatly wrapped gifts, and places them under the tree. I want to get a closer look at the name tags, but I play it cool. I don't want to seem too eager.

"Is Alita asleep?" my mother asks, looking in the playpen.

"She's in her crib in the bedroom. I tried to keep her up, but she started falling asleep in her walker."

"I'm going to peek in on her," she says.

Jack and I sit on the couch while Larry makes himself comfortable in one of the chairs. He says something about the Bruins, and he and Jack talk hockey until my mother returns to the room.

"Do you want to open your present or wait for tomorrow?" she asks.

My smile is a reflex. I don't remember the last time I opened a Christmas present. "There's no way I can wait until tomorrow," I say.

Jack brings me the gift with my name on it. The package is wrapped in cobalt blue foil—my favorite color—and decorated with a silver ribbon. I know she curled the ribbon by sliding it along the edge of the scissors, as she showed me when I was a kid. Color from the blinking lights on the tree shimmer across the wrapper.

I want to tear open the gift, yet at the same time, I want this moment to last forever. Starting with one end, I patiently peel the tape away from the shiny paper. When the wrapping is loose, I fold the sheet in half and set it on the coffee table. It's too pretty to throw away.

On my lap is a flat white box. I remove the top and hand it to Jack. Under the silver tissue paper, there's a shiny blue fabric, the same rich color as the wrapping paper. I stand when I take it out of the box, letting it unfold against me. A silky sleeveless V-neck nightgown falls to the middle of my thighs. My mother is smiling.

"Oh my God, I love it," I say.

"That's really nice," Jack says. He's smiling too.

"Thank you," I say, looking at my mother. I'd forgotten about Larry for a moment, but he's sitting right next to her, and the reminder of him makes me look away.

"You're welcome. I'm so glad you like it," she says.

"I'm sorry I didn't get you anything," I say as I fold the nightgown and sit next to Jack. "I didn't know I'd see you." *Fuck, I didn't need to say that.*

"That's okay. Really," my mother says. "As I said, I have a lot to make up for."

"Well, I say, getting up from the couch, we should get to bed. Alita will be up at the crack of dawn." I look at my mother. "I didn't expect you to bring anybody. I planned for you to sleep on the couch, so I guess Larry will have to sleep on the floor."

"No," Jack says. "They can have the bedroom. We'll be fine out here." My head snaps in his direction. I can't believe he's offered my bed to my mother and this stranger. First of all, my mother shouldn't have brought this guy to my home. She didn't even ask me. Never mind that she's never given up anything for me, and I'm supposed to give my bed to her, and this guy? On Christmas Eve? The more I think about it, the angrier I become.

I open my mouth to speak but then remember—this isn't the person I want to be. What's one night? And as long as Jack is beside me, I can sleep anywhere.

"Okay, fine," I say. "But I want my pillow."

Jack moves Alita from her crib to her playpen so she'll see our familiar faces in the morning. Once my mother and Larry are behind the closed door of my bedroom, I change into my new nightgown. Jack and I lay a comforter on the floor near the Christmas tree. We have another blanket to cover us. He pulls a cushion from the couch to use as a pillow. Once we're on our makeshift bed, Jack turns to me, propping his head up on his hand.

"It was nice of you to let them have the bed."

"Yeah, well, I wouldn't have If you weren't here."

"But you could've said no, and that says something about you."

"I'm a sap?"

"No, that you're bigger than all you've been through," he says. I wish that were true. I want so badly to be the person Jack thinks I am. Still, I love him for believing the best in me. With my head on his chest and my leg draped across his thighs, I fall asleep thinking this is already the best Christmas I've ever had.

My mother is the first one awake. I can hear her making coffee in the kitchen. I recognize the sounds of her pouring boiling water into a mug, the opening of the refrigerator for milk, and the clinking sound of the spoon as she stirs. The task belonged to Chrissy and me when we were kids. We'd boil the water before waking her and Walter so we wouldn't have to wait to open presents. Alita must have heard her too. She's moving around in the playpen. Jack is looking at me when I open my eyes. He's smiling, as usual.

"Finally," he says. "It's Alita's first Christmas."

"Yes," I say, smiling back. "It is."

Alita is standing with her arms outstretched when we sit up. Jack pulls her onto the blanket with us. My mother comes into the living room with a steaming mug of coffee and sits on the couch. Larry must still be sleeping.

"There's nana," I say to Alita. Even though Alita doesn't know her grandmother, she goes to her when my mother puts her arms out. She pulls Alita onto her lap, holds her hands, and chants, "trot trot to Boston, trot trot to Lynn, look out little Alita, cause you might fall in." As she sings the last word, my mother opens her legs and lets my little girl fall backward through them before she pulls her up to start over. Alita's laugh fills the room, and she looks expectantly at my mother for the song to begin again.

I wait for a break in the singing before I turn to Alita. "Do you want to open your presents?" I ask, even though she has no idea what I'm talking about. My mother hands her to me, and we sit next to the tree. Jack moves to her other side.

We begin with the packages my mother brought. I hand the gifts to Alita, Jack starts tearing the paper, and Alita pulls at it. The sound of the paper tearing makes her laugh every time. In one package, there's a pink dress that will fit her by spring, and in the other, a teddy bear. It's hard for me to imagine my mother shopping for these things, although they seem to have been meant for Alita.

We're halfway through the present opening when Larry strolls into the room. My mother snuffs out her cigarette. "Do you want a cup of coffee," she asks him, already on her feet and heading toward the kitchen.

"Sure," he says as he plants his ass in one of the living room chairs and lights a cigarette.

A few minutes later, my mother, the dutiful girlfriend, comes back into the living room with a cup of coffee for Larry and then returns to the kitchen.

I HEARD THE bathroom door close fifteen minutes ago. I'm trying to focus on Alita opening her presents and Jack's attention to her, but I can't. I lean my body far enough to my right to see the bathroom door. It's closed. She's been in there too long, and I know what that means. I hand another present to Alita. When she starts to gnaw on the corner, Jack takes it away and tears the paper. She laughs again. I lean to see the door.

"What's up?" Jack asks.

"My mother's been in the bathroom for a long time."

Jack shrugs. "Okay," he says. "When you gotta go, you gotta go."

"I guess," I say. Okay. It's not a big deal. At least, I don't want it to be. But I know what my mother does in the bathroom. What if she's overdosed? The panic rises in me faster than I can tamp it down. I can feel my heart pounding against my chest. I jump up and rush to stand at the bathroom door, where I hold my body still and listen.

Silence.

My rap on the door sounds loud and sharp.

"Yeah." She responds right away. I immediately feel the muscles in my shoulders soften.

"Are you okay?" I ask.

"Of course, I'm okay." She sounds annoyed.

"You've been in there for a long time."

"I'm not feeling great," she says. I know what that means, too.

We've had many similar through-the-bathroom-door conversations over the years, except this time, the bathroom door is mine. I don't shoot dope. No heroin or needles are allowed in my apartment. She doesn't get to make the rules here—I do. I'd tell her that, too, if she'd only come out of the bathroom.

A few minutes later, I force myself back into the living room, where I sit on the couch instead of the floor. From here, I can watch Alita and the door. I light a cigarette and wait.

Jack reaches for my hand and gives a gentle tug, a silent request for me to rejoin him and Alita. He's trying to distract me. When I refuse to budge, he squeezes my knee and turns his attention back to Alita. I'd be mad if I weren't so grateful for him.

We're done opening presents by the time my mother emerges from the bathroom. Jack is sitting at the kitchen table next to me, peeling potatoes for our Christmas dinner. Alita is almost done with her breakfast. Larry is quiet in the living room, although I couldn't give two shits about what Larry is doing. My mother says nothing about having spent forty-five minutes in the bathroom. Instead, she takes the Wellspring House-gifted spiral ham out of the fridge and puts it in the oven before sitting with

Jack and me at the table. I can't help but notice that her pupils look like pinpricks. I should say something to her, I think. No. I'll wait and talk to her when Alita goes down for a nap.

Jack breaks the silence. "I've never met anybody like your daughter," he says, smiling at me.

"Of course not," my mother says. She smiles too. It's enough to disarm me.

Jack tells my mother about Alita, how she loves to bounce, and what a great sleeper she is. My mother tells Jack about Pokie and Nonni, my invisible childhood friends, and about the surgery I had to correct a lazy eye. As they exchange stories, I decide not to say anything that will ruin Christmas and our limited time together.

AFTER DINNER, MY mother is ready to go. She must have been gathering her things while I was changing Alita's diaper in the bedroom.

"It was so nice to see you and Alitabug," she says, smiling at us. I'm standing in the living room, holding Alita on my hip.

"You're leaving already?" My chest tightens, and the lump in my throat makes it hard to swallow. I don't want her to go. It's barely past lunchtime. "I thought we would have a chance to talk."

"I wish I could stay longer," she says, leaning to kiss Alita's cheek. "I'm going to see Philip." She told me my brother was living with his father again. Now I know why.

She's already called a taxi.

Twenty minutes later, although expected, the sound of the horn startles me. Jack and I are sitting on the couch when my mother comes in from the kitchen. Larry thanks me and goes outside.

"I'll call you again soon," she says, walking toward me. I stand because I know she's expecting a hug. I can't return her embrace. I want to, but when she wraps her arms around me, my body won't respond. I don't know when or if I'll see her again. It doesn't make sense that I'm angry and sad at the same time.

"I love you more than I can say," she says before blowing Alita a kiss and closing the door. The threat of tears keeps me from responding—I refuse to cry today. This is Alita's first Christmas and our first with Jack.

My mother's gone now. I need to put her out of my mind and focus on the good. I'm still standing when Jack puts his arms around me.

"Are you okay?" he asks.

"I will be," I say.

"Damn straight," he says. "You've got me."

A FEW DAYS AFTER Christmas, Jack and I are alone in the apartment. I'm grateful for a quiet night. The lights from the tree are making the room glow, and there's a pine-scented candle burning on the coffee table. I'm lying on the couch, singing softly along to the radio, waiting for Jack to join me after putting Alita down for the night.

"I have court next week," he blurts as he comes back into the room. He says it quickly, as though he's got to get the words out before he has time to change his mind.

"Okay," I say, sitting up. "Alita will be in daycare, so I can go with you." I'm sure it's no big deal since I'm just hearing about it now. And I don't know anybody who hasn't caught a criminal case at some point.

Jack sits down and looks at me. "I have to tell you something."

I can tell by his expression that I won't like it. I hold my breath and wait for him to continue.

"I'm going to jail," he says.

I exhale in relief. "No way," I say, even though I have no idea what he's been charged with. "That's not going to happen." I lean my head on his shoulder.

"What makes you think that?" he asks.

"There's just no way, after the shit-storm of a life I've had, that whatever makes this world go around would have given me the gift of you, only to take you away."

"I wish it were different, but my lawyer says there's no way around it."

"He's wrong. He's got to be."

"Yeah, well, I wish you were my lawyer," he says, slipping his arm around me.

"Maybe someday," I say. We both chuckle before falling silent.

A few minutes have passed when I speak again. "I have something to tell you too."

"Okay." He shuts the radio off and turns to face me. The silence is unnerving.

"There's some stuff you don't know about me—things I used to do for money," I begin. I'm looking at my hands, inspecting my fingernails for something to nibble. He puts his hand on mine. I glance up to gauge his reaction.

"It started with my Aunt Julie when I was eleven," I say, holding my face in my hands. I stopped when I went to live in the foster home with Becky and Greg." He knows about them. We sit for two hours while I tell him as much as I'm able. He asks a few questions, but mostly, he listens. There are some things I leave out, stuff I'm sure I'll take to my grave, but I've said a lot.

When I'm done, I lean forward and rest my elbows on my folded legs. Jack leans back.

"That's fucked up," he says. His eyes are wet. "I can't believe what those people did to you, your own family."

His reaction catches me off guard. I didn't expect him to feel sorry for me. His sympathy makes me feel a new, overwhelming sadness for my younger self. My eyes fill quickly, and as much as I don't want him to see me fall apart, I'm powerless to stop it.

When he pulls me to him, I sob into his chest. I'm still taking in huge gulps of air when I'm finally able to speak. "I thought you'd leave once you knew."

He tightens his arms around me. "I told you, babe, I'm not going anywhere."

35

GUILTY

~1989~

I have no idea how many times Jack has stood before the judge, but I'm guessing more than a handful based on how pissed the guy in the robe sounded today. "I'll give you one final continuance," he had said. "But this is the last one. On the next date, we will proceed with the plea and sentencing. Is that clear?" Yes, I thought after hearing the word sentencing. It had suddenly become crystal clear: Jack was going to jail.

Before court today, all I knew about Jack's case was that the charges were serious enough to warrant a ten-thousand-dollar cash bail. Still, I was positive he wouldn't be going anywhere.

We were quiet on the way home and said little during dinner. Jack wants to tell me about what happened. Although I really don't want to know the details, it seems important to him, and I need him to know that nothing he can tell me will change how I feel. I'm ready to listen now that Alita is down for the night.

Jack settles into his spot near me on the couch, lights a cigarette, and takes a drag before he begins. "I took a bunch of Valiums," he says. "The rest is what I've been told because I don't remember any of it. I guess we broke into a house—me and another kid—and a lady was at home. We scared the shit out of her." He doesn't try to hide his face when the tears come. "The next thing I know, the cops show up and arrest me." "That's crazy," I say. I don't know what else *to* say. I can't imagine the Jack I know doing something like that. He's the guy who helps strangers carry groceries to their door.

"Yeah, the whole thing was pretty bad," he says, blowing out a puff of smoke.

I sit up and tap a cigarette out of my pack. "What does your lawyer think you should do?"

"He thinks a plea is the best way to go. I could end up spending twenty years in prison if we take it to trial," he says as he lights my smoke.

My stomach tightens. "Are you going to plead guilty?"

"Yeah," he says.

"But how can you do that when you don't even remember doing anything wrong?" I ask.

"Well, I'm the one who took the pills," he says. "It'll be okay. "I promise."

I don't know about that, but Jack hasn't let me down so far. I take a deep drag from my cigarette and repeat his words in my head before curling up against him. It'll be okay.

IT's MID-MARCH, a little more than a month since we were last at the Salem Superior Courthouse. I've been dreading this day. I'm sitting between Jack, and his sister Dottie, on one of the galley benches. There are so many of us, Jack's supporters, that we fill two entire rows of seating. Jack's parents, and a couple of other sisters, are sitting with us. Two more sisters, and some friends of the family, are in another row.

We sit quietly while waiting for Jack to be called and take a collective deep breath when his name is finally announced. He squeezes my hand, stands, tucks his button-down shirt into his pants, and moves toward the microphone where his lawyer is waiting. The old hardwood floor creaks beneath his sneakers, and the sound echoes throughout the large room.

As Jack takes his place next to his lawyer, the judge begins to speak. I have to strain to hear what he's saying over the noise from the creaky benches and floorboards. The lawyer says something, and then the judge asks Jack some questions, like whether he's on any medication and if he understands what's going on. The white-haired judge pushes his glasses down and looks over them when he asks: "Do you agree that you are guilty?" The room is silent.

"Yes," Jack says.

"You'll have to speak up for the recording," the judge says.

"Yes," Jack says again.

"Okay then, I accept your plea."

For the next ten minutes, the judge lectures Jack about his crime and how the worst kind of offense is one that infringes on the sanctity of somebody's home. "For those reasons," he says, "I'm sentencing you to two to twenty years in the state prison. You are remanded into the custody of the court officers."

Jack's knees buckle as a chorus of cries and gasps echoes throughout the room. His lawyer grabs hold of his arm to keep Jack upright. A court officer runs to help.

When Jack is steady, the officer cuffs his wrists behind his back. Those of us on the benches look at each other; none of us know what to do next.

The court officer leads Jack to the back of the courtroom, to an empty room near the exit. This is the last time we'll see him outside of prison. Jack's parents, sisters, and friends say goodbye and hug him one last time before they leave us alone.

"I'm sorry," he says, looking down to where his arms disappear behind him. "I wish I could hug you."

"Me too," I say, barely above a whisper. My throat is tight. Jack is still standing in front of me, yet I can already feel his loss.

"I'll call and write as soon as I can," he says. He leans close to me for privacy from the guard. "I love you, Gail. Don't ever forget it." I know he means it, but I also know that love is never enough. My mother loves me too.

36

GUTTED

~1989~

Jack had only been gone for a few weeks when everything went to shit. I'd been having such a hard time with his going away that I decided to throw a big party for Alita's first birthday. We needed something to celebrate.

People from all my various families—Walter's, Phil's, and most recently, Jack's—gathered in my kitchen. I bought a cake and decorated the room with pink and white streamers. We sang happy birthday, and everybody took turns holding a chocolate-frosting-faced Alita for pictures. She smiled the whole day. Even though Jack wasn't there, we were getting through.

I cleaned up and put Alita in her crib when the party was over. I'd just curled up on the couch with a cup of tea and a cigarette when I heard Walter crying on the street outside. From the window, I could see a small group of people encircling him and his father.

I soon learned there'd been a fight at the Crow's Nest, a barroom down the street. Rich, Walter's only living brother, had gone there after leaving my apartment. Nobody could say what the brawl was about, but Rich was airlifted to Boston with a severe head injury. He died two days later. Just as when his brother Kevin died, Walter has been on a bender since getting the news.

Rich's death made us all stop celebrating life, and I started to spend much of my time alone. My communication with Jack was my one saving grace. I'd seen him often during the first couple of months of his incarceration.

His sister Dottie would drive, so I didn't have to worry about gas money. But it became near impossible to find somebody to babysit for the length of a jail visit. The prison is an hour away, and in addition to the time it takes to get processed in and then the visit itself, it'd take a good five hours altogether. Bringing Alita along for a visit was even more difficult than finding a sitter, so our visits became few and far between.

At first, Jack and I talked almost every night on the phone, but I couldn't keep up with the bill. One month of collect jail calls cost half my five-hundred-dollar monthly welfare check. After the disconnection notices started coming in, he began to limit his calls to a few a week. The long periods between our communication felt unbearable. Still, I waited for his call. I rarely left my apartment in the late afternoon hours for fear I'd miss him.

It had been a few months since Rob's passing, and I needed to hear the sound of Jack's voice, which is why I rushed to answer the phone when it rang.

"Hello," I said, out of breath.

"Gail?" said the voice of a man I didn't recognize.

"Yeah. Who's this?"

"This is Artie, Kathy's ex."

My heart started to race. I hadn't heard Kathy's name for years. She'd been dead for at least a year. Although not from an overdose like I thought after I'd seen her shoot up in the bathroom that one time, it was AIDS that got her in the end.

"Oh," I said. "Long time no see. What's up?" There was certainly no good reason I could think of for him to be calling me. I kept my voice calm as I wrapped the telephone cord around my finger until the tip turned white.

"I have some pictures of you, and I thought you might want them," he said.

I felt a sudden rush of heat on my face and a dip in my belly. "From where?" I asked as I walked to the kitchen window and back to the sink.

"A hotel, I think," he said.

I remembered it all at once: Artie, Kathy, and the others—all of us high. And me, standing naked in the middle of the room. I might have been on my way to the bathroom when there was a flash, then another, maybe even more. It was so long ago—at least five years. I couldn't have been more than fourteen.

"Oh my God, how did you get them?" I asked, with a rise in the pitch of my voice. I'd tried so hard to put the past behind me.

"Not sure how I got ahold of them, but I've kept them for a long time."

The thought of him looking at me—touching pictures of me—made me feel sick. "Well, yes, I want them. Of course, I do. When can I get them? Where are you living? I'll meet you." I was starting to panic.

"I'm not sure when," he said.

"I really want those pictures."

"I'll call you tomorrow and let you know when we can hook up."

"Give me your number so I can call you in case you forget," I said.

"I don't have a phone. I'll call you tomorrow, though." He sounded like he was enjoying himself, having control over me.

"Promise?" I asked. I waited for some affirmation that he would follow through.

"I promise," he said before the line went dead.

I couldn't sleep that night. Every time I closed my eyes, I saw the hotel room, the table with all the cocaine laid out, and my naked body. I thought about what I should've done back then—maybe grabbed the camera and smashed it. But I was just a kid. When he called, though, I could've demanded a phone number or an address...something. I'm not a kid anymore.

Finally, I let it go. I had to. Like everything else, it was out of my hands.

It's been a month since Artie called, and it doesn't look like I'll hear from him again. I still hope for his call every day. I wonder where the pictures are—when or if they'll reappear. It'll probably happen when things are going well in my life. Of course, there's nothing I can do about that either. For now, I need to put the whole thing out of my mind and get through the day. The only way I can do that is to stay high.

PRESCRIPTION PAINKILLERS ARE relatively easy for me to get because of all the pain I have in my body. I've always had pain in my back due to a slight curve in my spine. My belly hurts all the time, too, probably because I'm anxious. It can't help that I don't eat very well.

My gynecologist has been giving me opiates for cysts and menstrual cramps—Percocet and Vicodin. He must know I take more than I'm prescribed. I always run out before I'm due for a refill and call his office with reasons as to why I don't have any left: somebody stole them, I dropped them in the sink, or the pharmacy must've short-changed me. Sometimes he gives me more; sometimes, he doesn't. Today, unfortunately, he didn't.

Tonight, I'm alone without any lubrication, nothing to make the chore of being in my head any easier. I'd settle for anything at this point—a line, a joint, an upper, a downer, or even a drink. I've been sitting in the same spot on the loveseat for over an hour, with my back to the window and the harbor. The room is starting to get dark, yet I refuse to get up to turn on a light. I wish the day would hurry up and end. Now that it's almost summer, they seem to go on forever.

I feel the rush of hope when I hear the cordless receiver's muffled ring between the cushions beside me. I keep it, my only connection to the outside world, close at all times. It could be Jack, Artie, or somebody with something to get me high. It's only eight-thirty, still early enough to get some relief.

"Hi," my mother says. I haven't heard her voice since Christmas. "I don't want you to worry, but I have some news." She inhales deeply and continues. Her voice is calm. "I'm okay, but I tested positive for HIV." She doesn't hesitate long enough for me to respond. "I won't bore you with the details, but I had some weird symptoms, so I got tested. I got a second test, to be sure. There's no question—I'm positive."

"What does that mean, exactly?" I ask. I don't know anything about HIV.

"HIV is the virus that causes AIDS. I haven't had an opportunistic infection, so I don't have AIDS yet, which is a good thing."

Opportunistic sounds like it should be a good thing, too, but next to the word infection, I'm assuming it isn't. "What are you going to do?" What I want to ask is whether she's finally going to stop getting high.

"I'm taking medication, and my T-cell count is really good."

"What does that mean? I ask.

"It means my body can still fight any sickness." She pauses and says, "maybe I'll never get AIDS." Given the bad luck in our family, that sounds like a fantasy; just like every time she told me she would stay clean or we wouldn't get evicted again.

"I'm sure heroin doesn't help." I don't like how sharp the words sound, but I can't stop myself. Heroin has always come first.

"Actually, I've been doing well—clean and sober since I found out," she says. "It's been three weeks. I'm renting a great little house in Lynn."

"That's good." I want to be excited, but clearly, it's too little, too late.

"I'm thinking about coming back that way," she says. "I want to be closer to you and Chrissy. And Alita, of course. I know Philip would love that." The possibility makes me both excited and anxious. She hasn't lived in Gloucester since Philip hurt his finger and got taken away. It's been a few years now, and although I want her nearby, she's never been able to stay clean in Gloucester. Then again, she hasn't been able to stay clean anywhere.

"Philip's back with you?" I ask.

"Yes. That poor kid has been through so much," she says.

"We all have," I say.

"Drug addiction at its finest," she says. "I'll call you soon to figure out a time to get together. I love you more than I can say."

"I love you too."

And then, silence. The air in the room feels thick and heavy. Stifling. I take a deep breath, hoping it will somehow fill me up. It doesn't. I feel hollow.

Gutted.

Of course, this is how the story of my mother would end. I've been waiting for her to get clean and be my mother for as long as I can remember. Now she's going to die.

If I didn't have my little girl to think about, I'd find a bunch of pills, swallow them, and drift gratefully away from this shitshow of a life, once and for all.

37

SCORE

~1990~

I'm sitting at the end of a raised gynecology table in Exam Room One with my feet dangling, waiting for the doctor. Underneath the paper blanket, I'm wearing only a johnny and my socks. The *People* magazine on my lap is open to a story advertised on the cover in large, bold print—AN AIDS MYSTERY—about a woman diagnosed with AIDS after dental surgery. The dentist had the virus and passed it to this patient. It was her picture that caught my eye in the waiting room—a pretty, short-haired college student. She looks too young to have AIDS, although, at forty, my mother is also too young.

If only I could focus enough to read the small print. Maybe I'd learn something about what's happening with my mother. She was officially diagnosed with "AIDS" when her T-cell count dropped to eighty a few months ago, just a little more than a year after her diagnosis. She's living in Gloucester again, so I see her occasionally. The visits are still rare, although now, ironically, it's not good for *her* to be around *me*. She's clean, and I'm not.

I felt okay when I woke up, but the cold sweats from opiate withdrawal began at around ten. From there, it only worsened as nausea, muscle spasms, and irritability set in. I tried to get something to manage the symptoms but couldn't find anything—not even a joint. It doesn't help that my phone was shut off, and I can't call around. Coming here was my last resort.

It's always so cold in this office. I swear they keep it this way to deter us from coming in; those who know that Dr. Filbert Hutchinson is quick to write prescriptions for various heavy-duty painkillers. Calling for something would have been easier, but the odds of getting a script are much better in person.

A gentle knock on the door startles me into character. As though I've just stepped onto a stage, I put the magazine behind me, furrow my brow into a pained expression, and roll my shoulders forward into a slouch.

The doctor ambles into the room and closes the door behind him. He's awkward and timid. His belly beats the strides he makes with his short, stumpy legs. He might be taller than me, but it's a close call. I imagine he was picked on in grade school.

As soon as he's close enough, the doctor reaches to shake my hand without looking me in the eye. It helps ease my guilt about why I'm here to know he doesn't really see me.

When I lie back, Dr. Hutchinson performs his exam. He uses the speculum and then presses on my belly. I wonder if he can smell the chemicals seeping from my pores, remnants of my last methadone high two days ago.

"Does this hurt?" he asks.

"No."

"Here?" he asks as he moves his hands across my abdomen.

"Ouch," I say.

"On a scale from one to ten?"

"An eight," I say. It's an exaggeration but not a lie.

"Did you give a sample?"

"Yes," I say meekly. "It's in the bathroom." He'll check for a urinary tract infection and pregnancy. It's part of this game we play.

"You can get dressed and come to my office when you're ready."

DOCTOR HUTCHINSON GLANCES at me when I enter the room and then looks down at his desk. I follow his gaze and scan the area in front of him for his prescription pad before sitting across from him. I've barely settled in when he speaks.

"You're pregnant," he says. Although his expression doesn't change when he says the words, his tone reeks of disapproval. Of course, he disapproves; I'm a twenty-year-old single mother strung out on pain meds.

"No way," I say. It's not that I don't believe it; I just don't know what to do with the information. I've been on birth control for years, but I hardly ever remember to take those little white pills. *When was my last period, anyway?*

"I can't keep you on narcotics, given your current situation," he says, his eyes meeting mine for the first time today.

Now he's going to put his foot down? I don't think so. Not after the bomb he's just dropped on me. We're locked in a staring contest—a battle of wills. "I'm in pain," I say.

"I understand, but strong painkillers aren't good for the baby," he says.

"It's probably worse for the baby if I suddenly stop taking them after being on them for months." The time for pretense has passed, and I've come too far to leave here empty-handed. I needed the pills before the pregnancy news, and now I *really* need them.

He finally breaks. Leaning forward, Dr. Hutchinson picks up a pen, scribbles on his pad, hands me the script, and storms out of his office. I wish I could tear the piece of paper in half and leave it on his desk to show him I'm not the pill junkie he thinks I am. But I can't. My stomach clenches. The tightness in my chest threatens to rise into my throat and rupture into a mess of snot and tears, but gratefully I'm able to push back down. Another time I might allow myself to give in to this shame and contempt for who I am, but not today.

BARRY, MY NEW boyfriend of one month, is right where I left him. He's sitting in the passenger seat of the little red diesel Ford I purchased a couple of months ago for fifty bucks and a quarter-ounce of pot. Jack and I haven't officially ended things, and I had intended to stay faithful, but two-to-twenty is a long time. It's only been two years, and the loneliness was already more than I could handle. I'm done making promises I can't keep.

The prescription is still in my hand as I slide in behind the wheel. Barry smiles when he sees the piece of paper.

"Score!" he says.

"Not really," I say. I close the door and sit still, staring straight ahead through the windshield. I can't look at him.

"Why. What's up?"

"I'm pregnant," I say. I smile when I say it because that's what I do when I get nervous.

"Holy shit, that's fucking awesome!" he says. "We're gonna have a baby!"

"Seriously? Are you crazy?" I ask, turning to him.

"What?" he asks. "You don't want a baby?"

I reach for a cigarette and start the car. We sit idling in the lot. Maybe I want another baby, but not now and not with Barry. I barely know the guy. We met a month ago while I was working as a gas station cashier. He came in for a loaf of bread. Tall, thin but built, wavy dark hair, eyes the same shade of blue as mine—just my type. "You have beautiful eyes," he said on his way out. I smiled. When he returned a few minutes later, I gave him my address.

Although the job didn't last, Barry's been waking up next to me since we met. He's smart and quick-witted. He taught me how to play spades, a popular team card game he mastered in prison. "Shot down like a plane in flames," he says to the losing team. He makes me laugh, and up until today, that was all I needed from him.

But now, sitting in this parking lot, it occurs to me that I don't know his favorite color. He doesn't know mine. I doubt he even knows my birthday. We're both from Gloucester and have some acquaintances in common, but besides that, he's a stranger who sleeps in my bed.

"So what's the scoop? What did he give you?" he asks.

I look at the prescription for the first time. "Thirty Vikes—extra strength." Vicodin. Exactly what I need. Barry and I barely speak on the way to the pharmacy. I can't talk to him until I get some medicine into me.

My neck and shoulders begin to relax the moment the smooth white pills hit my palm. My body knows relief is on the way. I hand Barry three tablets and put the bottle in my pocketbook, out of his reach. I take my three before leaving the pharmacy parking lot.

When we get back to my apartment, I move quickly up the back stairs, through the entryway, kitchen, living room, and short hallway to my bedroom. Barry doesn't follow me. That's good because I need to be alone.

As soon as the door clicks behind me, the tears come. I curl up—knees to chest—on my unmade bed. My head is spinning. A baby. Two kids. Two kids with different fathers. I don't even know who the father is. It's too close to call. Jack and I were together while he was at a pre-release just a few weeks before Barry showed up in my life. I haven't had a period since. The baby can't be Barry's; it just can't be. Jack will never forgive me. Even if he could have accepted all of my faithlessness, having another man's baby is just too much.

It's been half an hour, and the Vicodin is doing its job. My palms aren't sweaty anymore. I'm just starting to doze when I hear Barry yell from the other end of the apartment. "Gail, we got company!"

I jump out of bed when I hear the urgency in his voice. In my rush to move, I bump into the dresser and cause a tub of loose powder to crash to the floor in a puff of white. "Shit," I say out loud. "That'll be a bitch to get out of the rug." I don't have a vacuum.

I open the bedroom door to a large man wearing jeans and a navy-blue windbreaker standing almost directly in front of me. He speaks before I have a chance to say anything.

"Gloucester PD," he says, pointing to a badge clipped to his belt. He walks around me and looks in my bedroom.

"Anybody else here?" he asks.

"No," I say. "Why are you here?"

"We've got a warrant," he says, flashing me a document. "We're here to search your apartment. We've gotten some information that you've been dealing drugs."

A wave of relief sweeps over me. If they'd come a week ago, I would've had a quarter pound of skunk weed. All I have today is a legal prescription for painkillers.

"Follow me," he says. I stay quiet on the way to the kitchen. Two other detectives have already started to search the living room. "Check the bedroom," he says to one of them, pointing his chin in that direction. "I think she hid something. There's a mess on the floor."

"No…" I start, but my voice trails off. I don't need to explain. They can search all they want. There's nothing to find.

"I'm gonna need you to have a seat," he says, pointing to a chair at the kitchen table.

Barry is already seated, his pupils barely visible in the ocean of blue surrounding them. It occurs to me that the police are probably here because of him. It can't be a coincidence—this raid and Barry being in my life. He's the one with the criminal record. He's been in prison, not me. And now, I may be having his baby.

I look at the detective who's babysitting the two of us. "Of all friggin' days," I say. I found out I'm pregnant today."

"Congratulations," he says. I can tell he's being polite.

"I was planning to return to school in January for my third semester, but now I'm not so sure.

"You should," he says. "This is no way to live."

"I know," I say before a new threat of tears silences me.

I stay quiet for the next hour until the men leave. They didn't give up the search until after they'd emptied all cabinets, drawers, and closets and torn apart the furniture, only to come up empty-handed.

My apartment looks like it's been burglarized. Ransacked. Nothing is where it's supposed to be. I put the cushions back on the couch and sit so I can return the contents of my purse, which have been dumped onto the coffee table. Barry is standing nearby. I pick up the Vicodin bottle and shake out four more pills—two for each of us. For now, at least, we are in this together.

"The way this place looks is a perfect analogy for my life," I say as I hand him the pills. "We need to clean this up before I get Alita from daycare."

"It could've been worse," he says, smiling. His exaggerated movements annoy me, the way he tips his head back and drops the pills into his open mouth. I don't say anything, but as far as I'm concerned, this is as bad as it gets.

38

A MIRACLE

~1991~

A sudden, severe pressure in my abdomen startles me awake. This time, I recognize the pains of labor. My bedroom is dim. Early morning light seeps in around the window shade. The green numbers on my nightstand digital read seven-fifteen. I turn onto my back and lie still while I wait for the pain to pass. The only sound I hear is the ticking of the kitchen clock.

I'm alone. Barry's been gone for months—since January or February. Our entire relationship lasted for three months, and his exit was as smooth a transition as his arrival. Aside from the pregnancy, it's as though he was never here. I saw him a few times after the breakup, but it's been a while. I'm sure he's back in jail. I haven't seen Walter for a couple of weeks either, and the last time I heard from my mother, she was going into another detox.

As I reach to turn on the bedside lamp, a second wave hits. I roll out of bed onto my knees and use the nightstand to pull myself to my feet. The pain feels like a knot in my lower back that becomes a dull-aching squeeze as it moves to the front.

When I make it to the kitchen, I silently thank the Unitarian Universalist Church for paying the three hundred dollars necessary to restore my telephone service. Then I dial Mary, my parent aide. Our birthing plan, as she calls it, is for her to drive me to the hospital. Jack's sister Dottie is coming to get Alita.

Another contraction takes hold as I hang up with Dottie. It's seven-thirty-five—they're less than seven minutes apart. I wait for it to pass before making my way to Alita's bedroom. I need to get her ready. I think this might be another quick labor, and I'd rather not deliver this baby alone.

"Time to get up, sweetie. Baby Jack is coming today." I've decided on the name even though I still don't know whether Jack is his father. Alita sits up and rubs her eyes. It's not like her to sleep so late. With her clothes in my hand, I sit on the edge of her bed to wait through another contraction.

"Are you sad, Mommy?" she asks.

"No, my belly hurts," I say.

Alita takes her clothes from me and dresses herself. She seems to know I need her help.

Dottie and Mary arrive at nearly the same time. It's good they came when they did; by the time we make it to the hospital, the contractions are four minutes apart.

Being at Gloucester's hospital reminds me of when Alita was born and my first drug detox at fifteen. I've spent a lot of time in this building. Things are different now, though. I'm an adult—twenty-one in three weeks. I hope the nurses don't judge me like they did back then, but that's not my biggest concern at the moment. The pain is so much worse than my labor was with Alita, and I can't help but wonder if it's because of all the pills I took while I was pregnant.

According to the nurse, it's too late for an epidural. The baby is already on his way. The most they can do is give me a shot of Demerol, which is still more than I had during labor last time.

GRATEFULLY, MY SECOND birth was as smooth as the first. On the eighteenth of July, just three hours after my early morning contractions began, Jack, my healthy baby boy, was born.

That was a few hours ago. Now that we're alone for the first time, I hold the swaddled bundle in my arms. I unwrap his tiny body from the receiving blanket and study his perfection—ten fingers, ten toes. When I trace my finger along his jaw and chin, his mouth opens in search of a nipple. He will never find mine waiting for him to latch on. I caused him enough damage while he grew inside of me. Even then, I knew he could suffer terrible consequences if I kept using pills during the pregnancy—opiate addiction, mental deficits, or even disfigurement.

Fear plagued me every day, and still, I couldn't stop. Each month the doctor agreed to another ultrasound in response to my complaints of unusual pain. I needed to see my baby, to hear his heartbeat. The doctor and I never discussed how the pills could harm my son. Perhaps Dr. Hutchinson felt guilt of his own for his role as my prescription-writing accomplice.

I don't know how, or to whom, to give thanks for this healthy baby. I want to tell him that he's a miracle, but I don't know how. He needs to know how much he's wanted and that I'm sorry I didn't take better care of my body while he was growing in my belly. I want to promise him it'll be better now, but if I'm anything like my mother, I don't know if it's a promise I can keep. Though the bed beside mine is empty, merely thinking of saying something so adult to such a tiny person embarrasses me.

I fold the blanket back around him, pull him close, and whisper, "I'm happy you're here."

39

TAKE-HOMES

~1992~

It's been just a few short months since Jack stood at my door—fresh out of jail—wearing a new forest green sweater and black jeans, his face smooth under the shadow of a black baseball cap. It was the best kind of surprise. The last time I'd seen him was a month before when I brought the baby—whom he nicknamed Jackamo—for a visit at the jail. Jack hadn't known his release date then, and I didn't have a phone.

"Hey," was all he'd said.

"Hi. I was starting to think you weren't coming."

"That's crazy talk," he'd said, stepping into the entryway and wrapping his arms around me. "You can't get rid of me that easy."

He couldn't have come at a better time. I'd been the mother of two small kids for only a few months, and it was already too much for me alone.

During my pregnancy, I thought it would be easy to have another; after all, I'd been feeding, bathing, and clothing one kid for three years. I was wrong. Alita had been a ton of work before the baby came, but she's become impossible since his birth.

She started leaving our apartment in the middle of the night while I slept. The downstairs neighbor brought her back two times during the weeks after Jackamo's birth. I don't know what compelled her to go outside, but she was determined. A bolt lock didn't even hinder her. She'd figured out how to reach the latch by pulling over a chair to stand on.

Later in the summer, she decided to look in the back of the toilet. She was able to lift the top just enough to crack the tank when she dropped it back down. Toilet water flooded the bathroom and poured through the apartment ceiling below. The landlord charged me two hundred dollars—that I didn't have—for repairs.

Life became instantly better with Jack's help. We shared household chores and responsibilities. Once the kids were asleep, we'd settle in to smoke a joint and play cards or snuggle on the couch for a movie. It almost felt like it did in the days before Jack went to jail. I was happy and hopeful, even though we were still getting high. We often talked about putting down the drugs and having a normal life.

As though we needed a greater incentive, a month later, Walter brought us the news that Debbie had died. Drugs played a part in her death, and her life was over at thirty-one. In my memory and my heart, she was my sister. Her father and my mother connected us. But in reality, she was my brother's sister, not mine. Still, I couldn't have loved her more if we shared the same blood.

After Debbie's funeral, we stood next to her freshly dug grave and smoked a joint in her honor. As we smoked, I thought about when Debbie would bring Chrissy and me to Stage Fort Park when we were kids. We'd visit the playground for a few spins on the merry-go-round, walk along the dirt road to the cannons overlooking the harbor, and move through the pathways around huge boulders alongside the calm ocean water. I'd run and climb the rocks barefoot and scale the sides of every steep incline before stopping for a swim at Half Moon Beach. I remembered how she was the only person who'd ever made me feel like I mattered.

I wondered what would happen to her now-motherless kids. I wished I could be present for them the way she had been for me, but of course, it was more than I could do to take care of Alita and Jackamo. Blowing the last bit of smoke from my lungs, I recognized the insanity of paying Debbie tribute with a drug, the very thing that had killed her. What they say is true; I thought: Life sucks, and then you die.

When we got home, Jack and I had a serious talk about our using. We agreed to slow down, to make a real effort to put the drugs out of our lives for good. Together, we could do anything.

A few weeks later, shortly before Christmas, my mother surprised us with a visit. I took it as a good sign. It was the first time I'd seen her and Jack together in the nearly four years since I'd spent Christmas with them. The conversation was as easy as it had been the first time they'd met, and I was so grateful for the reunion that I kept reminding myself not to mess it up. We spent an hour talking and laughing.

Before leaving, my mother invited us for Christmas dinner. Now a few months clean, she and Philip are living in Gloucester. Chrissy will be there too. For the first time in eight years, since before I ran away to Texas, my mother, Chrissy, Philip, and I will be together on Christmas day.

As I step inside my mother's apartment, I'm swathed in warmth and the aroma of honey-baked ham. It feels like coming home. Philip is sitting in an easy chair in the corner of the room. My mother's newest boyfriend, Larry, is sitting on the couch. We've met before, but I don't make any attempt to get to know him. I doubt he'll last. Since Walter, my mother hasn't met a man intelligent enough to keep up with her.

The apartment is immaculate, as clean as any new place she's ever had. I recognize it at once as a reflection of how she's doing and whether she's getting high. I'm again reminded of how she makes the outside perfect so nobody looks close enough to see that she's a mess inside. It's hard to believe this is different from any other time she seemed to be doing well, but I'm hoping for the best.

Alita runs ahead into the kitchen, following the voices of my mother and her Auntie Chrissy. Jack takes Jackamo out of his seat, and we follow her lead. When we enter the kitchen, my mother moves toward us, away from the stove. She wipes her hands on a dish towel and reaches for Jackamo. Even though he's only met her a handful of times, the baby goes to her without hesitation.

She holds him with one arm and hugs Jack with the other. I'm still behind him, afraid to fully give myself to this moment.

When Jack steps aside for my turn, I can see her eyes are clear and bright. The eyes are always a dead giveaway when she's high. The dark circles are gone, and her cheeks are pink. Her hair is different, too; it's short now, above the ears. She's wearing earrings and a short-sleeved blue dress. When I hug her, I smell her favorite scent; rose water that comes in the cobalt blue bottles lining her kitchen window sill.

"I'm glad you made it," she says as she pulls away.

"Me too. You look really good." I reach for Jackamo so she can finish preparing the meal. I'm sincerely happy to be here, but I'm also cautious. It wouldn't be the first time I've gotten my hopes up only to have her relapse after a week or a month.

"Why thank you," she says, smiling as she curtsies and pretends to flip back hair that used to hang past her shoulders.

Alita is sitting on Chrissy's lap at the kitchen table. A woman my mother met in her treatment program is seated next to them. Lori introduces herself to me, and she and I talk while my mother is busy at the stove.

"Your mother's doing great," Lori says.

"Hopefully, it lasts," I say, immediately regretting my negativity.

"One day at a time," my mother says over her shoulder.

"Yup, that's what they say." My sarcasm is out of my control.

After dinner, the men, apple pie in hand, go into the living room to watch television. Alita sits on the floor next to Jack's feet with her coloring book, and Jackamo is asleep in his carrier. Chrissy has gone to eat a second holiday meal with the family who took care of her when my mother couldn't.

With the table clear, my mother, Lori, and I sit with a mug in front of each of us. Coffee for them, tea for me.

My mother lights a cigarette, takes a drag and looks me in the eye. "I love you, Gail," she says. "I know I haven't been a good mother, but I want you to know that I will be here for you now."

I want to believe her more than anything, but she must see in my expression that I don't.

"Getting AIDS has really changed me," she says. "I don't know how much longer I have to live, and I don't want to waste any more time. I haven't had a chance to tell you how it happened. Do you want to know?"

"Sure," I say, as I look at Lori, who nods in support of my mother.

"I was at a house in Lynn, a shooting gallery they call it. It's a place where people go to get high," she says.

"I figured."

"Anyway, there were four of us and just one set of works. We used bleach to clean it after each turn. Obviously, it's always a good idea to clean a shared needle, but especially in this case because we knew one of the people was HIV positive. By the time the syringe got to me, we had run out of bleach. I didn't want to go to the store to buy more because I was afraid they'd do all the heroin while I was gone. So, instead, I took my chances. It was like playing a game of Russian roulette, and I lost."

The story should sound crazy, and to most, I'm sure it would, but it makes perfect sense to me. If heroin had been my drug of choice, I would've done the same thing. Still, I don't know what to do with this information. It doesn't change anything. Time with my mother has always been limited. I've been expecting her to die my whole life.

THINGS BETWEEN JACK and I haven't been great in the weeks since Christmas. Despite all my good intentions, I'm getting high more than ever. Jack is too. Neither of us is who we used to be. He's so distant; I feel alone even when he's here. He's angry. Not just with me, it seems the entire world. His criminal record has made it hard for him to find work. It looks like he's got a spot on a tuna fishing boat, which will be great money if they make a catch. For now, though, I'm still responsible for the bills and food. I also can't be sure he hasn't been with other girls. He was corresponding with somebody before he got released from prison, and I'm sure they were still dating after he got out. I'm not convinced it's as over as he tells me.

My New Year's resolution had been to stay clean. I figured I could stop getting high since my mother did, knowing she'll die sooner rather than later. But we're well into February, and I still can't stop. I've been using methadone in between prescriptions. I have a connection who sells me his take-homes so he can buy heroin, the one drug I still refuse to do because it took my mother from me.

All I want is to be free from this shit, but the sickness that comes along with detox is way too hard to get through. I know I can't do it on my own. I need to go somewhere, and not just a four-or-five-day spin dry. I need more like a month, but I don't know what to do with the kids.

There's no way Jack can handle taking care of Alita and Jackamo, not in his current frame of mind. He hasn't been around for a few days, anyway. We got into a fight, and I don't have the gas money to look for him. My mother can't take them. I'm still not even sure I can trust her. Chrissy doesn't have the space, and she works during the day. Little Nana is too old to care for little kids. She hasn't even met Jackamo yet. Of course, Aunt Julie isn't an option. I heard she had another baby while in the psychiatric hospital and that the baby was taken by social services right after she was born. I wish I had the nerve to ask Becky and Greg, but I'm too ashamed to even speak to them while I'm getting high.

Even though I had no choice, I still can't believe I've asked social services for help. I always said it would have to be a cold day in hell before I'd let social services take my kids. I've been second-guessing my decision since making it. I wonder if maybe I can do it on my own. I didn't go into treatment when I got clean with Becky and Greg. But if I could've done it without help, I would have. At this point, I've been using for four years straight. It is a cold day in hell, for sure.

When the social worker arrives, Alita is sitting at the kitchen table eating a pop tart. I'm holding seven-month-old Jackamo.

The worker moves just far enough into the room to gather the bags I've packed for the kids. The small suitcase and Jackamo's diaper bag are on the floor next to the table. "Everybody ready?" she asks, her tone sickeningly upbeat.

Alita looks at me. I crouch down to meet her eyes. "It's okay," I say. "Remember what I told you. Mommy is sick. It's just for a little while so I can get better." As I speak the last word, I'm suddenly struck with an understanding so clear that I have to brace myself against Alita's chair—I have become my mother.

40

WHY NOT?

~1992~

I 've been clean since leaving the twenty-eight-day program. It'll be five months in a few days—the longest stretch since I was seventeen. Pulling into the driveway of my mother's new rental house, less than two hundred feet from Gloucester's Good Harbor beach, I can't help but smile. Our lives have changed so much.

I cut the engine and sit for a moment, welcoming the breeze that blows salt air through my car's open windows. It's barely noon and already almost ninety degrees outside.

Alita reaches for the door handle—at four, she knows how to unbuckle her seatbelt. There's no need to stop her. We've been here enough times for her to go in by herself. Jackamo starts to whine as soon as Alita leaves the car. He wants to go too. I look at him in the rearview mirror. His big blue eyes watch me, his chubby cheeks pink from the sun. His bangs are starting to stick to his forehead. I'm sweating, too, even though my hair is up and I'm wearing a tank top.

"I know, birthday boy. I'm coming."

I unstrap Jackamo from his seat, and although he can walk now, I carry him into the house.

Robin, my friend and sponsor is sitting on the couch with a friend of my mother's. Chrissy is at the peninsula. My mother and Alita are standing across from her in the kitchen, looking at Jackamo's birthday cake.

"Happy First Birthday, Jack." My mother points to each word as she reads them to Alita. I stand with my little boy on my hip and observe them. Even though I've watched my mother evolve into a grandmother, it still surprises me.

"Can I have some?" Alita asks.

"First, we have to sing happy birthday." My mother says. "And we have to wait for the clown."

"The clown?" Alita asks, her eyes wide.

"Yes, Billy the clown," my mother says.

"Can I see him? Alita asks.

"Of course. In a little while. Want to help me outside?" my mother asks as she takes Alita's hand.

They walk to the sliding door that leads to the deck. My mother moves with confidence—shoulders back and head high—as though she's been carrying herself this way her whole life. And she's the perfect picture of health. Nobody would ever know she has AIDS. In fact, she looks radiant. Her face is framed by her short hair, bangs draped above her sparkling blue eyes. A small opal earring dangles from each earlobe. Her beach-made bronze skin is pronounced against a white denim skirt that falls just above her knee, and a white sleeveless shirt exposes arms she kept hidden when they were lined with needle marks. I'm still amazed by this new version of my mother, the kind of woman I want to be.

"This must be little Jack," says Scott, a newly sober friend of my mother's. His voice jolts me back into the moment.

"Yes. One today," I say cheerfully, looking at Jackamo.

"Can I hold him?" he asks with his arms out. "My son is almost the same age, and I haven't seen him since I got sober." Jackamo leans in and reaches for Scott. I'm sure my boy misses being around a man now that Jack is back in jail for violating his parole.

I hand Jackamo to Scott and walk to the deck door. Outside, the red, yellow, and blue streamers hanging from the roof-line look like waves. The railings are wrapped to match. I watch as Alita helps my mother spread a paper tablecloth over a table on the deck and then places a birthday plate and plasticware in front of each chair.

Alita calls the fifteen of us to join them outside when everything is ready. Jackamo sits on my lap in the folding chair designated for the birthday boy. Chrissy, Philip, and Alita sit near us at the table.

Once everybody has settled in, Billy the Clown jumps out onto the deck, his big shoes flopping on the wood planks. At first, Jackamo is afraid of Billy's round red nose and polka-dotted suit. But after cake and ice cream, he lets Billy hold him for a picture. As I look around at the happy faces of all the people I love, I can't help but give in to the hope that my mother is here to stay.

JACK LISTENS QUIETLY while I tell him about the party. I try to picture him sitting comfortably on a couch instead of standing at a payphone surrounded by concrete blocks, with a line of men waiting to use the phone.

"Holy shit, babe, she planned the whole thing," I say. "All I had to do was show up with the kids. It's like she's somebody else—The Invasion of the Body Snatchers."

He laughs. "I guess she kind of is."

"It's crazy. Guess what?" I ask, although I'm too excited to wait for a response. "I'm going to North Shore in the fall. Paralegal studies."

"That's great, babe. You should be doing something in the law; God knows you love to argue."

"Ha ha," I say. "I'm not going to be a lawyer."

"Why not?" he asks without a hint of joking. "Then you can represent me someday." Even though I laugh, a whisper in my head repeats his words: Why not?

"It feels like things are finally coming together," I say.

"They are," he says. "And soon, I'll be there to help, so you won't have to do it all alone." Things have changed between us. Even though we got the paternity test results and Jack's not Jackamo's father, he loves my boy just the same. He's forgiven me, and we're better than ever.

"Both of us clean and sober," I say.

"Absolutely," he says. It seems a given that he'd stay clean in jail, but he's not the only person to tell me it's easier to get drugs on the inside than on the street. He's already told me he's done getting high; he wants to have a good life, too.

"I love you, babe," Jack says sweetly before we hang up. "We got this. Nothing is gonna come between us ever again."

41

THE THIRD ROOM

~1993~

I made the dean's list last semester. Turns out it's easier to learn without drugs fogging up my brain. It also helps that I've got a new apartment with plenty of space for the kids to play while I study. We can spread out. And with Jack back home, things are looking up. So far, he's kept his promise about staying clean. He shows up when he's supposed to and does what he says he'll do. We've also been going to twelve-step meetings together—my mother too.

Last Friday night, the three of us sat in a row, Jack to my left, my mother to my right; all of us clean and sober—a couple of months for Jack, a year for me, over a year for my mother. When I think about it now, I can almost feel Jack's hand resting on my leg and my mother reaching over to massage my neck. Between them, I feel safe and loved in a way I've never experienced.

My feelings for Jack are far from the infatuation-hormone-driven lust I used to mistake for love. This emotion is what I now know to be true love, the kind that has nothing to do with what I've done or failed to do but exists simply because of who I am.

I can tell my mother is changed, too. She's been giving more than taking these days. Over the summer, she organized a drive to collect new clothing to give to families affected by the AIDS virus. She called manufacturers and retailers for clothing donations and received so many that she needed a space to keep them. Now she has a place next to the Gloucester Police Station. It's a free store with a sign that says "Jackie's Clothes Closet" hanging on the door.

Also, as a client of The North Shore AIDS Health Project, a Gloucester agency that helps people affected by AIDS, my mother is given a Christmas gift each year. This year, she asked for a massage table instead of a trip to St. Croix, as she had for the last two years.

I asked her why she didn't want to take another trip.

"It's not that I don't want to go; I want to make people feel good," she said.

"But this is supposed to be a gift for you."

"I know," she said. "Making people feel good is a gift for me." I might have rolled my eyes—partly because I don't get it and partly because I resent that she's present for a bunch of strangers in a way that she's never been for me. Still, I'm glad she's different from before.

TONIGHT, JACK IS with the kids. My mother is going to tell her story. She and another woman, the chairperson, are facing the other fifty or so of us in the room. Only a few of the chairs are empty. She sits with her back straight, her hands folded on the table in front of her. Her posture reminds me of how she sat at her secretarial desk when I was young. As it did then, as though I am an extension of her, my chin rises, and I sit straight in my chair.

To those who don't know my mother well, she appears poised and confident. She's better at pretending than I am, but I can tell she's nervous. Her jaw is tight, as though there are rubber bands wrapped around the joint on each side. She looks around the room and then down at the table. Her hands are still, unlike mine. I'm a fidgeter, constantly moving. When my cup is empty, I will methodically break it into tiny Styrofoam squares.

Despite being November-cold outside, the old Essex elementary schoolhouse is so warm that I put my cup of tea on the floor and push up my sleeves. I'm sure part of the reason I'm hot is that I'm anxious about what I'll hear tonight. She's told me some things and some other stuff I know because I was there, but I don't know all of it.

My mother begins her share by describing her childhood. She talks about the extensive mental illness and alcoholism in our family. Then she tells the group about the first time she tried heroin, her failed romantic relationships, and how she couldn't be a mother to her children. She glances at me. Her eyes are wet, but she's holding it together. We both are.

"It's like there are three rooms inside of me," she says. "The first is immaculate. I'll invite anybody to come in because I'm proud of how clean it is. They can sit with me over coffee and chat about idle, meaningless things.

The second room, which is buried deeper than the first, isn't quite as clean. It's cluttered and dusty but not filthy by any wild stretch of the imagination. I'll invite a select few to visit in this second room because I'm still a little embarrassed about how it looks."

We take a deep, steadying breath together before she continues. The room is so quiet that it feels as though we're here alone, and this incredibly articulate woman is speaking only to me.

"The third room is buried deep inside, tucked away from the world; it's dirty and disorganized—filthy even. I won't let anybody in that room because for what exists there, I feel shame. It's the third room that kept me a prisoner to heroin for so many years. Today, with the help of the few people I'm learning to trust, I'm starting to clean out that room."

It takes a moment before slow applause begins to fill the silence. Maybe, like me, her audience wasn't ready for it to end. Perhaps they, too, wished she'd never stop talking.

EVERYTHING HAS BEEN going so well. It's early spring, so I'll be wrapping up the school semester soon. My grades are excellent. The kids are good, and Jack is working. I couldn't imagine anything going wrong until I heard my mother's melancholy voice on the phone.

"Little Nana is really sick," she said with a sniffle. "They think it's cancer." I could picture her sitting at Little Nana's kitchen table, the rotary telephone's yellow receiver in her hand. "It doesn't look like she'll make it past the weekend," she said. I instantly began to worry that this would shake my mother enough to make her get high, although it's a constant fear regardless of what happens. I've yet to let my guard down in the year and a half that she's been clean.

I was also surprised by the call, even though Little Nana is well into her eighties, and I've never known her to see a doctor. That she's been around this long must've made me think she'd live forever. Of course, I haven't seen her in over a year, so I have no idea how she's been feeling. It's not that I don't want to see her. In fact, I miss and think of her often. I don't visit because the dark, smoky rooms of her tiny apartment remind me of who I used to be. I never really forget, but it's easier to let the memories fade if I don't go there.

"I'll come tomorrow," I said before we hung up. Gratefully, being the middle of the week, there was still time for me to say goodbye.

I woke up this morning feeling prepared for my last visit with Little Nana. The kids are at school and daycare, and I'm just about ready to go when the phone rings.

"I'm getting ready now," I say, knowing it's my mother.

"It's okay," she says, "she didn't make it through the night."

I'm not sure what to do when the call ends. I lean back against the kitchen counter, letting it support me. I need a cigarette. Just one more day, I would've at least had the chance to say goodbye. When I look down at the phone still in my hand, I'm overcome with a sudden urge to throw it at the wall and watch it shatter. I lift my arm with the phone above my head. I'm sick and fucking tired of all this loss. It's not fair.

"Life's not fair," I hear myself say out loud, as though I've been taken over by somebody else. I put my arm down. I want to be angry, but I know it's not the truth of how I feel. The tears come despite me. Instead of fighting it, I sit in the closest chair and allow myself to feel the pain. I'm grateful to be home alone where nobody can see me this out of control. As I sit with my elbows resting on the table, head in my hands, every loss I've ever experienced moves through my thoughts. My body heaves with sobs while every goodbye makes a brief appearance on the screen of my mind.

When it's done, I stand at the kitchen sink, fill my cupped hands, and splash water on my face. There's no time to waste sitting here feeling sorry for myself. I have to go grocery shopping, and I have some calls to make. Good thing I didn't smash the phone; it's the only one I have.

IT'S GRADUATION DAY, just a year since Little Nana's death. My gown hangs on a railing in my bedroom. I've already removed the cap from its plastic wrapping and placed the tassel around the button. Everything is ready. Today is not a day to take chances. It may very well be the best day of my life so far. I'll have an Associate Degree in Paralegal Studies in just a few hours. Not bad for somebody who barely went to high school, I think.

I'm sitting alone at the kitchen table with a hot cup of tea in front of me when I pick up the cordless phone and dial my mother's number. When she answers on the third ring, I start talking.

"Hi," I say. "I'm so excited; I could barely sleep last night. Jack is dropping the kids at the babysitter's now. What time do you want us to pick you up?"

"I'm sorry honey, I can't make it," she says. She sounds tired.

"Oh," I say as my stomach tightens. "Why not?" I ask, slowly letting out my breath.

"I feel like shit. I think the shingles are back. I can't even get out of bed."

I know she's sick, and I feel bad about that, but I need her to be there. "What if you nap and then see how you feel?" I ask as I move my hand through the steam from my mug.

"I just can't do it, Gail. I have a card for you, though. Philip will bring it with him."

"Okay," I say.

"I'm so incredibly proud of you," she says.

"I know," I say. I'm trying to think of another way to get her to come.

"I love you more than I can say."

"I love you too. I wish you would come," I say.

"I wish I could."

EVEN THOUGH I'M twenty-three and have been a mother for six years, I feel like a teenager standing in this line. I imagine this is what my high school graduation would have been like.

The crowd quiets almost instantly when the music begins. Hundreds of eyes watch as the graduating members of the NSCC Class of 1994 take our designated seats in the middle of the gymnasium of a bigger state school. We sit and wait through speeches and awards for the procession to begin.

When they call my name, I make my way onto the stage to accept my diploma, magna cum laude. There's yelling and a loud whistle to my right. From the corner of my eye, I see my people: Jack, Chrissy, Philip, and a couple of friends. With them standing for me and with me, sharing in this success, I realize I belong here. I earned this. I suddenly feel like I'm on the inside of a clubhouse in which I've always felt excluded. For today, at least, I'm a member of this group, my entry made possible by the secret knock of education.

42

DON'T WORRY ABOUT ME

~1994~

"Jack is sick," Dottie said. "It's bad." She called right when I got home from work. She said he's at the Lemuel Shattuck Hospital in Cambridge, where prisoners are taken when the jail can't handle their treatment. He'd gone back into lockup a few months after our last breakup.

After hanging up with Dottie, I sat at the kitchen table, lit a Newport, and called my mother. She agreed we shouldn't worry. "Jack's a fighter," she said. "We all are."

I lit another cigarette when the call ended. I probably would've smoked a joint if I had one, so it's a good thing I didn't. I've been clean for almost two years now. If only Jack had stuck it out with me. His most recent relapse started near the beginning of summer. It seemed like a small bump on the highway of all the challenges we've overcome, and instead of going into detox, he went to Connecticut to stay with his sister, Francine. It was good for him to get out of Gloucester for a while.

Before the relapse, things had been better than ever. I'd gotten a job as a paralegal and was accepted into Suffolk University to continue my education. My mother and I met with the dean of students, who offered to give me two free courses as I worked my way out of student loan default.

Jack had returned from Connecticut in August, just in time to bring me to get my books and attend orientation. He'd also started making good money tuna fishing.

But near the beginning of October, I got a call from a drug dealer. As soon as I heard her familiar raspy voice, I knew Jack was messed up again. Jack didn't lie when I asked if he was getting high. Instead, he came to where I stood in the kitchen and wrapped his arms around me.

"I can't keep doing this," I said, feeling beaten and exhausted. We both knew he had to go. I'd never been able to stay clean with him using, and my kids needed me to be well.

"I know," he said. "I'm sorry."

Even after we ended our relationship, Jack came to see me every couple of days. Sometimes he'd stay for hours. He didn't mention anything about trying to clean up again, and I didn't ask.

DOTTIE AND I don't speak as we ride the elevator to the second floor of the cold, gray hospital. As we walk down the hallway, I hear the sounds of machines beeping and whooshing, along with the squeak of my rubber soles on the shiny floor.

Jack's parents and sisters are in the hallway outside Jack's room. There are too many of us for everybody to be inside at the same time, so we wait our turn. We don't have to wait long.

Dottie takes the lead. She doesn't hesitate in the doorway, but I stop short when I notice a change in the air. The hallway was cool, but it feels like a fever in here. I'm overwhelmed by the thick stillness. It feels so much like being underwater; I'm afraid I'll drown if I breathe it in. I ignore the voice in my head that's screaming for me to turn around, and I take another step. The heavy door closes behind me. Dottie stands next to the bed; another sister is on the other side.

It takes a moment for my eyes to adjust to the dim room. I'm surprised by how much it looks like any other hospital, with its checkered floors and chrome privacy curtain pipes that snake around the ceiling. For now, the curtains are bunched up near the head of the bed.

Jack is lying on his back on a bed with wheels with his head raised slightly. The padded side rails are up. I take a deep suck of the acrid air and walk toward him but stop at the foot of the bed where I can assess the situation. He's dressed only in a thin blue hospital gown. A white blanket covers him from the waist down. When I see the brown leather straps hanging loosely around his wrists, I assume his ankles are also restrained.

"Why are these on?" I ask, pointing to the strap. "It's not like he's going anywhere."

"He was thrashing around earlier," Dottie says as she wipes his forehead with a damp facecloth. "They were worried he'd hurt himself." Dottie used to be a nurse, so I trust she knows what she's talking about. It should make me feel better that the straps are for safety rather than confinement, but it doesn't.

When Dottie goes to the sink, I step closer to the head of the bed—close enough to see that Jack's open eyes are covered with a thin transparent film and are yellow where they should be white. I'm close enough to feel the heat radiating from his body. He looks terrified as he stares, unfocused, at the only place the bed's position allows. I need him to know I'm here, that we'll face this demon together, but I'm afraid to touch him.

I was driving the last time I saw Jack. He was walking near my apartment. When I pulled my car next to the curb, he smiled and opened the passenger-side door. His appearance startled me. The hood of his gray sweatshirt was pulled up over his baseball cap. He was even thinner than when I'd seen him the week before, and his cheeks looked hollow. The circles below his eyes were dark against his pale skin, and his eyes didn't look right.

"You look like you're going to die," I said.

"Don't worry about me," he said. He always said that.

"I can't help it," I said. "I love you."

"I love you too, babe," he said and smiled again before closing the door. As I pulled away from the curb, I watched him in the rearview mirror. The hoodie, no match for the early November chill, hung on his shoulders—his faded black, once tight jeans, now baggy. Still, I thought, I would know him anywhere, even from the back.

We all take turns sitting with Jack throughout the night. His sisters and parents talk to him as though he can hear them. They tell him they love him and that it's okay for him to let go if it's too painful to hang on. I refuse to tell him that. He has to keep fighting. That's what we do. I need him, and I can't imagine a world without him in it.

JACK'S EYES ARE closed when I return to the hospital the next day. They say he's in a coma. I think that's a good thing; it'll give his body a chance to rest and heal. I need to believe something positive. According to the doctor, Jack's liver is so full of toxins that there's no way to flush out the poison. His body is shutting down.

Of course, I know it's the truth. I know the smell in the room. I recognize it from just a few months before, when I visited my sister, I mean my brother's sister, Terry, in the hours before her death. Just like Rich, Debbie, and now Jack, she never reached her thirtieth birthday.

It's late Saturday when I get some time alone with Jack. I stand beside him and lightly touch the cold, damp facecloth to his cheeks, chin, and forehead. I run my other hand down each of the long thin fingers of his left hand, the one closest to me. I then trace the outside of his arm, stopping at his initials—J.M.—in amateur tattoo green.

With my knuckle, I move along his jawline, over a small mole on the left side of his face and another under his eye. I'm trying to etch every line, scar, and imperfection onto the slate in my mind that will always belong to him.

For the first time since I found out Jack was sick, I believe this may be the last time I'll see him. When I turn my attention to his face, I half expect him to open his eyes and say, "Don't worry about me," but his lids stay closed. He remains still.

Finally, with the same awkward embarrassment I felt when talking to my son for the first time, I take a deep breath and speak. "This isn't right," I say. "We should be getting ready for Christmas. Anyway, I can't believe I'm saying this, but I want you to know that you don't have to stay for me if you're in pain. I mean, I want you here more than anything. I can't even imagine what it will be like to know I won't see you again, but I'll be okay." I press my forehead against his cheek. "I love you so much."

Dottie brought me home late in the afternoon. She called shortly after to tell me that the doctor agreed to give Jack a hefty dose of vitamin E in the hopes that it would flush the toxins from his body. From the research Dottie's done, the treatment sounded promising. We discussed the possibilities and decided there was a good chance it would work. When we hung up, I felt hopeful. I was so relieved that sleep came quickly.

When my alarm sounded from far away, loud and incessant, I reached to shut it off. *No,* I thought, *I don't want to get up—just five more minutes.* It didn't stop. When my eyes opened, I realized the ringing was coming from the telephone, not the alarm. The digital clock showed it was a little after three in the morning.

"Hello," I said, groggy and confused. It was Dottie, and she was crying.

"My brother didn't make it," she said. "He's gone."

43

THE CHERRY TREE

~1995~

Early April brings weather warm enough to open the windows. I'm grateful for the change in seasons. The cold made it even harder to move through the grief of losing Jack. It felt like the pain would swallow me up. I'd been waiting for him to come home for so long that I didn't know how not to. I took a leave from school for the spring semester. Peter, my boss and friend, hasn't pushed me to come back to work. He knows I need time.

After Jack's funeral, I tried to find CJ, my and Jack's long-time friend. Since the day I met Jack on the highway when he and CJ changed my flat tire, the three of us had become best friends, a much less heroic version of the Three Musketeers. I wanted CJ to hear about Jack from me. I worried about how he might handle the news.

The last time I'd heard from CJ was by letter back in September. He was in a treatment program. It sounded like he was doing great, but the card I sent him was returned to me unopened. He'd left the program. We'd all done that more than once. I didn't have any other leads on how to find him.

At the end of December, less than two weeks after Jack's death, there was an article in the *Gloucester Daily Times*. A body had been found at a dump in Concord, New Hampshire. It took them a week to identify CJ's frozen body; his only identifiable mark was a tattoo of Yosemite Sam on his back. I remembered how excited he was when he showed it to me; his skin was still red and tender from the needle. He was twenty-five, just like me. I couldn't help but wonder if CJ had died the same day Jack got sick and if that was why Jack had been so afraid—perhaps he could see something we couldn't.

For months I dragged myself out of bed in the morning, got the kids ready for school and daycare, and crawled back into bed after dropping them off. I'm not sure I would've kept trying if not for Alita and Jackamo. I never came out and said as much, but my mother knew. A few months ago, she said, "If you kill yourself, your kids will always think it was their fault." Of course, she couldn't know this first-hand since her mother was still alive, but it made sense. It was probably something she'd told herself over the years. My mother's being here helps, for sure. I can't imagine missing her too.

I KNOW IT'S my mother calling as soon as I hear the phone ring. We've been talking every day. When she asks how I'm doing, I'm glad to tell her I'm feeling good. I didn't go back to bed after bringing the kids to daycare, and I'm cleaning the kitchen.

"I've been working on a poem," my mother says. She sounds excited. She's been taking writing classes at the community college since the beginning of fall. Now, in her second semester at North Shore, she's starting to recognize her talent for writing. She's always been good with words. "I'd like you to hear it," she says.

"Okay, let me get a cigarette," I say. "Hang on." I light up and get the cordless, so I can go outside and sit on the back stairs. "All right, I'm ready."

"It's called The Cherry Tree," she says. My mother takes a deep breath and reads:

> Wandering through the countryside, my daily nature walk,
> I chanced to meet a woman and stopped with her to talk.
> Tired eyes and frail frame, the spark of life near past,
> she's planting there a cherry tree; the task no doubt her last.
> Curious, I asked her, "Why do you bother to plant this tree?
> Soon you'll draw your final breath, the fruit you'll never see."
> "It's true," she said, "I'll see no fruit, for I am deathly ill.
> I'm planting here this cherry tree for Chrissy, Gail, and Phil."

44

I AM

~1995~

Halloween is four days away. Alita, Jackamo, and I are sitting at the kitchen table, eating dinner and discussing the upcoming holiday. "I can't wait to be a witch," Alita says before she shovels a spoonful of macaroni and cheese into her mouth.

"And Jackamo's a karate guy," I say. He smiles his most delighted smile. At seven and four, they're finally at the perfect ages to enjoy trick-or-treating.

When the phone rings, I leave the kids to their excited conversation. It's my friend Robin.

"The meals-on-wheels people weren't able to get into your mother's apartment with her dinner," she says. "The downstairs door was locked, and she wouldn't respond to their banging and yelling. Firefighters broke down the door. They found your mother unconscious on the second floor."

I can picture my mother on her living room couch with her favorite down pillow, a pack of Marlboros within reach on the ottoman, and the television on for company.

"They've taken her to Addison Gilbert," she says.

"I don't know what to do," I say as I bite at the thumbnail of my free hand.

"Why don't you call the hospital and ask them what's happening? I'm here for whatever you need," she says before we hang up. I know she means it.

The nurse who takes my call says my mother is being evaluated. "Her temperature has gone down a bit, but it was one hundred and six degrees when she arrived. It doesn't look good," she says.

"Should I come there?" I ask. I can see the kids from the living room eating, oblivious to what's happening with their grandmother.

"No. We're still trying to get her fever under control. She wouldn't even know you were here. Call back in the morning, and we'll have a better idea of what happens next."

I CAN'T SLEEP. I've been sitting on the couch for hours, smoking and thinking. My mother has been so lonely since my brother moved out in September. I wish I'd spent more time with her recently. Between the kids, work, and school, I've only been getting to her apartment once or twice a week. And, since Jack died, I'm afraid to be so close to death. He's been gone for ten months, and I'm just starting to regain some sense of normalcy.

I'm also replaying the conversations I've had with my mother over the last few months. She mostly talked about pneumonia, shingles, and her constant pain. She also told me unequivocally that she was ready to die.

"I'm not quite as ready for you to go as you are. We've missed so much time," I said.

"I know," she said.

"I want you to contact me from wherever you end up."

"Okay," she said. "I'll let you know when I get there."

"But how will you let me know without a body or a voice?"

"I don't know," she said. We were quiet while considering the dilemma at hand.

"It doesn't help that neither of us has been dead before," I said. We laughed.

"Maybe I can make something move," she said.

"That'll scare the shit out of me." We laughed again.

"I'll figure it out," she said. I had no doubt she would.

IN THE MORNING, a different nurse tells me my mother has been transported to Beverly Hospital, where I was born. The woman says Beverly is better equipped to handle "cases like hers." She sounds disgusted, as though she's been saddled with emptying bedpans. Apparently, Gloucester's hospital doesn't handle AIDS cases.

It's nearly eleven when I reach a Beverly Hospital nurse by phone, and time is running out. "If you want to say goodbye, you should come now," she says. Even though I knew this day would come, first because of the drugs and then AIDS, it still feels too soon. Rushed. We should have more time.

My apartment is quiet. The kids are playing a game in Alita's bedroom. I don't have a sitter, and my car is broken down. I dial Robin's number after I hang up with the hospital.

"The nurse said I should go now if I want to say goodbye. What the fuck. I don't want it to be today."

"I'll be there in fifteen minutes," she says, giving me just enough time to call for a babysitter and change from my nightgown into a pair of jeans and a sweater. I didn't even think to grab a jacket.

AN HOUR LATER, Robin and I walk through the automatic double doors of the Beverly Hospital. I'm wishing Alita and Jackamo were old enough to be here with me to say goodbye to their Nana, the grandmother they've come to know and love over the last few years.

The woman sitting behind a desk in the lobby directs us to an elevator at the end of a long, bright corridor. I'm moving as fast as I can without running.

Just before the elevator, to my right, I pass a large refrigerator filled with colorful flowers. It occurs to me that it's a strange sentiment—to give the gift of cut flowers, something that will die, to people who are in a place where life is so fragile. I look through the window of the gift shop across the hall at the magazines, chocolate bars, and hardcover bestsellers. I should get her something. No, I remind myself, there's nothing she needs now.

The elevator takes us to the second floor and a hallway identical to the first. The symmetry is soothing.

My mother's doctor is at the nurse's station. Dr. Stewart greets Robin and me and motions for us to follow him.

"Your mother is coherent," he says. "She fully understands what's happening to her. As you know, she has a terminal illness." No shit, Sherlock, I think.

"It won't necessarily end her life today, but she's had several opportunistic infections, which have caused her great discomfort." I'm sure he's talking about the recurrent shingles that, in recent months, had erupted on just about every part of her body. He continues.

"She has a lesion that's causing her lungs to fill with fluid. Inevitably, she won't be able to breathe anymore," he says. The doctor's voice is measured, his words carefully chosen.

Philip and Chrissy are walking toward us from the opposite direction. They meet us at the door in front of my mother's room. Chrissy's cheeks are red, and her eyes are swollen and wet. Philip looks both sad and angry, a combination I understand well. The doctor stops speaking for a moment while we greet each other. The hugs between us—Philip and me, then Chrissy and me—are as awkward as one would expect between siblings who've grown up mostly apart.

After a short conversation, Philip returns to the waiting room where he and Chrissy had been sitting. He's already said his goodbyes.

Chrissy, Robin, and I follow the doctor into the room. Bonnie and Kay, my mother's close friends, are near the window on the other side of the bed. They say hello and smile in a way that says: we're here, we know why, and it sucks, but this is what we need to do.

I move to the left side of the bed. My sister lingers behind me, and Robin leans against the wall at my mother's feet. My mother's head is elevated. She's lying on her back. She looks peaceful, seemingly pain-free, and so incredibly young. Even at twenty-five, I know that forty-five is too young to die.

Bonnie leans over and uses a facecloth to wipe away a thin stream of something dripping down my mother's chin. Aside from the trickling fluid, she looks like she could be asleep.

Dr. Stewart gently rests his hand on my mother's foot. The gesture makes me trust him completely—a trust that might have otherwise taken years to build. So many won't touch people with AIDS, even with a layer of cotton between them.

"Jackie, your daughters are here," he says. I watch her while he speaks, but instead of hearing his voice, I hear my mother's. She's singing Neil Diamond's "I Am, I Said." Neil breaks in for the chorus, and I, too, join the concert.

"Hi, Mom," I say out loud. My voice sounds far away. She opens her eyes for a moment, and when the corners of her mouth twitch, I picture her alive and greeting people with her smile. She's trying to do that now, even on her deathbed.

Dr. Stewart continues. "I was just explaining to Chrissy and Gail what we discussed earlier. I told them what's happening and that I can repair the damage for the time being. I also told them you chose not to have me perform the surgery. Can you let them know you understand what I'm saying?"

"Yes," she answers softly, with a slight nod.

"Yes, what?" he presses.

Stop badgering her, I want to say, but I know he must do this.

"I understand," she whispers.

"And you understand this means you will not leave this hospital."

"Yes," she answers. This time, she opens her eyes wide for a brief moment—proof of her lucid conviction.

ALL WE CAN do now is wait. As the day wears on, my mother's breathing becomes shallower; the fluid spills up and out of her lungs. Although she responds when we speak to her, she doesn't move when the phone rings. The rest of us jump when its abrupt, harsh sound pierces through the silence. I'm closest to the phone, but I don't know whether or not I should pick it up. The others look at me, none of us with an answer to the question we don't ask out loud—What is proper phone etiquette when your mother is dying?

I lunge for the receiver before it can ring a third time and disturb my mother, though I know it won't. "Hello?"

"Is Jackie there?" Big Nana asks in her deep, raspy voice that unnerves me even in adulthood.

"Oh, hi, Nana. Hang on a minute." I put my hand over the mouthpiece and lean toward my mother. "Mom, Big Nana's on the phone."

She doesn't open her eyes when she whispers: "Tell her I'll call her later."

A HANDFUL OF visitors have been here throughout the day—Aunt Sherry and a few of my mother's close friends. But at the moment, it's just my mother and me. I'm afraid to leave the room; I don't want her to die alone.

This is also the first time we've had privacy.

I move from where I've been sitting or standing during the four or five hours I've been here to the other side of the bed. From here, I can see the door. The window overlooking the parking lot is behind me.

"Mom," I say quietly at first. When she doesn't answer, I start to panic. "Mom!"

"Yeah?" she says, barely above a whisper. Her eyes stay closed.

"Remember that we talked about you contacting me—however you can." She doesn't respond.

"Mom." I wait. "Mom?"

"Yes, I know. I heard you. I will."

"Promise me." She doesn't answer. I need to hear her voice. "Promise." She opens her eyes. "I promise," she says.

I sit in the chair beside my mother, watching her as I wipe the fluid from her chin. Her face is relaxed, her jaw slack. Her lips are parted slightly. I'm struck by the differences between my mother, at this moment, and Jack, the last time I saw him alive. I can still picture the fear in his eyes and the way he fought. There's no fight here. Unlike Jack, my mother is ready to embrace death.

She hasn't spoken again. The fluid stream is steady now; it has nowhere else to go. Soon, there won't be any room for air in her lungs. I'm watching her drown.

I think about telling the doctor I've changed my mind. In my imagination, I ring the buzzer. "Tell Dr. Stewart to come quickly," I say. When he comes into the room, I tell him my mother isn't in her right mind. "She's not capable of making the decision to end her life. It's my choice," I say. "Repair the damage." He does as I ask, but my mother is angry when she wakes after surgery. In truth, I know she was more clearheaded than ever when she asked us to let her die. She's finally at peace. I can't take that away from her.

We're still alone in the room when my mother inhales for the last time. It's barely a breath at all. When she exhales, I hold my breath and wait. We are both not breathing until I have no choice but to exhale.

Five minutes.

Ten.

She's quiet and still. There's been a shift in the room. Or maybe something has changed in me; I don't know. The only thing I'm positive about is that my mother isn't here anymore. When I look at where she used to be, all I see is a body with a face that looks a lot like mine.

45

DAMAGE, DAMAGE, DAMAGE

~1995~

The familiar scents of rose water and eucalyptus wrap around me as I step over the threshold into my mother's apartment. It smells so much like her; I want to linger here forever, drinking it in. Also, the longer I stay on this lower level of the duplex, the longer I can pretend she's still up on the second floor, watching television in the living room or making coffee in the kitchen. But I have too much work to do to waste time.

Before I make my way upstairs, I take off my coat and drape it over the banister. At the top, I breathe deeply and move further into the main floor. From here in the hallway, I can see some of every room but the kitchen. I take my time and survey the area. It looks the same as it did when I was last here a few weeks ago when my mother was still sitting upright on the couch.

The thick beige carpet that stretches throughout the space is as clean as if it was just vacuumed, and as always, my mother's bed is made. With the bathroom door open, I can see a towel hanging over a rod next to the tub; it's probably the one she used for her last shower. Although I can see the back of a living room chair from here, I can't see the couch where my mother had been sleeping for the last few months. That's good. I'm not quite ready to go there yet.

Instead, I decide to start at the top and work my way down. I climb two more flights to the fourth floor, a small, square room with windows on every wall. With an expansive view of the ocean, I'm sure the room was built at a time when women watched for the return of their fishermen husbands.

I sit on the only piece of furniture in the room, an old loveseat, and think about my mother's death and the call I got from Aunt Sherry five days later. When I first heard Sherry's shaky voice, I was sure she was calling to talk about my mother's service. We still didn't have a plan. We still don't have the money. Besides a small social security check, my sister and I will somehow have to scrape the funds together.

"I have to tell you something," she said. "My mother passed away."

"You mean my mother," I said, confused.

"No," she said. "Big Nana. I went to see her this afternoon and found her on the kitchen floor. She's gone."

"Oh my God," I said. It was the only thing that came to mind. I told Sherry I was sorry, and we talked about the tragedy of our losses—her mother and sister, my mother and grandmother. We ended the call after agreeing to organize a dual service. I considered my feelings about the loss and wondered if I would've asked Big Nana how she was doing if I'd known that the day my mother died would be the last time I'd hear her voice. Probably not. For us, family meant shared blood; beyond that, we couldn't have been more detached.

I look around the small room again. Aside from Philip drinking beer and smoking pot with his friends, the space was rarely used during the two years my mother lived in the apartment. All that's left here now are a few empty red Solo cups and an ashtray. I wish I could just stay here, enjoy the view, and forget what needs to be done. But the kids are only at daycare until five. I force myself to stand and return to the business of packing up what used to be my mother's life.

Philip's old bedroom is on the next floor down. I look in briefly as I pass by. The room is nearly empty, so there's nothing for me to do here.

The air feels thick and heavy on the main floor, like a weight of emotion is trapped and lingering in these rooms. Maybe that's why I feel lost as I walk through them. At least, it's one of the reasons. I also don't want to move or change anything. This is my mother's home. These are her belongings, and she has so many of them—a surprising amount considering all the things we lost due to evictions. I have to keep reminding myself that this isn't her home anymore. These aren't her things. And although the landlord has given Chrissy and me some leeway, we still only have a couple of weeks to get it all done.

I take a right at the bottom of the stairs, into my mother's bedroom, and look around before tentatively opening the top drawer of her dresser. I close it without moving anything inside. I feel like a kid again, home alone, looking through her things for cigarettes and dirty magazines.

I move toward the closet. The door is ajar, swollen from years of exposure to the humid ocean air. I pull it open and take note of the neatly stacked boxes and clothes hanging inside before closing it again. I'll deal with that later, too.

At her desk, I slide into the kneeling chair and glance over the contents: an old Apple computer, a stack of notebooks, a bowl of paperclips, and a cup full of pens. Everything is arranged so neatly—too neatly to be disturbed. I should've known better than to start in the bedroom.

I go to the kitchen instead, where my mother's collection of empty blue rosewater bottles is lined up on the window sill above the sink. Beside them is a mason jar filled halfway with water and a rooting spider plant clipping. There's a mug, spoon, and small plate in the sink, and clean dishes in the strainer. A towel hangs from the oven's handle. Everything is exactly as she left it. I take two blue bottles and put them in a box in the living room I labeled "Take Home" with a black Sharpie.

The living room looks lived-in, as though my mother has gone on a quick errand and will return any minute. I light one of her Marlboros and sit on the couch where she spent her last days before the hospital. The fitted sheet is still wrapped around the couch cushions, and her feather pillow is against the armrest, still indented from where her head had rested. I pick up an empty mug from the coffee table in front of me and sniff inside—it still smells like coffee. I raise her pillow to my face and take in her scent. The tears have started up again. I think again of how I should've come to see her more often.

I'm considering coming back tomorrow when the red blinking light from the answering machine catches my attention. I take a deep breath, wipe my cheeks with the back of my hand, and get up off the couch.

I put her pillow in my box before pressing play. "Hi Jackie," says a man's unfamiliar voice. "Just calling to check on you, to see if you're feeling any better." His concern makes me start crying again. I make a mental note to return his call to tell him no, she isn't feeling better. But what do I know? Maybe she's feeling better than ever.

The button next to "Play" reads "Greeting." When I push it, my mother's voice fills the room. "Hi, this is Jackie. I can't make it to the phone but leave me a message and your number, and I'll call you back. Have a grateful day." I press it again. And again. I press it until I'm exhausted and can't see through my tears.

When I'm done, I take the miniature cassette tape out of the machine and place it with the other things I'm taking home. I've been here for at least an hour and have yet to fill a single box. I need to get the kids soon, and I still have homework. I don't want to fall too far behind in school and delay graduation. My mother wouldn't want that either, I reason, as I take my half-filled box and leave the apartment.

IT'S BEEN NEARLY two weeks, and my mother's apartment is finally beginning to empty. It's been slow going, but her bed has been disassembled, and the kitchen table and living room furniture are gone. Boxes are stacked in the bedroom and living room with designation markings—Chrissy, Philip, Good Will, and the one for me.

The trunk at the end of my mother's bed is one of the last containers I empty. Just like the rest of her apartment, the contents are neatly organized. On top of a stack of folded blankets, there is an equally neat stack of notebooks. I believe their placement is intentional, that she's left them here for me.

Most of the notebooks are regular, one-subject, and wide-ruled, but not the one on top. At first, I think she put that one there because it's the smallest. It's wire-bound like the rest, but the paper is thicker. On the cover is a replica of an oil painting—a sailboat on calm water, with rolling hills behind it and a blue sky with shades of pink around the sun. This is the one I open first. My heart skips a beat when I see her impeccable handwriting in the center of the first page. It says~

This Journal belongs to Jacqueline Brenner.

Date—Christmas 1994.

Journal? 1994? That's when Jack died—not even a year ago. This one is on top because it is the most recent, I realize. I know I don't have much time, but I don't care. The room is warm and comfortable, and I feel close to my mother, here with her thoughts.

I sit on the rug next to the trunk, fold my legs under me, turn the page, and read the first couple of lines. "Bonnie and Kay—thank you for this lovely journal. One of the many, many acts of kindness you've extended me since God put you into my life."

I stop reading and thumb through the book until I get to the last entry. It's dated May 29, 1995—just five months ago. I read on…

Same frame of mind as on Saturday, last entry. It's 5:00 in the morning—I haven't been able to sleep yet. Restless, thinking in circles. Having arguments with myself. And the biggest treat: Beating myself up mercilessly. There's so much damage, damage, damage. Most of my life has been a deception. Not primarily other people being deceived by me (though that's 100% true), but more so me kidding myself. I feel as though I'm at the end of my life or fast approaching the end. This may not even be the case, in fact, however, it's quite true to me. Being at the end is causing me to look over my entire life—things that I've done, etc. It's a very UGLY picture as I see it. This, maybe, is why I'm so sad. And sad is what I am.

TWO WEEKS AFTER my mother's death, a little bit less for Big Nana, two boxes of ashes—mother and daughter—sit side by side on a table at the Unitarian Universalist Church. No less than two hundred people have come to say goodbye. We'll soon scatter my mother's ashes at Good Harbor Beach, her favorite place. Aunt Sherry said Big Nana's ashes would be buried with Little Nana's. If there is an upside, it's that they're all together again.

46

THE SOCRATIC METHOD

~1997~

S uffolk Law School looks like any other academic building. In fact, with only six floors, it's even less imposing than Suffolk's undergraduate building, where I earned my bachelor's degree earlier this year. And yet, standing in front of the law school's obscure entrance, I can sense the history that moves in the air around it. I feel so far out of my league.

Gratefully, nobody knows me here—where I come from or where I've been. Aside from the poorly applied press-ons covering my stubby nails and the smell of cigarette smoke clinging to me, I'm pretty good at pretending I'm just like all these other first-year law students.

I'm also glad to be a night student, where many of us have to work during the day. At least we have that much in common. Three nights a week, I'll drive Alita and Jackamo to night care in southern New Hampshire from my apartment in North Andover, where I moved shortly after my mother's death. I now know the move was an impulsive way to deal with my grief, but at that time, just three months after her passing, it seemed like divine intervention.

I'd been looking for a phone number when I happened to come across a map of Massachusetts at the front of the telephone book. While looking at it, it suddenly occurred to me that a whole world existed outside the place I'd started and ended every day for most of my twenty-five years. I had a realization that I'd never felt safe in Gloucester. Between the drugs, constant loss, and random run-ins with guys from my past, I was always looking over my shoulder. With dark corners and painful reminders everywhere in the small city, leaving seemed like a logical choice—a clear message from my mother to get out of town.

So, on a Saturday, my best friend and confidant, Lani, and I set out on a mission. After driving inland for forty-five minutes, we came upon a town with freshly-painted houses and neatly groomed yards. The neighborhoods reminded me so much of Becky and Greg; I knew I'd found my home.

I don't regret the move, but since I've only met a few people in the area, I'm lonelier than ever.

In law school, unlike undergraduate studies, all first-year courses are the same for everybody and property is the first class on my schedule. . The third-floor classroom is fan-shaped, with stadium seating. The professor is the star of the show. Because I'm early, I can sit wherever I choose. As always, I find a seat close to the door, where my back is against the wall. This also puts me as far away from the professor as possible, so I'll be able to slip out to smoke if he doesn't give us enough breaks.

From my place on the top tier, I watch the rest of my classmates find their seats. Of the hundred-or-so students, some know each other, but many look as uncomfortably alone and anxious as I must. Although the Percocet I took before coming tonight certainly helps calm my nerves. Since my new boyfriend offered me one for a headache a few weeks ago, I've been taking them occasionally. Four-and-half years of sobriety down the drain. And if I'm being honest, the headache wasn't really painkiller-worthy.

Professor Brown is all business when he introduces himself to the class. He explains that throughout the year, we'll read a great deal of case law and learn through the Socratic teaching method, which is supposed to force us to think critically. I don't think I'll have any problem with that, as I already tend to be critical.

Before giving us a break, the professor looks around the room, meeting the eyes of as many students as possible, and says: "Look to your left and look to your right—one of these people won't be here by the time you graduate." As I do what he asks, I wonder which of the two sitting on either side of me will be missing at graduation.

During the break, I meet the other smokers in the class. They're always my people. There are five of us. One of the guys is sober like I had been. One of the girls is my age. She's a single mother, too, but she lives with her parents. All of them seem down-to-earth, which makes me think that having just a handful of friends here might be enough to help get me through it.

Professor Brown puts the Socratic method into action after a break. He starts firing questions around the room. He asks about objectivity and subjectivity—what they mean and how they relate to the law. I don't know. I can't even define the terms, never mind explain how they relate to anything. I'll look them up when I get home, but what concerns me is that I don't understand how all these other people know the answers. I have a four-year degree, just as they do; it's a requirement when applying to law school. And I graduated from Suffolk with high honors. Maybe there are things I didn't learn before college, high school stuff that I missed. I don't know. I just hope he doesn't call on me.

47

DISMISSED

~1999~

My second year of law school is the worst by far. I'm stressed all the time, and my grades are terrible. I'm sure studying more would help, but squeezing it in between taking care of kids, pets, and the apartment, is tough. It's hard to imagine I'll ever be a lawyer.

On top of everything else, traffic north of Boston was exceptionally brutal today. That's the biggest downside to going to school during the day instead of at night. I had to switch to days when finding night care for the kids became impossible. Another day-student disadvantage is that I seem to be one of the only students with a full-time job, which I'm sure is why I've fallen so far behind my classmates. Law school grading is based on a curve, and in the day section, I'm much closer to the bottom than the top.

After picking up the kids and stopping at the supermarket, we finally made it home. The stench from the litter box hits me in the face as soon as I open the front door. Its potency makes my eyes water. There are way too many cats living here.

At first, I had one little kitten. Roxy. My friend was moving into a no-pets-allowed apartment, so I adopted the little black fur-ball. As much as I tried to prevent it, Roxy quickly became an outdoor cat. She'd wait for the thump of footsteps on the porch so she could slip out when the door cracked open.

Alita was the one who noticed the changes in Roxy, the way her belly bulged and her nipples jutted out. The bigger she got, the more often she stayed inside, hidden under a bed or dresser. I got a cardboard box, lined it with a thick towel, and introduced Roxy to her new space. There, a week later, Alita, Jack, and I watched as Roxy gave birth. She stood looking into our faces with pained, pleading eyes, her breathing shallow, and walked in a circle three or four times before lying back down. She repeated the process, sometimes moving to another spot a few inches away, and started again.

After a time, Roxy crouched down—her front legs straight and her rear legs bent just like in the litter box—and pushed. The sac emerged slowly and then dropped gently onto the towel below. She turned quickly to tend to her baby. Each delivery went like this. Roxy didn't lie down until her work was done. After all four kittens were born, she only left them to fill her belly or use the box. I wished I could be half the mother she was.

As the kittens grew, feeding them took every bit of extra money I had, not that I ever had any money that I would classify as "extra," and training them was another issue. Even if I knew how to teach them to use the litter box, I'm as short on time as I am on money. But whatever time I didn't invest in training, I spent cleaning up after them. Now, I'm on the fast track to becoming a strung-out cat lady.

After putting my book bag down on the floor, I close the door to the bathroom and the smell. With the door closed, the scent isn't bad at all. In fact, minus the odor, I note that this room, my office, is mostly clean. I move on.

When I glance into my bedroom, I feel a pang of anxiety. The green-sponge paint on the walls makes the room look messy on a good day, but today, it truly is a disaster. Clothes are piled high on the bureau, and the bed is unmade. I close that door, too, and keep my eyes averted to the right, shutting the kids' bedroom doors as I pass them. All three bedrooms are on the left, as is the second bathroom.

In the kitchen, I find the usual sink full of dishes. I roll the yard-sale-find dishwasher across the room, fill it, attach its dangling hose to the faucet, and hit the start button. The pile of dirty laundry next to the washer in the back hall will have to wait—the dishwasher has first dibs on the water.

Thankfully, the kids didn't follow me inside. I need a few minutes alone. My back has been screaming for the last few hours, and my temples are beginning to throb. I haven't had any pills for a couple of days. I take the calendar off the kitchen wall and sit at the table with my most recent pill bottle in hand.

Sitting here, I can smell the narcotic chemicals oozing from my pores. Not only does my skin have a sickly sour smell, but it also hurts to the touch, like when I have a fever. My legs are starting to cramp, and I'm sweating even though I feel a chill.

No matter how many times I count back on the calendar, it's still too early for a refill. None of my doctors are an option—not the shoulder doctor, my primary care, nor the one who has been writing for the most recent pain in my abdomen. I'll have to use the rent money to buy something and make it up when I get my script. Since my only connections in North Andover are doctors, I call a guy I know in Gloucester. Johnny answers on the third ring.

"What's up? Anything?" I ask.

"Sure," he says. "What do you need?"

"Twenty," I say. "I can be there in an hour."

I'm determined to keep Jack and Alita separate from anything concerning my addiction, so I decide to leave them at home. I reason they'll be fine during the short excursion—ninety minutes round trip, plus an additional ten for exchanging pills and money. I'm sure Alita, at eleven years old, can handle anything that might come up. Jack is almost eight. We also know our neighbors, the people upstairs, and a family across the street. The kids can go to them with any potential problems. Not that there will be any. I'm so sure everything will be fine; I don't even bother telling the neighbors I'll be gone.

I pull in front of the Gloucester bowling alley, our designated meeting place, exactly forty-two minutes after leaving my street, an hour after the phone call. Record time, I think as I look at my watch.

It's a weekday, so there are other cars around, which makes me feel a little less conspicuous idling here in my black Chevy Lumina. I light a cigarette and try to see if any of the other parked cars are occupied. From my rearview mirror, I can see a dark sedan on the other side of the street, a hundred feet from where I'm sitting. The glare from the sun makes the windshield look like black onyx, which means it's impossible to tell whether anybody's inside.

I imagine Johnny tapping his key on my window. When I put the window down, he reaches in for the exchange. When the pills are in my hand, the police swoop in with the sounds of screeching tires and slamming doors. My first thought is whether I can get a few of the pills out and down my throat before they get to me. Then I wonder whom I can call to get the kids. Any other day I might call the fantasy paranoia, but today, I recognize it as a brief moment of clarity. It's only a matter of time before I get caught.

When I hear the sound of crunching gravel, I look to see Johnny pull his car in behind mine. He runs over to the passenger side and quickly slides in. I always forget how good-looking the guy is. He's a few years younger than me, mid-twenties, tall, dark, Italian. Maybe...no. Stop thinking that way. He's a frigging dealer.

"How you doin'?" he asks as I hand him the ten crisp, neatly-folded twenty-dollar bills.

I smile as soon as the clump of pills hits my palm because I know relief is coming. The tension in my neck is already starting to ease.

"Law school's kicking my ass," I say. I don't look at him when I respond because whenever he smiles, I start thinking about him that way again.

I hear him laugh.

"I'll keep in touch," I say as he steps from my car. I'm sure it will be sooner rather than later.

As I drive away, I shake three pills out of the cigarette cellophane and toss them down my throat with a swig of water. I pop two more before I'm halfway home. The whole thing took way less than ten minutes—I'm ahead of the game.

Twenty minutes later, my palms aren't sweaty anymore. I feel fantastic. Even though it's chilly outside, the front windows are halfway down. Zeppelin is blasting on the radio. I'm singing and thinking about everything I'm going to do when I get home: clean my bedroom, empty the dishwasher, and tackle that mile-high laundry pile. Maybe I'll make sloppy joes for supper. The kids love those.

Holy Shit...the kids.

I'm almost home when I'm struck with the sobering reminder that I left them alone. I turn the music down. I know I'm still high because my face is itchy, and my pupils are little black dots, but I can't feel it anymore.

And although suddenly in a rush to get home, I can't risk getting pulled over with drugs, so I keep to the speed limit.

I'm still a quarter of a mile away from my street when I see red and blue flashing lights bouncing off houses and cars. Fire and police—this can't be good. They're at the top of my street, which intersects with the street I'm on. A police car is parked diagonally across the road.

I take a left onto a side street. I have to get around the police somehow. At the next intersection, a block from my house, a second cruiser sits in the middle of the street. Its lights are flashing, and a uniformed officer waves me away. I put the passenger window down despite the illegal pills in my pocket.

"The street is closed," he says. "You'll need to go another way."

"There is no other way. I live down there. What's going on?" I ask. The cop gestures to a truck behind me, and the driver backs up.

"A house fire," he says.

"How will I get home?" I ask. I feel like I can't breathe.

"You'll have to walk."

I pull over to the curb, grab my pocketbook from the passenger seat, and run as soon as I'm out of the car. My purse bumps against my hip, and the keys jingle in my pocket whenever my feet hit the ground. As with the imaginary scene at the bowling alley, I'm envisioning the worst—my house has caught fire, and my kids have gone inside the burning building to get the kittens and Alita's ferret. No, I tell myself; *you're just being dramatic.* But the truth is in the lights flashing around me—*this is real.*

I'm out of breath, and sweat is running down my neck and forehead. Just one block away, I can see the fire engines near the end of the street where we live. I'm out of breath, and sweat is running down my neck and forehead. I still can't tell where the hoses are directed. My view is blocked by the backsides of a group of people watching the show. I curse them for being in my way.

When I reach the wall of onlookers, I can see Alita standing on our front porch. She's holding the video camera her father gave her last Christmas. Jackamo is standing behind her. I can also see the hoses fixed on the neighboring house, the one occupied by a family of hoarders. With the empty lot between the houses and the flames nearly extinguished, ours is safe. I lean forward, panting, with my hands on my knees, and make two promises to a God I'm sure doesn't care about me: I'll stay clean and never leave my kids alone again.

I'M FINALLY GETTING home from the day. It's already dark outside, even though it's only a little after five. I toss the day's mail onto my desk and head for the kitchen. My back and shoulder are throbbing, and I still have to make supper before homework. I'll be thirty next year and feel like I'm fifty. Thankfully, I got a Vicodin refill today.

I've decided to take only the pills I'm prescribed—no more buying them. The fire was over a month ago, and I'm trying to do better. I've also admitted that the drugs are the real reason my grades are so bad. Unlike undergrad, where I could do well without even trying, I need a clear head to get through law school, where I'm currently struggling for a D.

I thumb through the mail when I finally have a chance to sit down. There are a couple of bills and a letter from the Dean of Students at Suffolk Law. As soon as I see the return address, I know it's bad news.

I open the envelope and read: *We regret to inform you of your dismissal from legal studies at Suffolk Law due to poor academic performance....* My throat tightens. *No, this can't be.* But, of course, it can. And it is. I've been on academic probation since the second semester. Still, I thought I would somehow skate through. I read the letter two more times. It says I can appeal to the committee, whatever the hell that means, or reapply in two years.

My only option is to appeal. I don't know what I'll do if I can't finish law school. Other than having kids, becoming educated is the only worthy thing I've ever done. And the truth is, I'm not much better at being a mother than I was at being a law student.

48

PLUGGED IN

~2000~

Ronnie and I met at a local recovery group. I started going to meetings again after losing the Suffolk appeal. I needed to stay clean to get back into law school. After a few pill-free months, I was accepted at the Massachusetts School of Law, where I sat before a committee and told them about my drug addiction and relapse. They welcomed me to the school as a brand-new student without the credits I'd earned at Suffolk. As a condition of my enrollment, I agreed to start from scratch.

I became obsessed with Ronnie shortly after we were introduced. As was my typical strategy, I put myself where I knew he'd be until I finally asked him out. We went back to his house after our first date, and I stayed the night. We've been together ever since.

Ronnie proposed on the terrace of his Aruban timeshare less than a year after we met. Truthfully, the man isn't even my type. For one thing, he's got an angry disposition. He's also twelve years older than me, and he's the kind of Italian that wears thick gold chains like the Gloucester Italians I've been trying for years to forget.

Still, it was an easy yes. I know Ronnie loves me. He also has a good job, owns his home, doesn't ask questions about my past, and has been sober and free from crack, his drug of choice, for three years. We quickly decided on a June wedding, and we'll get married in just over a year.

Between law school and wedding planning, more than a month had passed before I noticed my period was late. At first, I was less than enthusiastic about being pregnant. I'd never been able to enjoy the experience without the pressure of every responsibility falling on me alone. But once the shock wore off, I realized that this time will be different. I'm a woman well into adulthood. I'm also not alone anymore, and Ronnie is excited. Childless at forty-two, he was sure he'd never be a father.

"SORRY FOR THE cold," the technician says as she squeezes a gob of gel onto my belly. It makes me suck in my breath. My bladder is painfully full for our first ultrasound. Ronnie moves closer to the side of the table and reaches for my hand as we watch the monitor. Finally, at eight weeks, we'll get to see our baby.

The woman is quiet as she moves her hand back and forth across my lower abdomen. I don't recall it taking this long to hear the rapid, repetitious sound of the fetal heartbeat. I look at the woman's stoical expression and turn briefly toward Ronnie, who is still watching the screen. He doesn't know this is unusual. I look at the woman again.

"Can you see the baby?" I ask. I'm starting to feel anxious.

"I'm going to do a vaginal ultrasound," she says. "Sometimes we can get a better view that way."

A few minutes later, she's looking from the inside. At least another five minutes pass before she speaks again. "I'll be right back," she says, and without explanation, she turns and leaves the room.

"That's weird," I say.

"I'm sure it's fine," Ronnie says.

I hope he's right, but he doesn't know what I know—I've been taking pills. I was clean when we met, but I stumbled across Ronnie's pills shortly after. We were standing in the kitchen when he opened a cabinet. My attention was instantly drawn to the familiar orange bottles inside. I quickly looked away so he wouldn't see me eyeing them, but before he closed the door, I was already trying to figure out a way to be alone with the pills.

As luck or fate would have it, Ronnie's father, who was working outside in the yard, called his name. The second I heard Ronnie's faraway voice, I opened the cabinet and read the labels on each of the six bottles. The two labeled "Vicodin" were chock full.

I took note of the bottle's position before removing it from the cupboard, unscrewing the cap, and slipping a single pill out of the bottle and into my pocket. You never know when you might need a painkiller. That is why Ronnie had them, after all; for pain. Why should I have to suffer? Just because pills happen to be my drug of choice? After returning the bottle, I went to sit in the living room, bringing a glass of water to quench my thirst. I swallowed the Vicodin before Ronnie made it back into the house.

Since moving in a few months ago, I've been helping myself to the rest of the bottle, replacing what I take with vitamins that resemble his prescription pills.

When the door opens again, a tall, thin man in a white lab coat follows the woman into the room. The woman stops a few feet from the door, and the man stands beside me. He doesn't smile when he speaks.

"I'm sorry," he says. "This pregnancy is not viable." I'm looking at him, but I don't understand. Viable? It takes me a moment to realize that he means my baby is dead. Like a tall wave I don't see coming, the understanding knocks the wind out of me. My hands automatically move to cover my face. I can't hide the tears I try so hard to keep private. Ronnie's hand is on my leg, a gesture of consolation I don't deserve.

The man leaves first. The woman waits a few moments for me to compose myself before she tells me to call my doctor so he can remove the fetus.

On the ride home, I want to tell Ronnie that it's my fault the baby is gone. "I've been using." That's all I have to say. It'll be okay if he loves me as much as he says. A lie isn't good for any relationship, especially one this big when we're months away from getting married. But I don't say anything. I'll tell him when I'm clean again.

MY WEDDING DRESS swings out and back with a thud whenever I open my bedroom door, where it hangs because it's too big to fit in the closet. The sound is a constant reminder that I am a liar, undeserving of being anybody's wife. Thankfully, it will only be here for one more day. We're getting married tomorrow. I should be full of joy, but all I can think about is where I can find some pills to carry me through the wedding and honeymoon.

The last script I had, for thirty Percocet, was filled on Monday and gone by Wednesday. I had planned for the pills to last at least through the weekend. I started looking for more before running out, but it's been two days, and I can't find anything. I'm already feeling sick. Since I started using Fentanyl almost a year ago, my habit has gotten so much worse.

I had just started classes at MSL when I tried Fentanyl for the first time. Before property class, I drove to Gloucester to meet my pill dealer, Martha, who was out of pills but had Fentanyl patches. The price was my final convincer—one patch cost less than five pills.

After leaving Martha's apartment, I stopped at a pharmacy and bought a small pair of orange-handled Fiskars. In the parking lot, instead of peeling the backing off the patch and sticking it to my arm or thigh as the package directed, I used the scissors to snip the corner of the clear plastic patch. I squeezed a dime-sized serving of the thick gel onto my finger and licked it clean, like a five-year-old with a Tootsie pop. I didn't think about how much of the drug could kill me until after I'd put the patch back in its package. By then, it was too late, so I waited with anxious anticipation.

The effect of the drug was gradual. As I drove south on Route 128 toward school, my scalp warmed and started tingling. The feeling worked its way down to my eyes, then my jaw, and smoothed out the tension in my neck and shoulders. Although I'd felt plugged in before, it was the first time I'd been turned on.

Just a few minutes after the first twinge, my entire body became wrapped in Fentanyl's warm embrace. By then, I was in class. I could hear Professor Salito lecture about adverse possession as I played solitaire on my Palm Pilot, but all I could think about was the patch and how I might be able to squeeze two more highs out of the thing, three if I were conservative. It was probably the closest I would ever get to feeling my mother's heroin high, and I finally understood how she could give up everything for the sensation.

I COULDN'T FIND any patches yesterday. I wasn't sure I'd find anything to feed my addiction until a friend hooked me up with thirty Darvocet, huge, bright orange painkillers. Although one of the weakest prescription-only pills on the market, they're better than nothing. At least I won't be sick when I walk down the aisle. I rushed to cop the pills between assembling wedding favors, honeymoon packing, and a French manicure.

Although I've never been married, I'm pretty confident this is not what my wedding day should feel like. I took three of the pills when I got out of bed this morning and another two before getting my hair done. They're not strong enough to get me high, but I'm not as sick as I would have been without them. Thankfully, Ronnie and Jackamo stayed at a hotel last night. They'll meet Alita and me at the church; she's waiting for me in the living room, and the limo is outside. For the moment, I'm by myself.

A bride stands before me in the bedroom mirror; I barely recognize her. Everything looks perfect—hair, dress, and nails. Of course, I know the truth. There is no perfection here. The white satin and lace dress and matching pearl jewelry are nothing more than a cover-up, a costume. The whole thing isn't all that different from when I wore the button-down shirt as a prop for the Jimmy & Hal show all those years ago.

I keep my eyes on the woman in the mirror and watch her swallow two more pills. Disgusting, I think before I make my way to Alita, the limousine, and my husband-to-be.

Ten minutes later, we pull in front of Saint Michael's Church. The outside of the recently remodeled building is pink stucco, and the inside is bright, expansive, and modern. The church wedding was Ronnie's idea. He's Catholic and wouldn't have it any other way.

My father waits at the entrance. He's giving me away. It just so happened that his Texas trailer burned down two years ago, and he's been living with Nana Raizin in Gloucester. I wouldn't have thought to include him in the wedding if he wasn't so close, since our relationship isn't much better than it's been my whole life. But it's part of the traditional show, and I'm all about appearances.

I don't think at all about what it would be like for my mother to be here. Those fantasies ended while she was still alive, and I refuse to let myself go down that dead-end road.

Once inside the vestibule, my father gives me his elbow, and I take it with my right hand. I dip a finger from my free hand into the small bowl of holy water and make the sign of the cross over my chest, as I've learned at Sunday church services with Ronnie. Every little bit helps, especially now that I'm locked into this ceremony, away from the limo, my purse, and the pills.

My three bridesmaids and the ushers walk down the aisle first, then Lani, my matron of honor and Ronnie's best man. Ronnie is already waiting at the altar. Organ music plays until all are in their places beside him—men on one side, women on the other.

Everybody stands when the music changes to our march-down-the-aisle song. I see Ronnie before he sees me—his back is straight, and his tuxedo is perfectly pressed. My hands are shaking. *Put one foot in front of the other.* My mouth is dry. *Just get through the ceremony.* Ronnie wipes away a tear as he watches me walk toward him. Everything appears exactly as it should. The ceremony is picture-perfect.

During the reception, I slip away—outside for a cigarette or into the bridal room—wherever I can be alone long enough to down a couple more pills.

After the last dance, we change into our post-wedding clothes and say our goodbyes. Alita and Jackamo will stay with Lani during our honeymoon.

I take the last three pills in the bathroom of the Boston hotel where we're staying overnight. We'll fly to the Dominican Republic in the morning. *That's it*, I tell myself after I swallow them. *I'm done with getting high.*

49

INDEPENDENCE

~2002~

The big day was a little more than a month ago. My secret honeymoon detox was rough, but I must've looked okay because Ronnie didn't say anything. And although I was more determined than ever to stay clean after returning home as a married woman; it became impossible with a pocket full of wedding cash. A week after we returned, I broke down and bought a patch. One high led to another. Now, I'm right back where I started.

We're going to Gloucester for the Horrible's Parade and fireworks later today. It'll just be Ronnie, me, and Jackamo. Alita is with her dad, and at fourteen, she's probably outgrown it anyway. For me, the parade is a July third family tradition. Every year when we were kids, Little Nana would walk Chrissy and me to the intersection of Prospect Street and Railroad Avenue, where we'd sit and watch the three-hour parade. Aunt Julie and Sherry marched in the parade one year, dressed as cave people, wrapped in loincloths with bones in their hair. I even made an appearance one summer as a brief member of the high school's color guard. We'd always stay till it was over, and the fire engines' procession signaled the parade's end.

I couldn't find any Fentanyl for tonight's festivities, but I scored twenty-five Percocet. There's no way I can get through a visit to Gloucester without the shield of something to help me cope. I never know who I'll run into. My body tenses whenever I hear my name in town: "Oh my God, Gail, is that you? It's been so long." It usually takes a moment to figure out how I know the person. If they're my age, I sometimes guess we went to school together. If it is an old classmate, I'll stay for a brief conversation. In every exchange, I'll somehow work in the fact that I'm a law student status, so they'll know I'm not a loser, after all. But there are others with whom I've gotten high or worse; that's what I worry about. Ronnie still doesn't know anything about my past.

WHEN WE STOP at Lani's house following the parade, I slip into the bathroom for a moment alone with my pills. Usually, I'd start with three, but I won't have another opportunity for a while. I pop five with the ease of experience I wished for when I was eleven, and Aunt Julie handed me five pills to take. Then I return to the group.

Lani's small living room is crowded with six of us, and the heat feels oppressive. It's been fifteen minutes since I took the pills, but instead of the familiar tingling in my head, my belly feels agitated, and my mouth is watery. I stand abruptly, put my hand over my mouth, and run to the bathroom.

My stomach turns as I lift the toilet lid. The pills haven't been in my system long enough, and pieces come out in my vomit. My need for relief is so overwhelming that if I didn't have more, I'd fish the remnants out of the bowl and take them again. Luckily, there is no shortage tonight. I rinse my mouth, dig five more out of my pocket, and wash them down with cold faucet water from my cupped hand.

With my face clean and my hair tucked behind my ears, I rejoin the others in the living room. I'm sure this hot, stuffy apartment is what made me nauseous. I have no doubt I'll be fine once we leave.

Outside, the soupy air feels just as suffocating. The temperature topped nearly one hundred degrees today, and with the humidity, the heat isn't burning off. My limp hair is sticking to my face, making me grateful for bangs. I light a cigarette and try to ignore the feeling of sickness creeping back into my stomach.

The boulevard is crowded with families. Mothers and fathers sit on beach chairs while their children run around them with plastic swords and sticky cotton candy hands. I move closer to the water, where the crowd is thin.

I'm standing near the railing, watching the dark ocean, when my stomach flips again. This time, the urge to vomit comes on quickly, almost too quick for me to find a place where I can avoid splashing anybody around me. I lean against a small tree with one hand and hold my hair back with the other.

Ronnie and Jackamo are standing a few feet away with the rest of our group.

"Here," Ronnie says, handing me a napkin when I'm done.

"Thanks," I say, turning away so he won't see the tears in my eyes. I'm not embarrassed because I got sick. I'm not upset that Ronnie will soon know about the pills or even that I put on a show for all these people. What worries me—what terrifies me—is that this is the first time drugs have ever failed me. The pills, patches, and pot have been my only loyal support for as long as I can remember. The relief they've given me over the years has probably even saved my life. If not for the respite of a high, there were days when I might have otherwise tried to kill myself.

My stomach feels hollow, scooped out like the guts of a cantaloupe. My head is spinning, not with the euphoric escape the pills should have provided but with the dreaded thoughts of what comes next. I could try again, there are still fifteen pills in my pocket, but I know better. Although I don't want to be done with the drugs, I'm fairly certain the drugs are done with me.

THE WAITING ROOM at my doctor's office is crowded, only adding to my anxiety. At six months clean, the idea of seeing her makes me nervous; I rarely visit without getting something that'll get me high. Unfortunately, there's no way around it. I've been sick for a few days, and it's not getting any better. I could deal with the scratchy throat and congestion, but I think I need an antibiotic.

I just have to keep reminding myself of everything I've been through since the Fourth of July when Ronnie and Jackamo left me at the Bay Ridge Hospital in Lynn. While I made it through the detox without any problems, I still had a fierce craving after leaving the hospital. I told myself: *Today, I won't get high. I'll get high tomorrow.* The day after that, I said: *I'll get high tomorrow, and if every day is today, then tomorrow will never come.* For months that was my daily mantra—*I'll get high tomorrow.* Thankfully,

Ronnie figured out I took his pills and stopped keeping any in the house. It's much easier to stay clean without any drugs around.

Even though I'm here at the doctor's with a legitimate illness, I feel like I'm being sneaky. As always, I thumb through a magazine while I wait. In the past, a magazine was a prop, an expression of nonchalance, but today, I need the two-year-old Family Circle to distract me.

When I hear my name, I stand quickly. Before, I would have taken my time getting up. I would've coughed, grimaced, maybe. I'd follow slowly behind the nurse who called me in and maybe make some small talk. Today, I'm trying to hold back my cough. I don't know how to be in this office while honestly sick.

As instructed, I undress from the waist up and wrap the paper shirt around my shoulders. I stay seated with my back hunched and my legs hanging over the table's edge because I would have lain down in the past. After all, that's what sick people do.

The doctor enters mid-cough. "That sounds nasty," she says, reaching for her stethoscope. "You probably have the flu," she says after a listen. "Although it sounds like it could even be a touch of pneumonia."

I almost smile. I *am* sick—*really sick.*

"I'm going to give you an antibiotic. Do you still use the same pharmacy?"

"Yes," is all I say. This is when I would've asked for something for the cough—something strong.

"Do you need some cough medicine?" she asks, as though she can hear my thoughts.

I hesitate for a moment, grateful she's nearly behind me and can't see me smile.

"No, thank you," I say.

50

LABOR

~2004~

We're having a girl. The pregnancy was precarious at first, but this baby is definitely stronger than the two I recently miscarried. I've been clean for two and a half years now, and every day I'm more excited about becoming a mother again. When Ronnie and I started trying after the first miscarriage, I told myself I'd give up if we didn't have a baby before I turned thirty-five. Well, I'm thirty-four, and as of tonight, November twenty-second, I'm four days overdue.

I haven't had much of an appetite all day, I'm restless, and I can't sleep. It's well after midnight, and I've been tossing and turning since watching today's recorded episode of *General Hospital*. I kept the volume low so it wouldn't disturb Ronnie, who has to get up early for work in the morning. He's always out cold by ten, and tonight is no exception.

I've been out of work for the last couple of weeks, waiting for the baby to arrive. The timing of everything has been perfect. When the downstairs construction was finished a couple of weeks ago, we moved Alita and Jackamo upstairs so Ronnie and I could be down here with the baby. We also outfitted part of the space as an office with a built-in reception desk and a small bathroom for my future clients.

Despite mediocre grades, I finished law school last December, just a few months before finding out I was pregnant. I could've taken the bar exam in July, but at five months along, I decided to wait and take it in February. I started studying at the beginning of fall, and instead of listening to classic

283

rock while painting the new walls, I played CDs of my own recorded voice, reciting outlines in each area of law. As I moved the brush along the woodwork, I heard all about federal court jurisdiction, the elements of a contract, and the rule against perpetuities. I'm determined to take this exam just one time.

I feel pressure in my lower back, the familiar pang of labor. Still, I want to be positive before we go to the hospital. They've already sent me home once.

It won't kill me to have a little patience; Serena will be here soon enough. The anticipation is killing me, though, especially when I say her name. It reminds me of my first college visit with Serena, my childhood friend, and her mother. It gives me hope for a future I never imagined.

The same goes for Serena's middle name, Ann, which was also an easy choice. It's both Ronnie's and my mother's middle name, and I wonder if it will somehow join our families; my in-laws don't seem to care much for my kids or me. Ronnie says they do, and maybe he's right, but I think he's just seeing what he wants to see. Although they've never said anything to me, I get the impression that they think their boy could do better than an unmarried single parent of two kids with different dads. I doubt it. Of all people, Ronnie's parents should know better than anybody that Ronnie is far from the biggest prize at the fair.

It's after one in the morning, and I can't wait anymore.

"Ronnie," I say, whispering. He doesn't move. "Ronnie," I say again. Louder this time. I'm sitting on my side of the bed with two pillows pushed against my lower back.

"What?" He lifts his head a few inches off of his pillow.

"It's time," I say. He puts his head back down.

"Time for what?" he mumbles.

"What do you think?"

"Jesus," I hear him whisper. "Can't you wait until the morning?"

"No, I can't wait. I'm in frigging labor. We have to go now."

He sits up and rubs his eyes. "Okay," he says. "I'm up."

51

LIBERTY

~2005~

I watch from the living room window as Ronnie's father backs his blue Grand Marquis into the driveway next to Ronnie's work truck. If the car had a light bar, it could pass for a police cruiser. It makes sense that he'd pick that car; Tom is a retired police officer. He looks like a cop, too—tall, thin, straight-backed, serious—just like the investigators who interrogated me when I was a teenager.

I stay seated on the couch while they get out of the car. Tom gets out first and walks around to the passenger side. Mary waits for him to open the door. Old school. Seeing both the car, and Ronnie's parents, makes my stomach clench.

It's been five years since I first met Tom and Mary, and I still feel like we're strangers. Even though I'm their daughter-in-law and the mother of their grandchild, they don't feel anything like family. It didn't take long for me to figure out that we have nothing in common aside from Ronnie and Tom's involvement in the legal system. But even that topic is limited.

"I was a police prosecutor," Tom said the first time we met. Ronnie had already told him I was in law school.

"Really? I always wondered how that works."

"I was in the courtroom all the time," he said. "I loved it."

"That doesn't sound good to me," I said.

"Why not?"

"It gives me anxiety." I didn't tell him I knew what it was like to be a defendant.

"It's easy," he said.

"I don't know. Bankruptcy is more my speed." And that's where the conversation ended.

Before they get through the gate, I rush past Ronnie and into the bathroom. Easing into an in-law visit in progress is better than showing them in. I've lived in Ronnie's house for nearly four years, and it still doesn't feel like my place. Thankfully, they don't often visit because I don't know what to do with myself while they're here.

It was Ronnie's idea for his parents to drive us to my swearing-in ceremony. I agreed, against my better judgment. He thinks the ritual will impress them in some way. I doubt it; although in the month since I found out I passed the bar exam, Tom has tried to extend our conversations when I answer his call.

Ronnie, Mary, and Tom are standing in the kitchen when I come out of the bathroom. They all turn to look at me.

"Hi," I say as I move to stand next to Ronnie in the only space left in the small area. We're all quiet for a moment. It's awkward as the four of us are rarely in the same room.

"Congratulations," Mary says and hands me a small white jewelry box. She's never given me a gift outside of the wedding and baby.

"Oh. Thank you," I say, sure I sound as surprised as I am.

"Open it," Tom says.

Inside, against a cotton bed, lies a delicate gold charm—the scales of justice.

"Thank you," I say again. This time, I keep my eyes on the charm. I don't know what I'm supposed to do next. Should I hug her? My mother-in-law is no more a hugger than I am. I glance at Ronnie; he looks elated.

A hug seems appropriate. I step forward and put my arms up. Mary is still and keeps her arms at her sides. Because she's a good five inches shorter than me, I end up patting her awkwardly on her back. The hug reminds me of the levitation game "*Light as a Feather, Stiff as a Board*" we used to play as kids. Of course, Mary is the board and probably light as a feather, weighing in at less than a hundred pounds. The thought makes me chuckle to myself.

TOM DOES MOST of the talking during the forty-minute ride into Boston. He tells us about their most recent trip to Florida and the sharp rise in his triglycerides. Ronnie responds with relevant questions. Mary is sitting in the passenger seat. She looks the same as when standing—her back is straight, and her hands are on her thighs, palms facing down. She only speaks when directly spoken to.

I sit quietly, looking out the window. I'm thinking about the day my professor mentioned "white trash" in estates class and how I felt when the class laughed. The memory makes my stomach turn. I remind myself that law school is long over now. My grades weren't great, but I passed and took the bar exam. And like the others sworn in today, I'll soon be licensed to practice law in the Commonwealth of Massachusetts.

"Gail," Ronnie says. He's looking at me.

"What?" I ask, irritated by the interruption.

"My father's talking to you."

"Oh. I was thinking," I say. Ronnie doesn't ask what I was thinking about.

"Do you know what you'll do first?" Tom asks, looking at me in the rearview mirror.

"No," I say, even though I do. There's a warrant for my brother's arrest out of Gloucester. It's been hanging over his head for the last few years, and because of it, he can't renew his license. Tom doesn't need to know that. All I know about the warrant is that he got charged with assault after a fight over a girl. I'm sure drugs were involved. Heroin has gotten ahold of my brother, just as it did his parents and a few of his siblings. He's been using it for at least five years now. Gratefully, Tom doesn't ask any more questions.

Ronnie holds my hand as we walk from the parking garage to Faneuil Hall, where the ceremony will take place. We're all dressed like we're going to church. I'm wearing a business suit that makes me look professional, even though it's bigger than any I've ever owned, thanks to the baby weight I haven't been able to shed. It didn't help that I'd already gained thirty pounds when I quit smoking the year before getting pregnant. The jacket is slung over my arm, where it'll stay until we get inside to the air conditioning. Ronnie is wearing a suit too, and I've got to give him credit; the guy sure knows how to dress.

We meet up with Chrissy and Philip in front of Faneuil Hall, the "Cradle of Liberty," and get into a short line with the rest of the lawyers-to-be and their guests.

The marketplace surrounding the hall is hopping today, which is no surprise; the late June weather is perfect. There's a steel band playing nearby. Four guys are sitting on plastic buckets turned upside down, each banging on his tin barrel. The music is so mesmerizing that I would gladly join the crowd circling the group if I didn't have such an important appointment.

When it's time, we file through double doors into a majestic two-story room with white pillars that extend from floor to ceiling. An open balcony wraps around the room. The walls are decorated with gold-framed paintings of important-looking men, and busts line the wall behind a podium.

I take my assigned seat in one of the wooden folding chairs a few rows back from the front of the room. When my last name changed from Brenner to Nastasia, my place in line changed too.

After the speeches, Maura S. Doyle, the Supreme Judicial Court Clerk, asks the new lawyers to stand. We recite an oath to uphold the Constitution of the United States and the Commonwealth from a card we were handed on the way in.

Then, when my name is called, I go to the front and sign the Massachusetts Roll of Attorneys. Ms. Doyle tells me the pen is mine to keep.

On the way back to my seat, I scan the rows of newly minted attorneys. Even now, I'm painfully aware that, although they don't look all that different from me, I still feel like an imposter.

FOLLOWING THE CEREMONY and photos, we all walk to Quincy Market for ice cream. For the first time today, Philip and I have some time alone as we walk side by side.

"So," he says, "now that my sister's a big-time lawyer."

"Yes, I know," I say, smiling.

"When can we go?" he asks.

"Sometime this week," I say.

"Monday?"

"I'll try." My schedule is tight, but I know he's eager to get it done.

"Okay," he says.

"I'm proud of you for facing this," I say, glancing at him.

"Thanks," he says, watching the ground in front of him as he walks. After a moment of silence between us, he looks at me. "You know," he says, "I really am proud of you too."

52

OVERCOMING

~2012~

I t's been nearly seven years since I represented my brother, my first client. This morning, just like most mornings, I sat in my favorite spot in the arraignment session of the Lawrence District Court, waiting for my case to be called. From there, I could see everything: the judge's bench to my right, the galley of waiting litigants to my left, and directly in front of me, the defense and prosecutor's tables, and a jury box occupied by a few of my waiting colleagues.

The modern courtroom is different from the older ones. The dark wooden tables and benches of courtrooms past have been replaced with the younger, lighter color of birchwood.

I'd been scrolling through emails on my phone when I heard the clerk call the name: "Arthur Higgins." My head snapped up. Artie? I wondered. I looked to the audience, where a man was already on his feet. Was it the same Arthur Higgins who took those pictures of me as a teenager? It was an unusual name, for sure. I'll never forget it.

But I didn't recognize the man. His hair was dark like Artie's had been, but so wasn't that of half the male population. I studied his face as he walked to the podium, but getting a good look with the twenty-or-so feet between us was impossible. I probably wouldn't have recognized him even if he'd been standing right in front of me; I was only fourteen the last time I'd laid eyes on him.

I got to my feet without thinking and stood, rooted in place, while the judge addressed the man's case. After just a few minutes, he was on his way back out of the courtroom. I decided I'd follow him. I'd ask him questions: Are you Artie from Gloucester? Do you remember me? Why didn't you ever call me back? Do you still have the photos?

My own voice interrupted my internal interrogation.

Then what? It asked.

The questions became directed at me. What if it was Arthur Higgins from Gloucester? What if he did remember me? What if he did still have the pictures? I paused long enough for him to make it to the door. The answer came when it closed behind him.

It didn't matter. Artie was insignificant. The pictures couldn't hurt me anymore. He could publish the photos on a billboard for all I cared.

I was still standing in front of my chair when the next case was called. I looked around the room again—at the audience, the tables, the lawyers waiting, and the judge—and wondered if I would be okay if they all knew the truth about me. Yes, I realized that would be just fine. I took a deep breath and sat back down.

NOTE TO THE READER

Every person who's touched my life has profoundly impacted me and changed who I am in some way, even Mary Lee, whom I haven't seen since I was five years old. I hope to have an opportunity to meet her again someday.

While investigating my ancestry, I connected with Aunt Julie's second daughter. We're in contact and plan to meet in person. I was also blessed with finding another cousin on my father's side—a family I knew nothing about until after turning fifty.

Sadly, Walter passed away in February of two-thousand-sixteen at just sixty-years young. In June of that year, my brother, Philip, lost his battle with addiction a few months short of his fortieth birthday. I'm grateful every day for the gift of his daughter LJ.

My sweet, beautiful sister, Chrissy, is happily married with two sons. Both of my nephews are in college.

Although I haven't seen Aunt Julie for several years, I know she is alive and well. For more than twenty-five years, she's lived in residential housing, where she's able to get the help she needs.

My father still lives in Texas, where he spends his days raising pigeons and his nights playing pool.

ACKNOWLEDGEMENTS

I began writing THE FRUIT YOU'LL NEVER SEE several years ago, and many people have helped along the way. As it's been so long in the making, I'm afraid I may neglect to mention some of them. If I do, please know that it is an oversight and not for a lack of gratitude.

First, I want to thank Dottie McKay Lima for, without her encouragement, I wouldn't have gotten past the first three pages. As we mourned the loss of her brother Jack, I wrote, and she listened.

Thank you to my children, Alita (Artemis), Jack, Serena, and my sister Chrissy, who have been gracious involuntary characters in my story.

A very special thank you to Deb Goldstein, my friend and writing coach. My first goal when we began our work together was to "finish this f-ing book." That I'm holding a completed manuscript in my hands is a testament to her stellar coaching ability.

I have never-ending gratitude for my friends and beta readers: Billie Hruby, Maura Gearin Harper, Sierra McGregor, Melissa Lezynski, Kristofer Alexa, Erin Matthes, Lisa Hart Martin, Stephen Petrovcin, Brenda Brenner, Christine Adley, Debbie Pollock, and KC Hruby, who was one of the earliest champions of my work.

I owe a huge debt of gratitude to my many teachers along the way. First, Alex Marzano-Lesnevich, the former Boston Grubstreet Memoir Incubator instructor, who convinced me that I was writing an actual book. And my Grubstreet classmates and workshop partners who helped shape this story: Michelle Bowdler, Gita Brown, Alicia Googins, Ananda Lowe, Jay Moskowitz, Catherine O'Neil, Kristen Paulson-Nguyen, and Lara Pelligrinelli.

Thank you, Emerson College, for the exceptional education and all my Emerson instructors, especially Jabari Asim, my teacher and thesis chair, and Richard Hoffman.

Also, a special thank you to Joyce Maynard, one of the best authors and writing instructors with whom I've had the pleasure to learn.

Finally, a very special thank you to Kenny Francis, my partner and best friend, who takes care of me so that I can focus on the things that nourish my spirit and bring me joy.

WWW.GAILNASTASIA.COM

Made in the USA
Middletown, DE
05 November 2023

41828393R00179